BOATS FOR FISHERMEN

BOATS FOR FISHERMEN

Tom Earnhardt

THE LYONS PRESS

To ***Dana, Izaak, and Rachel,***
a more loving and supportive crew
than any man deserves

and

To ***Captain Donald Willis,***
my family's hero and mentor
on and off the water

10 9 8 7 6 5 4 3 2 1

Printed in Canada

Library of Congress Cataloging-in-Publication Data

Boats for fishermen
p. cm.
ISBN 1-58574-121-3 (pb)
1. Fishing boats.

VM431 .B62 2001
623.8′202′0247991—dc21
00-45417

Contents

Foreword by John Randolph vii
Acknowledgments xi
Introduction 1

I
What Makes a Great Fishing Boat?

1 Bound by the Water 7
2 Understanding Form and Function in a Fishing Boat 17

II
Powerboats

3 Hull Designs for the Ocean, Bays, Flats, Rivers, and Lakes 37
4 The Mystery of Trim 57
5 Weight, Materials, and Construction Techniques 67
6 Interior Designs That Make Sense 81

III
Motors, Accessories, and Rigging

7 Power Options and Transom Configurations 97
8 Cutting the Clutter: Choosing and Rigging Only Necessary Accessories 115

IV
Protecting Your Investment

9 Trailering, Storage, Mooring, and Maintenance of Power Boats 141
10 Ropes, Knots, and Anchors 159

V
Human-Powered Boats

11 Great Rowboats . . . Skiffs, Dinghies, Prams, and Drift Boats 179
12 Kayaks and Canoes for Anglers 189
13 Quiet Propulsion: Push Poles, Oars, Paddles, and Electric Motors 207

VI
Safety and Etiquette for the Boating Angler

14 Angler Safety: More Than a Fire Extinguisher and Life Jackets 225
15 Angler's Etiquette: The Golden Rule 233

A Boating Glossary for Anglers 241
Index 249

Foreword

It's a case of too soon old too late smart. That describes my long learn-by-my-mistakes approach to fishing boats. More specifically fishing boats that work for freshwater and saltwater light-tackle fishing.

I've made all the mistakes: using (round-bottom) canoes to fish in the salt; using prams or johnboats in choppy seas; trying to fly fish from cluttered pleasure craft . . . the list of my horror stories is endless. But oh how I recall that day five years ago when I first fished in a Jones Brothers Cape Fisherman LT (light tackle). Tom Earnhardt and I fished for false albacore near Cape Lookout for a story that Tom would write for *Fly Fisherman* magazine. The weather would range from windless calm under bluebird skies to raging wind-driven rain with whitecaps beating onto windward shores.

How sweet it was. The boat rode evenly in a sharp chop and I could cast without my lines being blown off the front deck. I found hand-holding bars in the right places to control myself when the boat swung over the swells to chase bait-busting albacore. When we ran into the wind, bow waves and spray flared away and we were dry in the boat's console area. I felt safe: The boat had high initial and reserve stability; when I stepped to the side of the front deck to cast, it did not roll sharply but held steady. When we ran hard through the chop, it held on trim and without the spine-numbing bucking and diving that I have experienced with other near-shore fishing boats. As we fished that day, that boat taught me the elements of matching a boat's design to its function. It was the first time that I had ever fished in a great near-shore fishing boat. This one had been designed by the Jones brothers with Tom Earnhardt's help.

Tom Earnhardt began his boating experience in the same way that I started mine, fishing with a father from wooden boats with wooden lures. He too made mistakes, but, because of broad fishing experience, he came farther and faster than I did in learning his boat lessons. And as I read this book I realized why I have made so many mistakes in choosing and using (or misusing) the boats of my fishing experience. Thank you, Tom, for helping me emerge from the cluttered woods of ignorance.

This book is quite simply the *vade mecum* of practical advice for fishermen who want to choose–and use–a boat suited to their fishing. And that is Earnhardt's message: Boats are designed (hull, power, and interiors) to do specific things; it's a case of form suiting function. The information contained in these pages proves that if you do not understand the critical elements of boat form and function, you simply cannot make intelligent choices in what you buy and use. After five decades of making my mistakes, I feel strongly that all prospective boat fishers should read this book before buying a boat. The knowledge contained here will allow you to make intelligent decisions about the boat best suited to the light-tackle fishing that you will do. The information can also save your life, for fishing in the wrong craft can be extremely dangerous, especially if you suddenly encounter severe weather.

From prospecting for the right boat to boating use and care this book should be your road map. And when you find that boat of your fishing dreams you will discover how sweet the experience of getting safely to the fish can be. A good boat, you see, is our chariot of dreams. Tom Earnhardt explains why.

—John Randolph
November, 2000

Acknowledgments

I would first like to acknowledge advancing age as a major contributor to this book. Having lived in the time before depth sounders, electric motors, large outboards, GPS, and the extensive use of fiberglass and graphite, I feel I am better able to appreciate the characteristics of more simple boats and at the same time recognize the more significant advantages handed to fishermen by technology. Other than this perspective on things past, advancing years offer few benefits.

The seed for this book came from Lefty Kreh, a friend for over thirty years and perhaps the best fly- and light-tackle angler of this, or any generation. Five years ago after a slow morning of fishing, the conversation turned to the pros and cons of various fishing boats and their design. After suggesting that I take a shot at a book on fishing boats, he then asked several times a year, "How's the boat book coming along?" With Lefty's kick in the pants and early support of the idea by Nick Lyons, my publisher and grand friend, I finally made the time commitment. Even with Lefty and Nick the project never would have happened without the support and understanding of my wife, Dana Jennings, and without my life's inspirations and cheerleaders, Izaak and Rachel. No one man should be so lucky.

The text of this book in various drafts passed through the hands of Gladys Carney whose typing and English skills have improved almost every major piece of writing I've attempted since 1968. I want to also acknowledge the help and friendship of Don Thimsen, a friend and angler, who has almost singlehandedly dragged me into the world of computers, and who saved several "lost" chapters of this book from an eternity in cyberspace.

Unfortunately there is not adequate space to list all the fishing companions, guides, marina operators, and manufacturers who had an impact on this book. Suffice it to say, I had a wealth of resources from which to draw; therefore, any shortcomings are mine alone. However, the following people, all great friends, must be acknowledged because they provided photographs and important information. They are in alphabetical order: Paul Bates, gentle Virginian and great photographer; Brad Burns, great angler, writer, and passionate advocate for coastal conservation; Buzz Bryson, writer, angler, and tackle guru; Hal Chittum, flats guide, innovative retailer, and boat builder; Bob Clouser, superb smallmouth guide and creator of one of the world's most useful fly patterns, the Clouser Minnow; George Conway, respected boat dealer and an expert on small coastal craft; Theo Copeland, a pioneering river guide in the Southeast for trout and smallmouth bass; Henry Cowen, Southern-gentleman Yankee, angler, and inventive fly tier; Steve Coward, extraordinary mechanic and a great source of boat maintenance tips; Kevin DuBois, one of Virginia's best and most creative saltwater fly-fishermen; David Falkowski, angler and expert in kayaks and canoes; Bruce Foster, adventurer, guide with many talents, and great cook; D. L. Goddard, angler and extraordinarily creative fly tier; Rose and Donnie Hatcher, both great anglers and marina operators; Ed Jaworowski, professor, master caster, and photographer; Donnie Jones, builder of superb boats, fly-fisherman in training, and the hardest working good guy I know; Lefty Kreh, world-class gourmand and master of all things fishing; Barry Kanavy, wooden boat builder, photographer, and master guide on Long Island Sound; Eddie Nickens, superb writer and lucky fisherman; the Pasfield family, great people with a great marina; John Randolph, great editor, angler, fishing companion, and one of the people who has had the most profound influence on modern fly fishing; Roth-Built Boats, builders of classic New England sport fishing boats; Eddie Smith, manufacturer of great boats and a friend of ducks and fish everywhere; Ed Ward, world-class pig cooker and fountain of boating knowledge; Jim Wheeler, perhaps the man most responsible for popularizing the pram as a viable option for West Coast anglers; Donald Willis, hero to my family and master seaman; and Scott Wood, angler, tier, fly shop manager, and great paddler.

I wish to thank the people of The Lyons Press, especially Nick Lyons, the complete package—publisher, editor, superb writer, passionate angler, and mentor. Nick brings out the best in people. I also want to thank Jonathan J. McCullough, editor and coordinator of this project, for his suggestions, gentle prodding, and professionalism.

Finally, I can't stop without remembering my parents, Irwin and Ruth Earnhardt, now departed, who gave me a world of opportunity, on and off the water. Thanks also to my brothers, Gene and Jim, who have always been there for support and advice. I'm a very lucky man.

—Tom Earnhardt
November, 2000

Introduction

I have had love affairs with lots of boats, most of which I didn't own. The boats I have owned and the boats after which I have lusted have all had one thing in common—they were built to fish. Riding in a great fishing boat is not enough; I also like to look at them and touch them. On the highway I frequently look in the rearview mirror to better examine a trailered boat going in the opposite direction. At boat ramps, restaurant parking lots, and tackle shops I like to ogle fishing craft. It's not a fancy paint job, high-tech electronics, or large engine that excites me, but rather it's the hull shape, the interior layout, and superb "fit and finish" showing quality construction. Because I enjoy all types of fishing, I am as excited to find a lovely wooden skiff as a well-designed fiberglass center console.

Over the past thirty years, at least three dozen boats have been part of my family. Some of these boats were well loved, while others never really fit in. Over the same period of time I have traveled and fished in many parts of the United States and other countries. I have spent time with many extraordinary captains and watermen, people who love the water and work on boats every day. I have also spent hundreds of days at the family home on Harkers Island, where I am surrounded by wooden boats under construction and on the water. Within a few miles of this Outer Banks community there are a number of companies producing quality fiberglass fishing boats where I often spend time observing all phases of the building process. From this experience I have learned that a fishing boat is a thing of beauty only if it is well built and does its job well.

Angling and boating have entered a new age where the sound of ringing cell phones (mine included) often drowns out the cries of shorebirds on a calm day. We also live in a time when there is a never-ending list of options and accessories available for boats in fresh and salt water. A few add safety, comfort, and enjoyment to a fishing boat. Many, however, do little more than add useless clutter, thereby detracting form a boat's "fishability."

Fishability is hard to define but easy to describe. It is the secure feeling you get in a heavy chop or swell when you know that you are in a seaworthy craft. It is having the wheel and grab rails at the right height and in the right place. It is fishing in boats that have no rattles or bouncing hatch covers. It is the ability to store necessary gear and tackle securely. Most of all, fishability means space that is clean and uncluttered, because simplicity in design and ease of operation is the key to a great fishing boat.

In writing this book, it was apparent from the beginning that hard facts and personal observations could not be easily separated. Although I have tried to set forth objectively the many choices available to anglers in powerboats and human-powered craft, I have not shied away from expressing my opinion on a variety of issues. For example, I make no secret of the fact that I have little interest in big-money tournament fishing in fresh or salt water. The people who participate in them are often extraordinary anglers. My big gripe is with the high-speed tournament bass boats (60 mph and above) and the seagoing hot rods of the king mackerel circuit. It seems incredible to me that as inland lakes and nearshore waters become more crowded, tournaments seem to sanction, and encourage, speed. High speed on public waters is dangerous business. When getting to the fish faster than anyone else is the first priority, too much has been lost to call it fishing; catching a bass or a mackerel for the table or sport should be its own reward. However, I admit some of the design technology used on these high-speed fishing machines may ultimately provide some benefit for ordinary anglers, so I have therefore tried to overlook my prejudice and to pay compliments when they are due.

Because of the limits of space and my expertise, some restrictions had to be placed on the types of fishing craft to be covered. This book was written specifically for fly fishermen and light-tackle anglers who fish for sport or catch fish for the table. It covers only boats with rigid hulls (no inflatables are dealt with), and boats that can be carried on, or trailered behind, a passenger or sport utility vehicle. Particular attention is paid to "personal boats" for fishing or family use that can be run by an individual without the help of a crew or the assistance of dockhands. You will find my observations on single-person rowboats and kayaks, but I also deal with larger, seagoing sportfishing boats up to 27 feet in length. Because of weight and beam (width), these are the largest boats that can be practically and safely trailered by anglers.

The goal of this book is to assist light-tackle anglers who want to choose the right boat for their needs in fresh and salt water, and those who already have a boat but want to make it more "fishing friendly." Because choosing a boat can be a subjective and even an emotional decision, I fully expect you, the reader, to disagree with me from time to time. In the end, however, by making suggestions and sharing my pet peeves, I hope that I will provide you with the information necessary for you to find a boat. I also hope that as your angling journey continues, you will look at, lust after, and learn from every boat you see.

1

WHAT MAKES A GREAT FISHING BOAT?

1

Bound by the Water

No other man-made thing can take you closer to God, man, and fish than a good fishing boat. I had more meaningful conversations with my father on fishing boats than all other places combined. Although Dad and I spent lots of time on the water in the 1950s and the 1960s, we did not have a boat of our own. Our ticket to the world of fishing was a green 5-horsepower Johnson outboard motor that stayed in the trunk of the car wrapped in an oily quilt. Knowing that we had a motor, Dad was always able to find a boat that we could rent or borrow. We plied the shallow waters of North Carolina's Currituck Sound, explored many of the TVA (Tennessee Valley Authority) lakes in North Carolina and Tennessee, caught crappie and stripers in the Santee-Cooper Reservoir in South Carolina, and visited Florida's St. John's River in search of giant largemouth bass. That old Johnson kicker was behind us when we searched for shad and stripers on North Carolina's Roanoke River, explored the brackish waters of South Carolina's Low Country, and when we first sampled the angler's smorgasbord of the Outer Banks.

During that period of my life, almost all the boats in which we fished had two things in common: They were all made of wood, and each contained a coffee can. My first job at each destination was to select a boat from the local rental fleet and begin scooping water. For a time I thought that water in a boat was a sign that it leaked. I soon learned, however, that boats needed water to swell their planks to remain seaworthy. It was also my job to find a board suitable to serve as a paddle, and an anchor, since most wooden rental craft came without either. I learned quickly that a cinder block, a window weight, or even a properly tied rock could serve as an anchor.

The rental fleets of the mid-1950s offered variety and surprises. The ideal boat had a flat bottom and a vertical wooden transom (the flat, stern end of a boat), which was notched in the middle for mounting a 5-horsepower outboard. At some destinations we were limited to wooden skiffs with transoms that were high in the middle and angled away from the boat. These boats were designed with a little "rocker" at the rear to raise the whole stern slightly out of the water to eliminate drag. Boats of this design were rowing skiffs that were never intended to be powered by an outboard motor. On a high transom the shaft of the little Johnson was not long enough to reach the water, which left the propeller high and dry. To solve this problem, I remember having to sit right by the motor on the port side of the transom while my dad sat on the starboard side manning the tiller. Our combined weight was usually enough to push the stern of the boat and the motor shaft down far enough so that the propeller could bite.

We were never concerned about the speed of a boat, just its ability to get us to the fish—eventually. With a 5-horsepower motor, only a few wooden boats 14 to 17 feet in length could actually get on plane. At full throttle most of our rental craft could

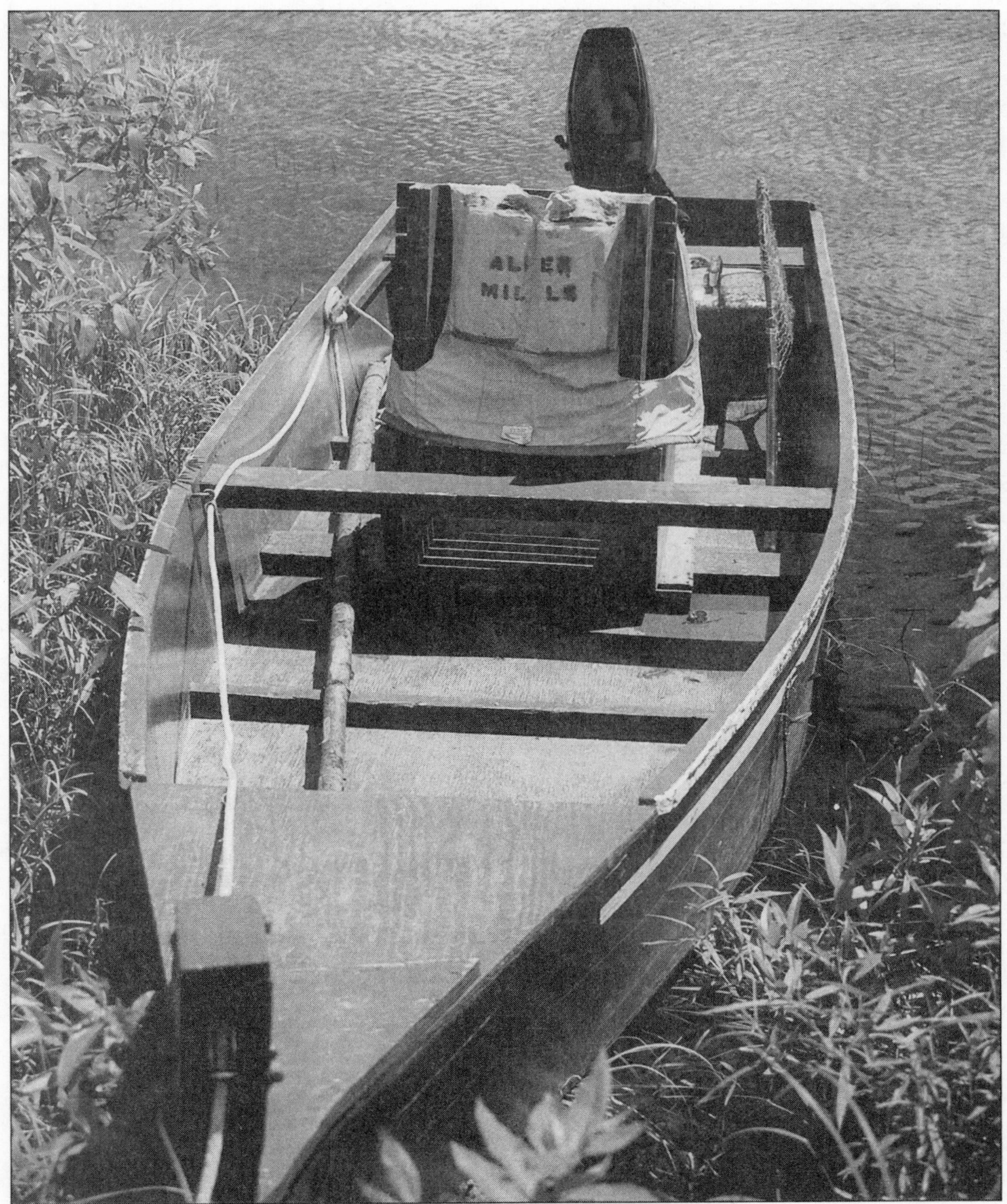

Bruce Foster

Some of my best fishing experiences and conversations have taken place on slow, wooden boats.

only reach a fast jog. Today, when I cross, in minutes instead of hours, the same bodies of water I crossed with my father forty years ago, I think of great conversations and fishing strategy sessions, not wasted hours.

It was on those slow trips across large lakes and lazy coastal rivers that we had the time to look, listen, and learn. On one trip in the late 1950s, my father and I drove from North Carolina to Palatka, Florida, a small town near Jacksonville on the St. John's River. I was equipped with a fly rod, the latest spinning gear, and an oversize fishing ego, even for a thirteen-year-old. On most of our trips we fished without a guide, but on this trip we met a man with whom Dad had fished on several earlier occasions. His name was Jedidiah, a strong black man with forearms bigger than my legs. Like most teenagers I was clueless as to Jedidiah's age, or about the age of any adult over forty. My best guess was that he was somewhere between fifty and seventy, but regardless of his age, he was a man with experience who lived on the St. John's and knew it like the back of his hand. With his eyes on the shoreline and a short paddle in one hand, Jedidiah would scull our wooden rental boat along the edge of water hyacinths looking for pockets that held largemouth bass. His paddle never seemed to come out of the water. Although electric motors now provide quiet propulsion for many of the craft on which I fish, I have never had a smoother, quieter trip along the shoreline than the one provided by Jedidiah.

My personal tackle cache consisted of a metal South Bend fly rod with a Pflueger Medalist reel, and a Mitchell 300 spinning reel slung under a Shakespeare "Wonderod." In my personal tackle box there were a few early plastic worms, some L&S Bassmaster jointed minnows, some Heddon Sonics, and several hot new Mepps' spinners. I also carried a small box of streamers and poppers that I copied from pictures in a Joe Brooks book on bass fishing. I tried several offerings without success before Jedidiah began offering me lures from his own small wooden box. Among his offerings were some dull, even rusty, old spoons tipped with chunks of pork rind. Later in the morning he offered me a wooden topwater plug with almost no paint on it. Finally he offered me a large, jointed wooden plug adorned with bent treble hooks. Each time Jedidiah made an offer, I rebuffed him and told him I had something else in *my* box that I wanted to try. I don't know how many times I had rejected Jedidiah's help when my father's voice shattered the silence: "Damnit! Damnit, Tommy. This man is many times your age; this is his home, and these are his fish. You haven't heard a word he's said all day. If you can't learn from a man like him, then life for you will be tough."

I had never heard my father sound so serious or so frustrated. He rarely shouted and had never cursed at me in that way. The next half an hour that boat became smaller and smaller as I sat between Jedidiah and my father, fighting back tears. At some point I swallowed my pride and asked Jedidiah for advice, and a lure or two. Some of the best lessons of my life were learned in boats, especially slow ones.

Speed and "Modern Boats"

Just before I went off to college in 1964, Dad retired the 5-horsepower Johnson and bought a 14-foot fiberglass "bass boat" and a trailer while on a trip to Oklahoma. The new rig was powered by a hot 9.9-horsepower outboard. Although we could tow the boat wherever we wanted, and we carried our own paddle and anchor, I secretly missed the hunt for the perfect rental boat and the old Johnson.

A couple of years after my graduation from college in 1968, Dad traded up to his ultimate fishing boat, a 17-foot tri-hull with a 50-horsepower engine. With our "modern" boats we were able to travel farther, faster, and in style. Even though we had reached the status of fishing-boat owners, instead of renters, I know for a fact that we did not catch any more fish, and certainly didn't have any more fun.

Not long after we became "boated gentry," my father died. The passage of time dulls many things, but not the lessons learned in small boats. I am, and will forever be, bound by the water to my father and his many friends. Although I have used and owned many fishing boats on my own over the past thirty years and have a passport filled with visas to exotic destinations, I still haven't forgotten those early lessons. For example, although the sophisticated boats I now own are either self-bailing or have bilge pumps, I still like to carry a coffee can, just in case.

No Delegation of Responsibility

In those early days spent in simple boats with simple outboards, I learned to troubleshoot and solve common boating problems. Those were the days before full-service marinas and "mechanics on duty." I knew that safety and seaworthiness were my responsibility; however, as boats got more complicated and marinas began to cater to the needs of our fast-paced lives, personal know-how seemed less important. Along with countless gadgets, most boats came with a folder full of warranty books, which also tended to lull us into a false sense of security: "It's a $25,000 boat, so what can go wrong?"

Twenty years ago I was forever reminded that safety cannot be delegated. Two friends and I waited at a marina near Morehead City, North Carolina, for the arrival of my new 19-foot center console. The dealer had told me in a phone conversation a day earlier that everything had been checked out and that my new boat was ready to go. He also told me that all the safety equipment for my old boat had been transferred, and that the gas tank had been capped off. When the sleek center console finally arrived, my friends and I performed an appropriate christening ceremony as the dealer let the new boat slide off the trailer into the water. The two friends and I jumped into the boat with rods in hand and marveled at my fishing machine. It fired up with one turn of the key, and I let it idle for a few minutes while the dealer gave me the obligatory spiel about breaking in the engine. After answering a few questions, he told me he would leave the trailer in the marina parking lot.

I eased her out of the marina and headed for Cape Lookout—a twenty-minute run. The September water was clear and warm. There was almost no wind. At the end of the cape jetty I cut the engine and slipped the anchor overboard so that we could jig for gray trout, or common weakfish. Ten minutes had passed when we noticed that something was not quite right. Because the transom seemed low in the water, I opened a rear hatch to look for the bilge pump. Both the bilge pump and battery were covered with a foot of water. Since the battery was underwater, the bilge pump didn't work, the radio was useless, and the motor wouldn't crank. In the minute it took to get our life jackets out of the forward compartment, the transom disappeared beneath the waves as the three of us stood watching from the bow. Moments later, the bow, too, disappeared beneath our feet. As the three of us bobbed in the swells in our life jackets, the boat lay on the bottom in thirty feet of water.

At the marina I had been assured that the boat was ready to go. In the dealer's haste to please me, and in my haste to hurry the maiden voyage, I had forgotten who was ultimately responsible for the boat and the safety of the passengers. If I had taken a few minutes to check, I would have noticed that the hose connecting the boat's livewell to the transom was not connected. During the twenty to thirty minutes in which I ran the boat on plane out to the cape from the marina, the boat did not fill with water. It was only after we anchored and sat for ten minutes that water rushed through the hole in the transom, covering the battery, making it impossible to start the engine or call for help. Fortunately, because there were other boats in the area, we were rescued quickly and the Coast Guard was able to recover my boat by snagging the anchor line. No one was injured, and the boat and motor were replaced by the manufacturer.

Back at the marina it would have been easy for me to absolve myself of all responsibility by hiding behind the fact that the dealer had launched the boat and said that it was ready to go. My years on the water had taught me that water offers opportunity, but it can also be unforgiving. As the owner/operator of a boat, I was responsible for making sure that everything was shipshape. I had failed in that responsibility.

Why Search for a Boat That Fishes Well?

I now have two young children, Izaak and Rachel. Nothing in my life is more exciting than to be reminded by them that it is time to go fishing. Whether we are chasing sunfish or bass in freshwater, or croakers and bluefish in the salt, we are bound together by the water. I am fortunate that I often have several different boats available to me. Since I learned a long time ago that conversation is diminished by speed and noise, I barely put a boat on plane when my children are with me. I am also cognizant that for me and my children, lots of gadgets—speedometers, tachometers, depth sounders, radios, and radar—can be a hindrance to that bond with the water. Don't get me wrong; there is a very important place for new technology for fishing success and for safety. My concern is that we sometimes allow speed and gadgetry to define our relationship with the water.

Whether rightly or wrongly, I believe that God provided boats for man's fishing enjoyment. Unfortunately, many people do not know God's will and use boats for frivolous activities such as waterskiing and day cruising. However, boats, like people, can be redeemed, and any boat can be made into a fishing boat. That is not to say that all boats can be *good* fishing boats, just that any boat can *serve* as a fishing boat.

For those who love to fish, with a fly rod or any other form of light tackle, there are few greater joys than fishing in a boat that truly enhances the experience. Because I have been in extraordinary boats and boats with no redeeming characteristics, I believe that it is the goal, the Holy Grail, of all who fish to find the best

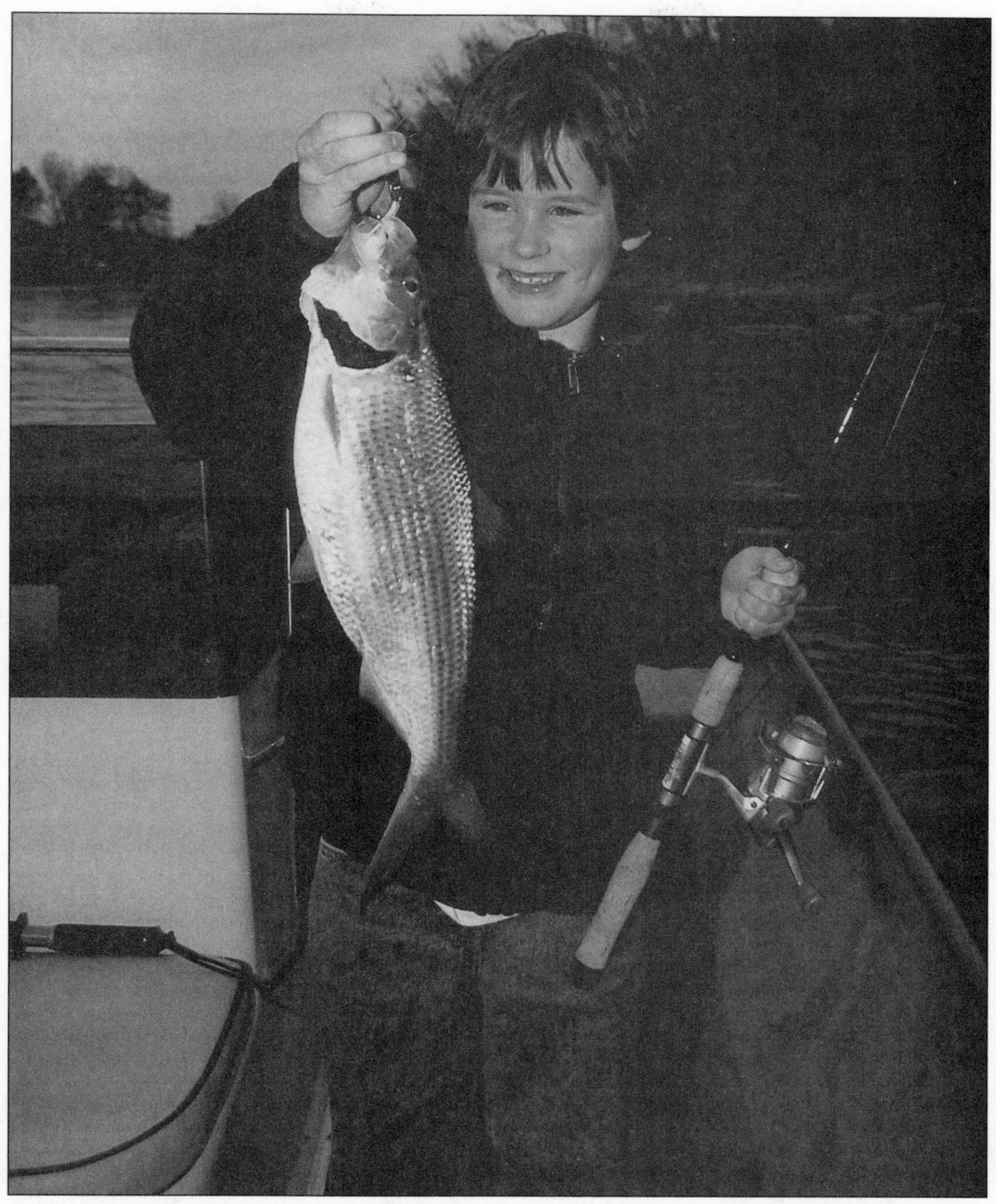

A good fishing boat can enhance the life of any person, no matter what their age.

boat for the fish they seek and the type of water conditions they are likely to encounter. In the pages that follow, I will share with you what I believe to be the essential elements that must come together to make a boat that fishes well.

The right boat should be the Holy Grail of every angler. A boat always expands angling horizons.

2

Understanding Form and Function in a Fishing Boat

When I look at magazines and go to boat shows, I sometimes believe there are now more boat manufacturers than there were boats just a few decades ago. Along with more manufacturers, the variety of boats for anglers has also noticeably increased. Each type of boat, including bass boats, center consoles, prams, kayaks, and canoes, is often available in a variety of styles, sizes, and materials. I can now go to a local boat show in my home state of North Carolina and see boats developed in other parts of the country and the world. As our horizons in sportfishing have expanded and our tackle has improved, our appetites for specialty boats have increased. Form follows function.

The Florida Keys flats boat, developed for sight casting for bonefish and tarpon, is a classic example of a niche boat that was soon embraced by anglers seeking other species. The basic flats boat design with poling platforms and push poles has now left the Florida Keys and can be found on shallow water flats

Barry Kanavy

Henry Cowen

Flats boats designed for use in the Florida Keys are now used by northern anglers in search of striped bass and by anglers on inland reservoirs.

anyplace in the world where light-tackle anglers seek game fish. Anglers seeking redfish and seatrout in coastal shallows of the mid-Atlantic now commonly use flats boats, craft seldom seen in the region just a decade ago. These versatile boats are also used in the "skinny" water (water less than knee deep) of inland reservoirs by anglers seeking stripers, smallmouth bass, and even carp. Flats boats have been transported by anglers for use around remote Pacific atolls. Even on the cold-water flats of Cape Cod and Martha's Vineyard, it is not at all uncommon to see small flotillas of flats boats being poled across shallow, sandy bottoms. After the basic design escaped the Keys, anglers and boat-builders began making subtle changes to better adapt these boats to the waters and fishing needs of different regions, especially along the Texas coast. Form follows function. Form also evolves to meet particular needs.

Almost the same metamorphosis has occurred with drift boats. Although I had seen pictures of them in magazines, it wasn't until the 1970s that I was a passenger in drift boats on rivers in Montana, Idaho, and in the Pacific Northwest. These tough, lightweight craft have the stability and high, flared sides of a dory to keep passengers dry. They also possess enough "rocker" (a curved-bottom design in which the ends turn up like a banana), which helps eliminate drag and allows them to be pivoted and maneuvered easily by a good oarsman. Western drift boats made of fiberglass, wood, or aluminum have found their way into large rivers everywhere. They are now common on the large rivers of the eastern United States such as the Delaware, Susquehanna, and North Carolina's Roanoke. The same boats are also seen in the rivers of Chile and Argentina. As with the flats boats, anglers in other parts of the world have begun to tweak their drift boats to adapt them to local needs. Again, form follows function.

Even in areas isolated from each other, similar craft have arisen out of necessity. In the early 1990s I fished some great

Western drift boats, whose heritage is part dory, can be found on trout rivers on the East Coast and in South America.

rivers in central Siberia in boats that were virtually identical to the large cargo canoes I had seen in eastern Canada. Clearly, boatbuilders in remote areas of Siberia near the Mongolian border had never seen pictures of Canadian riverboats, and it is unlikely that any of my Soviet friends had ever traveled outside their country. The craft I saw on large rivers in both Russia and Canada were long (perhaps 25 feet), stable, had relatively flat and narrow bottoms, and could be propelled by a low-horsepower outboard engine. Even with low-horsepower engines, they were able to move against fast currents going upstream. The length of these boats made it possible for their operators to "bridge" rough water. Thus, although good boat designs from

Bruce Foster

Long, slender boats and canoes, such as these on the Miramichi, are used on rivers around the world.

one region will be appropriated by angler/boaters in another, it is also true that similar boat forms can evolve independently in different parts of the world to match similar water and fishing conditions.

Once you begin to understand the basics of hull design and interior layout, you can then choose with confidence a boat for your angling style and local water conditions. Boats are often chosen by anglers for fishing they *might* do rather than for the fishing they *normally* do. Just because a boat appears on Saturday-morning television on a regular basis and looks great on a tropical flat does not mean that it will work well in rough ocean inlets, or that it will be adequate for bass and walleye fishing on a large inland reservoir. Form must follow function if you are to get maximum enjoyment from your fishing boat.

Choosing a Fleet of Boats

I am one of the many anglers in this country who happens to love all types of fishing. Every year I spend time on rivers, farm ponds, large reservoirs, coastal flats, and the open ocean. I imagine that some of the water conditions in which I fish are similar to those encountered by you. If money, space, time, and the survival of my marriage were not issues, I would have a fleet of specialty craft made up of boats, each specifically designed for my angling needs. I would not be burdened by a "compromise boat" that performs many tasks marginally well, but no tasks perfectly. Even though a personal fleet of eight to ten boats is a complete fantasy, I still think it is important to focus on the *ideal* boat for specific situations. By doing this you will better understand your design requirements, even if you ultimately have to choose a compromise boat. My fleet of specialty boats would have to include the following:

Aluminum Johnboat

Hickory shad begin to make their annual runs up the coastal rivers of North Carolina in late February. I break out my fly rods and light spinning gear and hope for good water conditions. By mid-April hickory shad give way to white shad, which are in turn followed by striped bass. All self-respecting light-tackle anglers on coastal rivers need a good aluminum johnboat with a welded hull to deal with rocks, stumps, and fluctuating river levels. My johnboat would be powered by an outboard motor with a short shaft, or perhaps even an outboard with a jet drive. It would have horizontal rod racks to protect my fly rods, and raised carpeted casting decks both fore and aft to make my

Lefty Kreh

A tough aluminum johnboat can take a lot of abuse, and take you to a lot of fish. Here, Bob Clouser (left) and Irv Swope cruise the Susquehanna.

metal craft more quiet. A 16- to 18-foot welded-aluminum johnboat is tough, but also light enough to be launched and retrieved easily on substandard boat ramps found along coastal rivers.

Pram

During the same time that shad and stripers are coming up the rivers, action in farm ponds and millponds in my region begins to heat up for largemouth bass, crappie, and a variety of sunfish. Since most farm ponds are not big enough for an outboard, and many millponds exclude powered vessels, I would have to have a good wooden pram in my fleet. A pram is a light, small (8 to 10 feet in length), stable rowboat that can be

Jim Wheeler

A pram will slide into a pickup truck and take you to stillwater action.

launched easily from a pickup truck, trailer, or car top. Prams can be rowed quietly and serve as the perfect fishing platform for fly and conventional tackle. Although a small aluminum boat with an electric motor would work in the same waters, a wooden pram with oars is quieter and far more sexy. There are not enough good wooden rowboats in the world today.

Modified-V Center Console

In the late spring and early summer, big bluefish and striped bass school up around the riprap and pilings of the Chesapeake Bay Bridge Tunnel. For this kind of fishing, my fleet would have a 20-foot fiberglass center console with a sharp forefoot to open up heavy seas and enough "Carolina Flare" to keep spray away from passengers. She would weigh just over 2,000 pounds and would be powered by a 150-horsepower outboard mounted on the transom. The boat would have the right amount of freeboard (the distance from the gunwale, also known as the gunnel, to the water) to handle heavy seas. Boats with excessively high profiles (too much freeboard) can be blown around easily by coastal breezes, a problem known as the "sail effect." Most important, my modified-V hull would provide a stable fishing platform at low speeds, while drifting, and at anchor. Deadrise (the angle of the boat's "V" measured at the centerline) at the stern would be 11 to 14 degrees. The boat would have a console high enough to offer some protection from the elements while under way, but low enough so as not to grab lines and plugs. The grab rails on my boat would be small and fly-line friendly, and all of the hardware, such as cleats and running lights, would be recessed to make movement in the boat easier and safer.

The Bass/Walleye Boat

Within a few hours of my house, in virtually all directions, there are large power and flood-control reservoirs. These lakes can offer excellent largemouth bass, hybrid, and striper fishing. In the higher elevations, many of the lakes hold good walleye and smallmouth bass populations. Although an 18-foot fiberglass bass boat makes a great fishing platform, with wide, stable fore and aft casting decks and low freeboard, I actually prefer something a little different. Some manufacturers are building bass/walleye boats that have the same raised decks, but with a little more freeboard and more V at the bow. These boats can easily handle the rough water that can arise on a large reservoir. My bass/walleye boat, also 18 feet in length, would be powered by an outboard between 90 and 115 horsepower. Such engines should provide top end speeds between 35 and 40 mph, plenty for any fishing trip. Like any good bass boat, it would have a

This 18-footer with higher freeboard than a typical bass boat can be used for bass, walleye, and coastal fishing.

There are plenty of great bass boats on the market that run well with smaller engines. Bass boats don't need 200-horsepower engines.

bow-mounted electric trolling motor to maneuver along shorelines.

I am fully aware of the 20-foot rigs with sports car–like interiors and 250-horsepower engines capable of pushing them in excess of 70 mph. Although many of these "muscle boats" are extremely well made, I prefer to leave them in the showroom. Fine boats, yes, but not necessary for angling enjoyment or safety on any lake.

Drift Boat

In my part of the country there are several excellent trout rivers and smallmouth bass rivers that can be fished well only with a good drift boat. The western drift boat, also known as the "McKenzie" drift boat, is a wonderful craft for anglers who like to move with the current over several miles of water. The

Theo Copeland

Drift boats, like these on the Watauga River, provide a perfect platform for trout and smallmouth angling.

Watauga River on the North Carolina–Tennessee border, and the New River in West Virginia are both great stretches of water where drift boats can be used for trout and smallmouth. On slow stretches and in unproductive water, drift boats can be rowed easily, even by a desk jockey like me. In rough water they can be maneuvered around boulders and through tight places because their designs make quick turns and maneuvering possible. Casting is made easy for anglers because of knee braces both fore and aft of the oarsman. Finally, these boats have the ability to take anglers through white-knuckle rapids with a high degree of safety. As will be discussed later, these craft have many of the same design features as the seagoing dories of New England. I would use my drift boat only a few times a year, but no other boat compares when fishing large, fast rivers.

Flats Boat

During the hottest part of the summer, from mid-July through mid-September, coastal flats and marshes are seen by many as inhospitable places. It is during this time, however, that I like to pole quietly along the edge of the great Spartina marshes of our region. Redfish, also known as red drum or channel bass, love to search the shallows for crabs, shrimp, and mud minnows. Only a flats boat will do the job here. I would want a flats boat 16 to 18 feet in length and no more than seven hundred pounds (without engine). An outboard of 50 to 70 horsepower would serve my purposes well, especially since my boat would have trim tabs to get me on plane more quickly and at lower speeds.

A flats boat, as has already been mentioned, has a very low profile and is not affected by the wind. My flats boat would draw no more than eight inches of water with the outboard motor tilted out of the water. Even though I have often taken aluminum johnboats in the marsh, the flats boat would be made of

Hal Chittum

Flats boats for redfish should be able to work in extremely shallow water.

fiberglass or composite materials, which tend to make less noise (less hull slap) while being poled.

Many so-called flats boats available today are 18 to 22 feet in length and wear outboards with 150 horsepower or more. Such large flats boats, with their heavy engines, often draw well over a foot of water and are, for me, no fun to pole. They often work fine with twin electric trolling motors, but I would want a boat I can pole.

Canoe

During the summer months, some of the rivers in eastern North Carolina offer some extraordinary fishing for long-eared sunfish. Although many prefer a fly rod with popping bugs, traditionalists like to fish for long-eared sunfish with a cane pole and crickets. These beautiful fish are found in the tannin-stained rivers that meander around giant thousand-year-old cypress trees. On such rivers the best way to get around is in a canoe. I'd have a beamy (wide) 17-foot canoe with a tiny bit of V in the bottom. Such a boat would track well when covering longer stretches and provide the stability necessary for casting to these jewels of the backwater.

Flat-Bottomed Skiff

Because I have two children under ten years of age, a kid-friendly boat is a must. No boat works better in protected coastal waters for family fishing than a flat-bottomed open skiff. These boats are incredibly stable and offer kids "room to roam." The design is based on traditional coastal work boats that, depending on the region, may be called a pirogue, bateau, punt, or garvey.

Along with being great family boats, an open flat-bottomed skiff also makes a fabulous drift boat for flounder. They are also

A flat-bottomed skiff is a stable platform for drift fishing and family fun.

a top choice of anglers specializing in weakfish, locally known as sea trout. The freeboard on these boats is greater than the freeboard of a flats boat, but less than the freeboard found on a modified-V center console—just the right height for playing and landing flounder and sea trout. My skiff, made of fiberglass, would be 18 to 19 feet in length, and powered by a 50- to 70-horsepower engine. I admit that this member of my fleet would get you a little wet going through a chop, but no other boat offers more open, stable casting space while drifting or at anchor.

A 25-Foot Walk-Around

After Thanksgiving, water conditions on the North Carolina coast can range from balmy to savage. Most anglers hang up their tackle and foul-weather gear with the first cold blast of winter. It is during this time of the year, however, that my answering machine is often filled with messages about the giant

A rig with a walk-around cabin and twin engines is good for any season, especially when the weather turns cold and nasty.

stripers and bluefish just outside Oregon Inlet. The last boat in my fleet would be a 25-footer with a "walk-around" cabin, which has some of the attributes of a center console and a small cabin cruiser. I much prefer a walk-around to the more common cuddy cabin because a walk-around allows anglers easier movement from bow to stern. Even though I like open boats and clear decks, I am a realist. In December and January I don't mind using a fly rod or spinning gear off the bow or stern of a boat with a cabin. After catching a large striper in cold weather, I want to celebrate with a cup of hot coffee out of the weather.

My big boat would have 14 to 18 degrees of deadrise at the stern and a sharp, flared bow, both of which are necessary for Oregon Inlet, one of the nastiest on the East Coast. This is the only boat that would require significant power. For this boat I would want twin 150- to 200-horsepower outboards. Because winter fishing often takes place when water temperatures are 50 degrees or below, I'd want the insurance policy of an extra engine to get me out of trouble and back home.

Only in my fantasy fishing world can I have a fleet with all the boats I want and need. In the real world most of us are limited to one, or perhaps two good boats, to fill our fishing needs. There is no perfect boat for all fish and all water conditions. There are boats, however, that will give you a broader range of options than other boats. Be sure that in choosing a "compromise boat" you don't end up with a boat that is unsuitable for your favorite kind of fishing and the water conditions that you normally encounter. Remember: Too many anglers buy boats for the fishing they *might* do, rather than for the fishing they *usually* do.

Before moving on, I make only one request: Unless you are very familiar with a boat, try it before you buy it. It seems absolutely incredible to me that many people buy boats, especially powerboats, costing many thousands of dollars, without ever taking them for a test run. Give yourself time to buy the right boat. You should insist on running the boat you intend to buy, or a factory demo. Run the boat at all speeds. Turn the engine off and walk around. Is it the stable platform you want? Does it have enough freeboard, or too much? Are the storage areas adequate and accessible?

In the chapters ahead I will discuss in some detail your choices in powerboats and in human-powered boats. I will examine hull designs, interior layouts, and accessories. All of these topics will be reviewed with one thing in mind: fishability. I will try to give you the tools to cut through the hype and hoopla so that you can find the right boat for your needs, or modify your present boat for even greater fishing enjoyment.

II

POWERBOATS

3

Hull Designs for the Ocean, Bays, Flats, Rivers, and Lakes

For many boating anglers, the least understood yet most important feature on any craft is the hull. The wrong hull can jar your teeth, pound your knees, leave you soaked, and turn you green. The right hull can give you a soft, dry ride, a stable angling platform, and security. The hull makes the boat!

Almost all small-powered fishing boats have planing hulls, as opposed to displacement hulls, which are found on many large boats. The bow forefoot (the sharp, cleaving front of the bow) of boats with displacement hulls, such as trawler yachts, stays in the water. I know that there is a category of semidisplacement hulls in which the bow forefoot almost clears the water. In my world, fishing boats either get on plane or they don't. Hulls are either displacement or planing, and I see little reason to nitpick about the gray in-between. With planing hulls the forward part of the bow clears the water, allowing much of the hull to move over the water, not *through* it. The planing qualities of a hull are determined by a combination of its design, weight, and available power. Anything, even a rock, can be planed if enough power is applied, but not all hulls are made for planing. Planing hulls are generally faster than displacement hulls. As a boat rises on plane, less of the surface area of the hull is affected by water resistance. High-performance planing hulls are designed so that very little of the hull is touching the water at top speeds.

Planing hulls appear to be a relatively simple combination of straight, curved, or rounded surfaces. When you add speed, weight, and waves, each of the different planing hull shapes will react in a different way. In the late 1980s a friend of mine pulled into a marina near my house with a gorgeous green-and-white center console about 23 feet in length. When he and his angling partner asked if I would like to join them for a day of fishing on his new boat, I jumped at the chance. The boat was powered by a large single outboard and was by all standards a deep-V design.

Even at the marina I noticed that the boat leaned to the left and then to the right as people moved back and forth across the deck. When under power, a shift of one person caused the boat to heel over excessively. When we finally reached the ocean, the constant side-to-side motion of that boat would have tested the stomach and sea legs of even the toughest Navy SEAL. To this day, I have never been on a fishing boat more "tender" than that center console. Because it had a deep hull and pitched excessively, was it prone to turn over? It may surprise you that a "tender" boat like that one has what is known as a great deal of *reserve stability.* This boat with its deep, narrow hull, however, had almost no *initial stability.* That deep-V center console was never going to turn over, but it was going to roll unmercifully in almost any water.

The opposite of a deep-V hull with great reserve stability would be a lightweight flat-bottom boat. A flat-bottom boat with low, straight sides possesses great initial stability but almost no reserve stability. Think about standing up in a light, flat-bottomed johnboat. In calm water you can probably walk around such a boat while it remains seemingly stable and completely flat. However, such a boat can be "stiff" and snap, or turn over easily, once enough weight and force is applied to one side, or when it is placed at an excessive angle by a wave. Ideally, most good fishing boats, especially those used by light-tackle and fly anglers who move around while casting, possess a combination of initial stability and reserve stability. For the angler, boats that possess only reserve stability can get you drunk, while those possessing only initial stability can get you dunked.

Boats with Flat Bottoms

Now that I have raised the issue of stability, let me quickly add that each hull form has its strengths and weaknesses, and each is

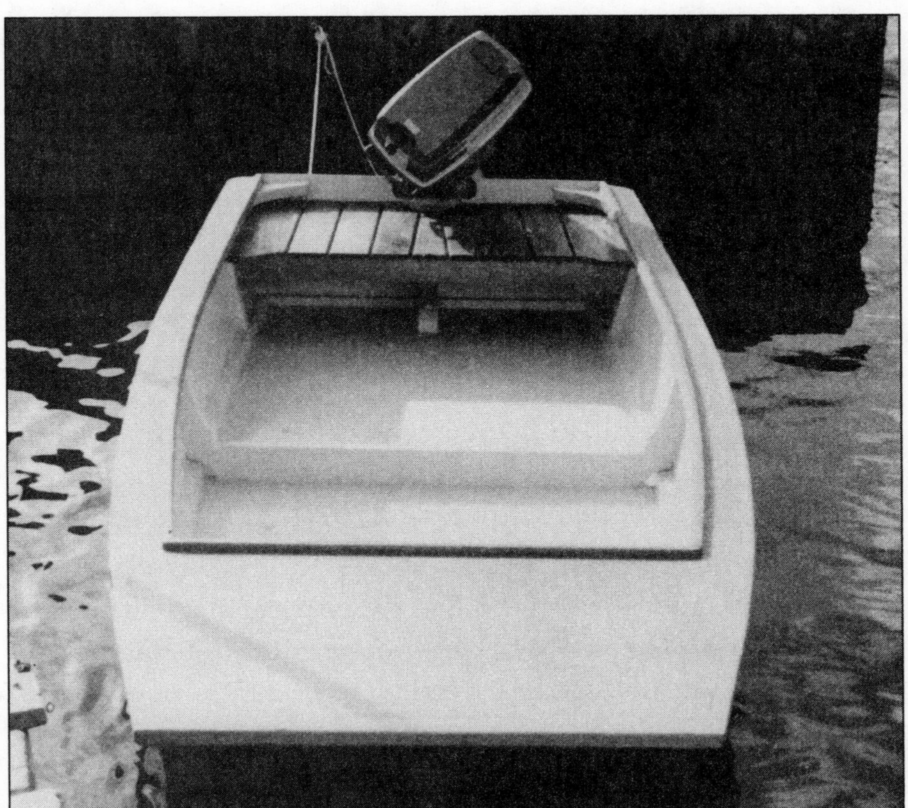

Barry Kanavy

Flat-bottomed wooden craft have long been used as workboats and for fishing.

D. L. Goddard

One of the most popular flat-bottomed boats in use today is the aluminum johnboat.

well suited for certain types of water and fishing conditions. Flat-bottom boats have been around since man first sat on a floating board. There are many old forms of flat-bottom boats, such as the scow, a flat-bottom boat with vertical sides. Many people are surprised to learn that the dory, with its pointed bow and high, flared sides, is also a flat-bottom boat. Another old design is the punt, an old flat-bottom design with a little "rocker" (a slight upturn) at the bow end and slightly rounded sides. All of these old boat designs were originally made of wood. Many of the popular fiberglass flat-bottom boats available today are variations of the old punt design. It should be noted that many boats in the flat-bottom category may have a slight "V" or a slightly rounded bottom.

Just because a boat has a flat bottom doesn't mean that it possesses only initial stability. Punts, with their rounded sides and lifting bow, can possess some reserve stability as well as initial stability. Dories have initial stability, but also excellent reserve stability because of their flared sides. Few small boats have a greater reputation for seaworthiness than the dory.

Flat-bottom powerboats occupy an important niche in the angling world. Weight distribution and design can give them some reserve stability along with their tremendous initial stability. They are ideal platforms for the fly rodder and light-tackle fisherman because they have lots of open space. They can be run on plane with relatively low horsepower motors since there is no "cutting" hull resting deep in the water that needs to be lifted out and held on plane. For several years, I operated a 19-foot fiberglass flat-bottom boat with a 50-horsepower, and now a 70-horsepower, engine with wonderful results. It is a great fishing platform and family boat that also offers excellent fuel economy and the ability to run in relatively shallow water.

Along with many benefits, there are a few problems that come with a flat-hulled powerboat. The most noticeable problem is their tendency to pound in a chop, because they do not have a sharp bow or V bottom to cut through the waves. Longer flat-bottom boats tend to pound less in a chop since they can bridge waves without pounding. Over the years I have noticed that flat-bottom boats under 17 feet—whether fiberglass or aluminum—tend to be more prone to pounding in a normal chop. Those 19 feet and over do a better job of bridging chop, thus providing a smoother ride.

Another problem with some flat-bottom boats is their tendency to slide in a turn. This can be especially dangerous around other moving boats in a confined area. Some boatbuilders utilizing different solutions have solved the problem. One solution is to incorporate several straight-line strakes (raised ridges) running the full length of the hull, which give the hull a little "bite." Another solution is a skeg (a small keel-like fin), which also enhances the operator's ability to turn and maneuver.

Many variations of the flat-bottomed boat can be found in fiberglass.

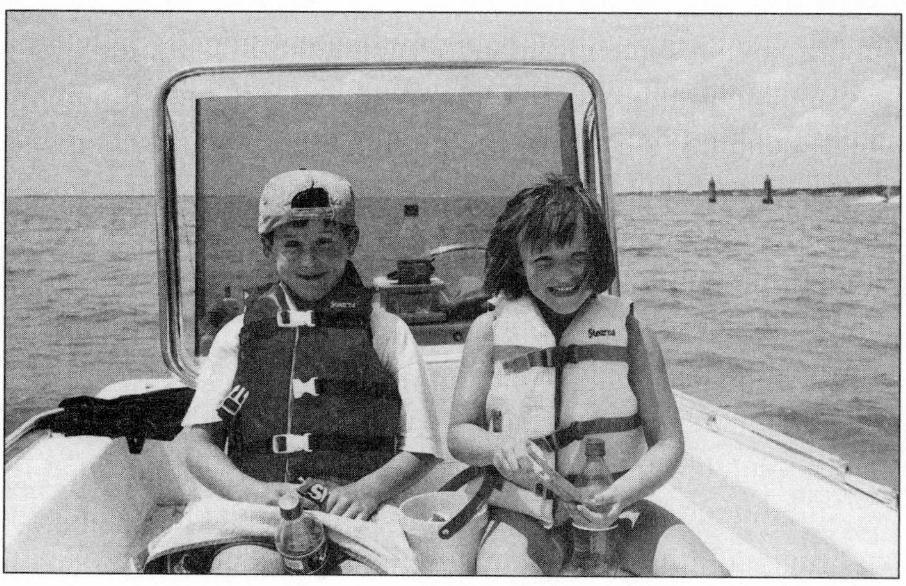

Flat-bottomed skiffs are great fishing boats, but they can work equally well as a family picnic boat.

While discussing flat-bottom boats, I must mention again the low-cost and extremely durable aluminum johnboats. Whether welded or riveted, aluminum johnboats occupy an important position in the world of light-tackle angling. Because they are not as heavy as a similar-size fiberglass flat-bottom boat, aluminum johnboats can be run with even less horsepower. Also, because they weigh less, they draw less water (have less displacement) and therefore have the ability to operate effectively in obstacle-strewn rivers. Please remember, however, that because these boats are lighter, have less displacement, and possess little reserve stability, they are more prone to capsize if too much weight is shifted to one side.

Finally, a chapter on powered flat-bottom boats would not be complete without some mention of powered dories. Both in the Northeast and in the Northwest some boatbuilders have

This model has a small finlike keel to give it "bite" so it will not slide in turns.

Dory-type boats have flat bottoms for stability and flared sides to keep the sea out. They also require less horsepower than a V-hulled boat.

taken the old flared-side dory form and added an outboard motor instead of oars. Again, because it is a flat-bottom boat, a powered dory does not need a tremendous amount of horsepower. These are excellent boats in light to moderate seas, and provide a safe, seaworthy option for the small-boat angler.

To V or Not to V

The next time you pass a four- or five-story dry-stack boat storage building, ask for permission to go inside and look at hulls from underneath. The vast majority of boats will have a V hull of some type. Boats will have a sharper V at the bow than at the stern. When you look at the sterns of a number of boats, you will notice that the angle of the V at the stern, the deadrise, will

Most of the boats in this dry-stack storage facility have V-hulls, from modified to deep V. The chine, the flat or turned-down area where the sides meet the hull, and the strakes, ridges on the hull, help provide lift.

vary from boat to boat. Those with a sharper V, an angle of 18 to 20 degrees or more, will be considered deep-V hulls. A deadrise of less than 15 degrees will be considered a modified-V or semi-V hull.

While looking at boats in the dry-stack facility, also look at the chines and strakes. The chine is where the sides of the boat meet the hull. The design of the chine has much to do with dryness and stability. Strakes are elongated ridges running lengthwise from the bow toward the stern that can add lift to help bring the boat on plane more quickly, and also provide a drier ride.

A true deep V hull carries extreme deadrise from the stern all the way to the bow. Again, angles of approximately 18 degrees or more at the stern are considered to be deep-V hulls. These boats are noted for their soft rides in choppy seas. Because so much of the hull is underwater while at rest, a boat with a deep V requires more power than other boats to lift it and keep it on plane. The engine or engines must literally push or lift much of the heavy, wedge-shaped hull out of the water as it gains speed. Even where the hull weight of deep-V boats has been lightened by the use of modern high-tech materials, significant horsepower is still required because of the hull shape.

In order to guarantee a stable ride at medium and high speeds, almost all deep-V hulls now utilize trim tabs on the transom on each side of the engine or engines. Trim tabs are flat metal plates, attached at the base of the transom, that can raise or lower the bow, and provide lateral stability as the boat moves under power. Without trim tabs, deep-V hulls have a tendency to lay over on one of the flats of the hull while under power. When a boat flips or changes from side to side, the motion is called "chine walking," and is not much fun. However, chine walking on well-designed deep-V hulls equipped with trim tabs is not a common problem.

Deep-V hulls were originally developed for rough offshore racing. They will soften a tough ocean, but for me they do not offer the type of fishing platform that I most enjoy. As a light-tackle angler, much of my fishing is done from a slow-moving, drifting, or anchored boat. It is under these conditions that a deep-V hull does not perform well as a fishing boat. Remember, these hulls possess tremendous reserve stability, but offer little initial stability . . . too much rock and roll.

Modified-V Hulls

A significant portion of all powerboat hulls falls into the modified-V category. There are so many variations of the modified-V hull that it would be hard to get complete agreement from any panel of experts as to which boats actually fit into this category. Generally speaking, however, modified-V boats have a sharp, cleaving bow with significant deadrise, but when you reach the stern of the boat the V, or deadrise, has diminished to somewhere between 5 and 15 degrees. The effect of less deadrise at the stern means that the boat has more stability at rest than when moving slowly. A modified-V hull has both the initial stability of a flat-bottom boat and some of the reserve stability of a deep-V hull. Owners of modified-V hulls like to think that their boats offer the best of both worlds. There is a lot of truth to this line of thinking. A modified-V hull and its variations have many of the sea-calming qualities of a deep V, but also provide the stable platform found in flat-bottom rigs.

Remember also that because the hull is flatter at the stern, less horsepower will be required than with a deep-V hull, and the modified V should also run and float in shallower water. The 20-foot center console I am currently using has 14 degrees of deadrise at the stern. Even with 150 horsepower bolted to the transom, it still floats in water approximately twelve inches deep

A modified-V hull has a deadrise of less than 18 degrees.

with the motor tilted up. For many light-tackle anglers, especially those who fish coastal inshore waters and large inland lakes, a modified-V boat is often the "compromise" that works. Boats with modified-V hulls are available with low freeboard and high freeboard, depending on the type of water in which it is to be used.

As with deep-V hulls mentioned earlier, most well-designed modified-V hulls also have properly positioned running strakes that help provide additional lift. Many boats also have flat chines or even slightly reversed chines that help knock down the seas while running. In all V boats the position and shape of the chines has much to do with stability at low speeds and whether the boat will give you a dry ride. Also, as with deep-V hulls, many manufacturers install trim tabs on modified-V boats to help them get on plane more quickly and to help anglers adjust the attitude (trim) of the boat while running (more on trim in the next chapter).

Performance Hulls and Planing Wedges

Another variation of the V hull, both the deep-V and modified-V form, is the planing wedge or "pad" modification. Beginning at the middle of the boat and extending back to the stern, the V of the hull is actually cut off or flattened, leaving a long, fairly narrow wedge. Some high-performance hulls used by tournament fishermen in fresh and salt water utilize the wedge, or pad modification, to gain extra speed. When you see one of these boats running wide open on flat water, the front half of the boat is often com-

Tournament-type bass boats often utilize a "pad" modification.

pletely out of the water. The boat is actually planing with only the wedge, or pad, in contact with the water. To give lateral stability, the boat is supported by port and starboard trim tabs.

The wedge is most often seen on high-performance bass boats. Some of the larger flats boats also utilize the cut-down V, or wedge, to enhance speed. Virtually all of the boats in this category require large engines.

Flats Boat Hulls

Twenty years ago I could tell you what the hull on a typical flats boat looked like, but not anymore. Manufacturers from Texas to New England are now making flats boats that utilize a variety of hull designs. Some flats boats are fiberglass flat-bottomed skiffs or aluminum johnboats with poling towers. Some are modified-V boats with significant V at the bow and a slight (5 to 8 degrees) deadrise at the stern. Many have a V bow with deadrise diminishing to almost nothing at the stern. As mentioned above, a few so-called flats boats are simply tournament-speed hulls with the pad or wedge design. Some boats designed for use in shallow water have tunnel-drive hulls (a concave indentation from the stern to the middle of the boat) that allow propellers to turn in very shallow water, behind the tunnel and not beneath the hull.

Regardless of what hull form is utilized, any self-respecting flats boat should be able to *float* with the engine up (along with anglers and gear) in ten inches of water or less. There are lots of boats being marketed as flats boats with hulls that need fourteen inches of water just to float. This is especially true of flats boats that utilize heavy, six-cylinder outboards and also carry a couple of fifty-pound trolling batteries. Heavy engines can make a stern squat and draw more water.

The flats-boat hulls I enjoy fishing the most have a V bow and little deadrise at the stern. They pole well, run shallow (if not too heavy), and track straight. All good flats boats need a pair of trim tabs to help them get on plane quickly.

Tri-Hulls or Cathedral Hulls

Tri-hulls, or cathedral hulls, have been around for a long time. They provide a wonderfully stable platform, track well in the water, and have a lot of initial stability and adequate reserve stability. There are very few anglers who have been around the water for more than twenty years who couldn't immediately identify the hull of an old Boston Whaler. The old Whaler hull and similar hulls of other manufacturers are still very popular in fresh and salt water. My first great fishing boat was a 17-foot tri-hull with a 50-horsepower motor. It provided a spacious, stable platform for fly fishing and plug casting. I fished it with an electric motor at the bow in many large reservoirs for both largemouth bass and stripers. It was also light enough that I was able

Tri-hulls are stable fishing platforms but offer a wet ride.

to pole it from the bow around coastal marshes while searching for redfish and spotted weakfish. With its three small V hulls in the water, it took me to artificial reefs as far as ten miles offshore to catch king mackerel, amberjack, and even a sailfish. My little tri-hull had a livewell and adequate rod storage for both conventional gear and nine-foot fly rods. Another bonus of the tri-hull was that it didn't need a lot of horses to get it up to speed.

It was such a good fishing boat that I hardly realized I got soaked every time I took it out. Yes, the big drawback to tri-hulls is that they pound in rough water and can produce a tremendous amount of spray. I also blame it for my bad knees caused by the pounding I took over a five-year period. Still, I wish I had it back!

Catamarans

Outboard-powered catamarans have been around the fishing world for a long time, but it is only in recent years that they have gained great popularity in American waters. Catamarans are finding their greatest use in coastal waters and in large lakes because of their ability to offer a smooth ride in a heavy chop.

I have both operated and been a passenger on a number of catamarans, often referred to as sea cats, in the 20- to 27-foot range. All of them were powered by twin outboards. These boats offer the angler incredibly smooth rides and plenty of room to roam, since the decks on these boats are often eight feet across.

Depending on your perspective, their height off the water is either a drawback or a benefit. Because the deck sits over two hulls with a tunnel between them, it is possible to feel that you are fishing off a pier high above the water. The decks on conventional boats are generally much closer to the water. If you enjoy catch-and-release fishing, you will find it difficult to reach a fish with your hands unless you go to the platform between the engines. In their defense, however, I have lots of friends who like the height of sea cats and feel they offer great visibility, since you are almost as high off the water as you would be on a poling platform of a flats boat.

One characteristic of the catamaran-type hull that I have never gotten used to is the "riding on rails" feeling. When you

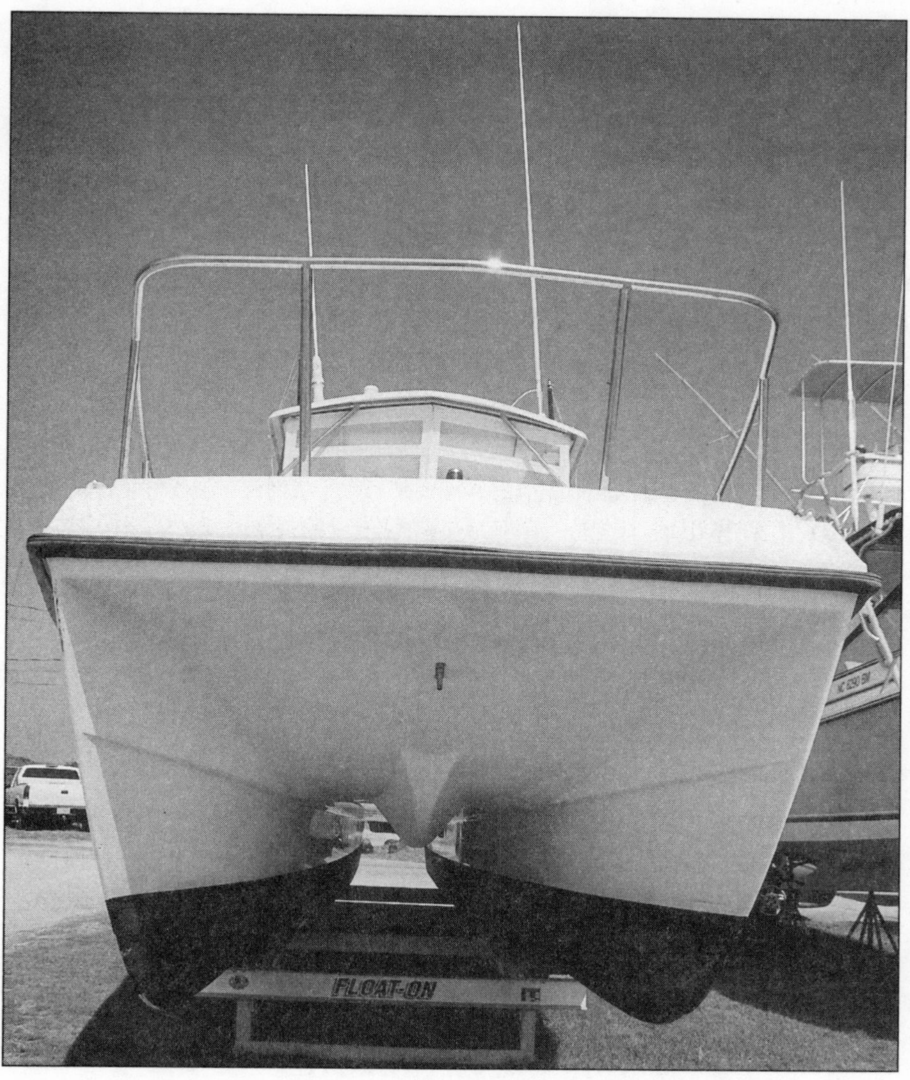

Catamarans give a smooth ride in heavy chop, but have a different "feel" than monohulled boats.

turn a sea cat, it does not lean into the water in the same way that a monohull makes a turn. In a turn, the deck of a catamaran stays level. During my fist rides on catamarans, I felt as if I was going to be launched from the deck each time we turned. Like anything new, the ride of the sea cat takes some getting used to. Once you get used to the ride, however, catamarans provide space, stability, and comfort. What more could an angler want, except maybe a deck closer to the water?

Sea catamarans are not cheap, and don't forget that they normally require two engines. Again, however, in their favor, catamarans do not generally require the high-horsepower engines usually seen on a large, deep-V hull. Also, even when one of two engines is disabled, many sea catamarans track well.

Round-Bottom Boat

The least common hull shape utilized by small powerboat anglers is the round-bottom hull, although round bottoms are common on canoes and dinghies. The round-bottom hull, also known as a U-shaped hull, provides less pounding than a typical semi-V, and much less than will be experienced on a flat-bottom or tri-hull boat. Round-hull boats have a "slower roll" in big seas and offer little or no "snap" as compared with hulls that have a chine where the sides come together with the hull. Round hulls in a planing powerboat typically have very little deadrise at the stern. Even though a round-bottom boat will have a slow roll in big seas, anglers should feel good knowing that they possess plenty of reserve stability, although not as much initial stability as most of us would like. If you live in an area where rough waters are common, don't pass up the opportunity to look at round-bottom hulls and their variations. These are safe, soft-riding fishing platforms.

Each of the major hull types and their variations mentioned above occupies an important niche in the world of light-tackle angling and fly fishing. Some hulls, most notably the modified-V, are more adaptable than others to different types of fishing and water conditions. Please remember, however, that no matter how well your hull is designed, poor distribution of the weight of fuel tanks, livewells, batteries, and gear can cause a hull to perform poorly. In the next chapter we will look at trimming a boat properly so that you can get maximum advantage from your hull.

4

The Mystery of Trim

As discussed earlier, most of the small powerboats used by sportfishermen have planing hulls. No matter what shape of hull you have chosen, never forget that there are always forces working to keep your boat out of trim. Remember when your heavy uncle Albert and his equally heavy friend insisted on sitting near the bow of your boat? Their weight caused the bow to plough and the stern to rise. When the bow of a boat is forced down by weight and the stern rises, it will not handle well. Boats in this predicament are often said to feel "squirrelly." Also, remember the time you placed two trolling batteries in the stern of your boat, and filled the stern baitwell? That extra weight, along with uncle Albert and his friend, who moved to the back of the boat, caused the stern to squat and the bow to rise. Whenever there is poor weight distribution in a boat, there will be trim problems.

A number of years ago a good friend of mine had a boat with two permanently installed fuel tanks, one on each side of

Roth-Built Boats

In most powerboats the point of balance is approximately three-fifths the length of the boats' waterline, aft of the bow.

his boat under the gunnels. When heading home after a day on the water, I often saw his boat ahead of me leaning to the left or to the right. If the boat was heeling over to the right, it meant that he had used fuel from the left tank. With the right tank full, and heavy, and the left tank empty, the boat was out of trim. This type of problem also occurs when a couple of your buddies insist on sitting on the gunnel on the same side of the boat, causing the boat to heel over. These are problems of lateral trim.

Most of the time problems of trim in a fishing boat are merely a nuisance. However, a poorly loaded lightweight boat is a safety problem. The operator of a fishing boat has the responsibility to make sure it is properly trimmed before leaving the dock. All sources of weight must be considered and secured: extra gasoline tanks, an ice chest full of drinks, tackle boxes, water in livewells, trolling-motor batteries, camping gear, and your uncle Albert. Weight should be carefully distributed fore and aft of the boat's center of buoyancy. In most fishing boats, this is a point of balance approximately three-fifths the length of the boat's waterline aft of the bow, *not* the center of the boat. Look at the location of seating in most boats, whether bass boat, center console, or johnboat. The primary seating area will usually be behind the boat's physical center and directly over the center of buoyancy. Proper trim of any fishing boat begins with a good loading job. Also, don't forget to unload the entire boat periodically. Storage areas in most boats tend to accumulate extra anchors, bottled drinks, extra oil, reels, and tools that add weight and make the boat more difficult to trim.

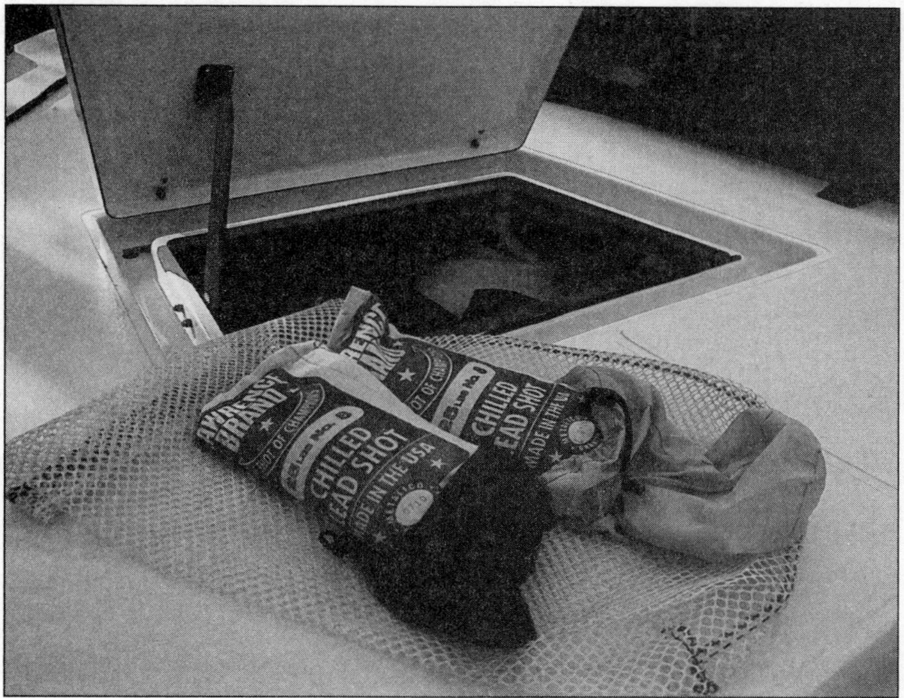

To trim his flats skiff when poling alone the author places 100 pounds of lead shot in the bow. Without added weight the boat would be stern heavy.

D. L. Goddard

Whenever possible, weight should be placed close to the centerline of a boat.

Trimming the Motor

Most of the powerboats used by light-tackle anglers are pushed either by an outboard or an inboard/outboard unit. Many boats now come with power trim, which allows the operator to change the angle of the drive unit and the propeller. Outboard motors that do not have power trim can usually be adjusted manually.

Under perfect conditions, which rarely exist, when weight distribution in your boat is ideal, the driveshaft and propeller will be at a 90-degree angle to the forward motion of the boat. When you have too much weight on your stern, you can lift it out of the water by "trimming in" the drive unit and propeller. When the motor is trimmed in, it is no longer vertical but *angled toward* the transom. Also, when the motor is trimmed in, it can help the boat get on plane faster.

During situations in which you have too much weight in the bow and want to lift the bow out of the water, you can "trim out" your lower unit. A trimmed-out motor will be *angled away* from the transom. If the motor is trimmed out too much, the boat will begin "porpoising," a constant rising and falling of the bow while under way. The great thing about power trim on your engine, whether it be an outboard or inboard/outboard unit, is that you can constantly adjust the trim of the motor in response to a change in weight distribution, or to raise the bow when you encounter heavy seas.

Trim Tabs

One of the most significant accessories that can be added to a powered fishing boat is a set of trim tabs. Trim tabs can either be electric or hydraulic. They are especially useful in helping a boat get on plane more quickly by adding instant stern lift. They can be especially useful for a flats boat that needs help in getting up on plane in shallow water. The stern lift is also important when you want to get out of a "hole" when running a tricky inlet.

Trim tabs can be extended out from the transom or placed in slots under the transom.

Another extremely important use of trim tabs is that they help to maintain lateral trim. If your boat is heeling over to one side because of the extra weight of an angler keeping the boat out of trim, you can adjust the tab on one side to level the boat. Trim tabs are also useful in adjusting the attitude of the boat in undesirable sea conditions. For example, you can raise the bow on one side of the boat to give you and your passengers more protection when heading into quartering seas.

Almost any planing hull, whether a flat or V hull, can benefit from trim tabs. Tabs can more than pay for themselves in fuel savings alone. A poorly trimmed boat is a gas-guzzler. By using trim tabs to correct problems of "squatting" or "plowing," the engine doesn't have to work as hard, which makes it more fuel efficient. Also, since trim tabs extend the running surface of a boat, most boats can stay on plane at speeds several miles an hour below normal planing speed, again providing greater fuel efficiency.

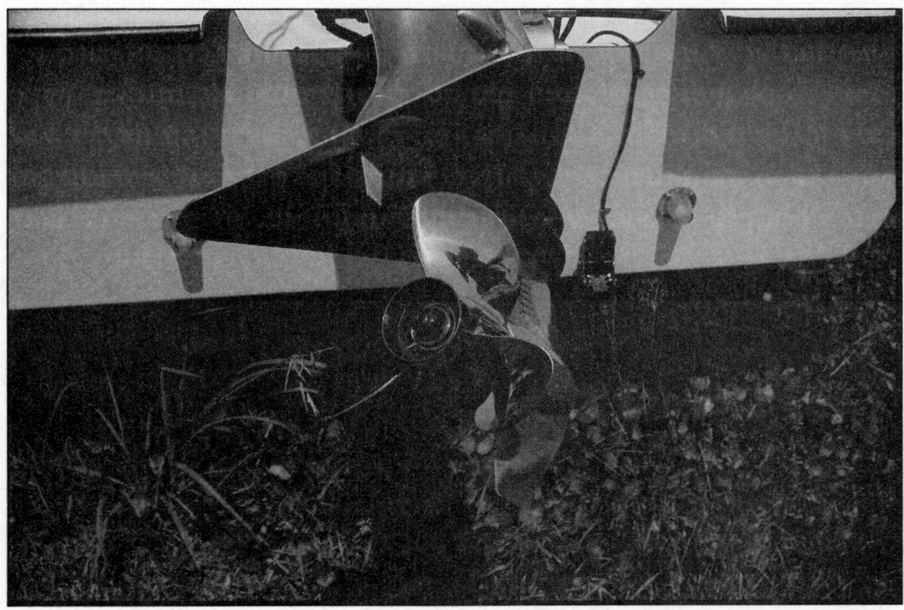

Attachments are available for the anticavitation plate that can add extra lift, much like trim tabs.

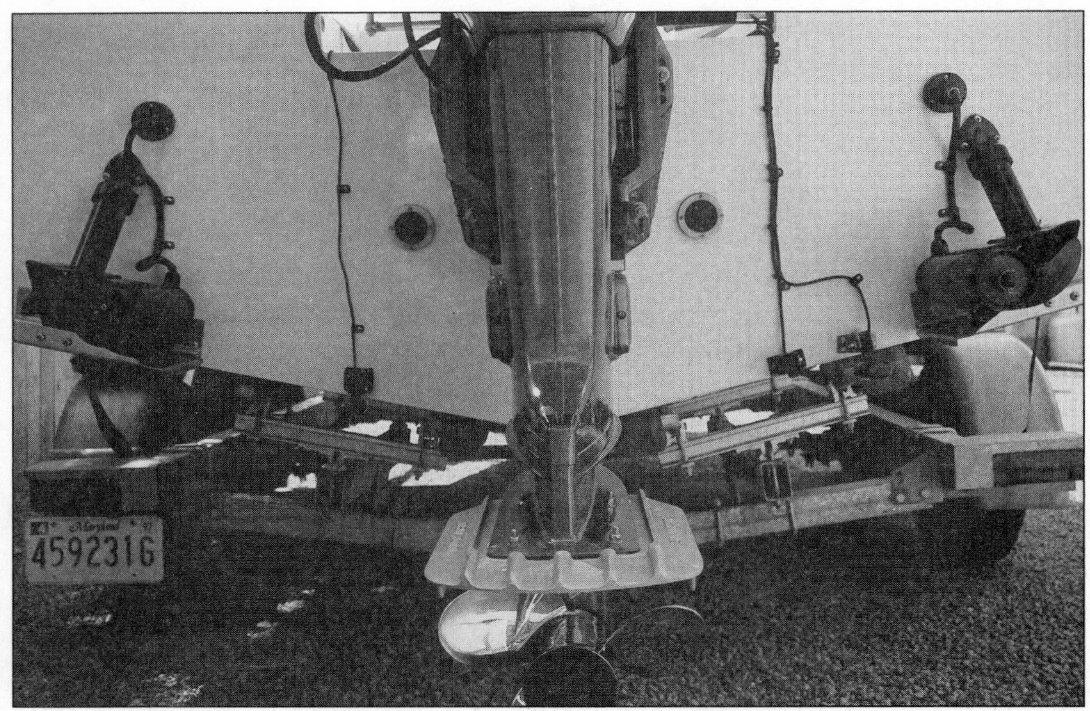

Bruce Foster

Although I am a strong proponent of trim tabs, tabs can be used by manufacturers to cover up flaws of a poorly designed hull or interior layout. For example, I have also seen boats that were permanently out of trim because the gas tanks were put in the wrong place, or the boat's console was too far forward or too far aft. Trim tabs should be used to improve a boat's performance, not to cover up flaws.

The Mini Rudder

At least one other trim problem is seldom considered by most anglers using outboards or stern drives. It is the torque problem. When propeller blades turn, they produce forward motion. The torque of the engine produces some extra side thrust, which can manifest itself in several ways. The unwanted side thrust can

Adjustment of the mini rudder can often solve torque related problems.

cause the boat to turn instead of maintaining a steady course. If you constantly have to fight the steering wheel of your boat to maintain a steady course, then you probably need to adjust your mini rudder. The mini rudder can be found under the anticavitation plate of most outboards or inboard/outboard units. If the boat tends to pull to the right, push the rear edge of the mini rudder to the right. If the boat pulls left, the mini rudder should go left. When the angle of the mini rudder is properly adjusted, you should no longer have to fight the wheel and the boat will maintain a steady course by itself.

A poorly trimmed boat can make for a sorry day of fishing. With a little effort, the ride and fuel efficiency of almost any boat can be improved. By redistributing weight, trimming your motor either manually or automatically, manipulating trim tabs, or adjusting the mini rudder, you can correct problems of trim. All your energy can then be devoted to fishing.

5

Weight, Materials, and Construction Techniques

Tied to a mooring stake behind my house on the North Carolina Outer Banks there is a 17-foot juniper skiff. Its owner, Captain Donald Willis, has used the boat almost without interruption since he and friends built it in 1964. This wooden boat, made of juniper strips, brass alloy nails, and a couple of coats of white paint, has all of its original wood. It gets an occasional cleaning and an extra coat of paint every couple of years, but because it is a working boat, it gets very little attention. But we've just entered a new millennium; wooden boats are out, right? Wood is old technology, and it rots. Try telling that to Captain Willis.

Now that we are in the "dot com" world and everything is lighter, smaller, and faster, I'm sure that you have heard that the early generation of fiberglass, commonly known as E-glass, and the old polyester resins that hold it together, are also out. They are too heavy and not as strong and stiff as the new materials now available to boatbuilders. However, if you look around a

Donald Willis's wooden skiff, made in 1964, is ready for work every day.

little bit, you will still see plenty of fiberglass fishing boats more than a quarter of a century old, bearing such names as Hewes, Ranger, Grady-White, Rabolo, Seacraft, and Boston Whaler. I mention Donald Willis's wooden boat and the boats of several manufacturers only to illustrate that a well-made and maintained boat can have an incredible life span, often significantly longer than the original owner wants to keep it.

That's why I get a chuckle out of reading the claims of manufacturers in magazines and listening to the spiels of salesmen at boat shows, both of which would have you believe that old technology is out. The boasts go something like this: "Our boats contain no wood, so they will never rot. They contain the same materials used to stop bullets and to make airplane wings. Nothing on the market compares . . ."

I am not a slave to old technology, and I am excited about the new materials available to boatbuilders. Although the latest high-tech materials and resins can add strength and reduce weight, I believe it is more important to focus on the builder and the designer of the boat. Quality materials can become a good boat only in the hands of a skilled builder or manufacturer. The same is true with other tools of the fisherman. For years fly fishermen and spin fishermen have been dazzled almost yearly by claims of faster, lighter rods made of high-modulus graphite held together by the latest resins. The fact is that even though most manufacturers are quite competent and make a very good rod, there are still some inferior, poorly designed rods on the market made with the latest materials. The same was true when bamboo was the king of rod-making materials. Some rod makers produced fishing tools of Stradivarius quality, while others working with bamboo produced rods that wouldn't make good tomato stakes.

Weight and Stiffness

I am currently using a 16-foot flats boat made from a variety of the latest materials including S-glass, graphite fiber, a foam core, and vinylester resins. It is a remarkable boat that can float in only four inches of water with the engine up, and its light weight (hull weight is around four hundred pounds) allows even an out-of-shape angler to poll it easily across coastal flats or along the edges of an inland lake dotted with bluegill beds. Do all flats boats need to be this light and draw so little water? Absolutely not. Boats made of more conventional materials and weighing a bit more should in no way be considered inferior craft. Heavier, wider flats boats, especially those equipped with electric motors, are preferred by many guides and anglers. The real beauty of the new materials is that they give builders the *option* of reducing weight, increasing strength, and improving performance when properly utilized.

Lightweight materials are also making it possible to reduce horsepower, and therefore fuel consumption. Although it is true that a lighter, stiffer hull needs less horsepower to perform well, an absence of weight can also create problems. Earlier in this book I discussed initial stability and reserve stability. An important factor in stability is weight. Weight in the right places, especially centered and below the waterline (ballast), can increase the stability of any fishing boat.

I've been in many situations where heavier is better. I like the soft ride and wave-cutting qualities of a heavier hull for rough water conditions. For example, I believe that a 21-foot boat with a modified-V hull, weighing around 2,400 pounds, will provide a better ride in a heavy chop than a boat of similar size and hull shape weighing hundreds of pounds less. In lighter boats I sometimes feel tossed about like a cork. Without weight and ballast, some extremely light boats tend to snap back into position too quickly. Again, however, it all depends on the needs of the angler and the water conditions that he or she is likely to fish.

Listed below are many of the materials commonly used to build fishing boats today. By weighing the pros and cons of various materials and construction techniques, I hope to add to your understanding of boat construction, and to help you make a better-informed decision the next time you write a check for a new fishing craft.

E-Glass

Although fiberglass was developed at the end of World War II, it wasn't until the mid-1960s that it became the premier material for building small fishing boats. Until then, wood and aluminum had been the materials of choice, but with fiberglass and resins, a builder could produce one identical hull after another from the same mold. Until very recently, people had little or nothing to complain about, since fiberglass was tough, long last-

Quality fiberglass hulls are "hand laid." Note that the darker areas in the mold mean extra glass and resin for strength in strategic places.

ing, and most important for weekend fishermen, it required very little maintenance. The fiberglass used to build fishing boats, known as E-glass, came in a variety of forms. It was, and still is, available to the boatbuilding world in many forms. E-glass can be fabricated into finely woven fiberglass cloth that is relatively thin and strong. A coarser E-glass cloth used in boatbuilding is called woven roving. Another common form of this material is known as chopped-strand mat; this is not a cloth, but it serves as an excellent filler and binder.

Quality fiberglass hulls are "hand laid," meaning that workers lay the right amount of cloth, roving, or mat into a mold with the right amount of resin. The fiberglass and resin are then rolled into the contours of the mold, hard enough to ensure adhesion, with tools that resemble paint rollers. If there is too little resin, the glass materials will not be properly "wetted" and will not adhere to the mold. If too much resin is used, the hull will be unnecessarily heavy. It is common for quality hulls to be made with alternating layers of glass cloth or roving separated by layers of chopped-strand mat. Many manufacturers also use a chopper gun to shoot chopped strands of fiberglass and resin over glass cloth or roving. Chopped-strand mat or glass fibers from a chopper gun can provide thickness and help bind woven layers of glass together. When E-glass cloth, roving, and strand mat are bound together in the mold by the right amount of polyester resin, a very formidable hull can be built. When a hull is built only with layers of fiberglass and resin, it is considered solid fiberglass.

From the very beginning, one of the major problems with solid E-glass hulls was that they were too flexible, an undesirable trait for hulls. The most common way of stiffening glass hulls was, and is, to add stringers that run the length of the boat hull. Stringers and the cross members separating them are much like the joists under the floor of your house that keep it from flexing when you walk on it. Marine-grade plywood wrapped in fiberglass is the most commonly used stringer material. When done right, plywood wrapped in fiberglass and resin should not rot. Some builders have developed stringer systems made of fiberglass and no wood. Both systems can work well. Builders have sought other ways of adding additional stiffness to hulls. It was soon found that when foam flotation is extruded into the spaces between the stringers it could provide multiple benefits. Closed-cell polyurethane foam provides flotation, is an excellent insulator, helps deaden sound, and provides additional rigidity by spreading the stringers.

Another method used to stiffen fiberglass is the use of "cores" laid in between layers of fiberglass. One of the early core materials, which is still widely used, is balsa wood. Now there are also expanded PVC foam cores, which provide lightweight

Hulls are stiffened with stringers, such as these made from marine-grade plywood and wrapped in fiberglass. The white is foam flotation.

strength that doesn't absorb water. When cores are used between layers of fiberglass, the result is a lighter, stiffer hull than can be produced with solid fiberglass.

It is important to remember that "old technology" E-glass is still an extraordinary building material. With it good builders can create strong, stiff hulls using a variety of stringer systems, coring, and foam flotation.

S-Glass, Kevlar, and Graphite

As has already been alluded to a number of times, there are newer, stronger, lighter, stiffer, and more expensive materials available to boatbuilders. For example, S-glass is a new generation of fiberglass that is significantly stronger and stiffer than its older cousin, E-glass. This glass is most often used in a unidirectional format. Fibers are aligned together in one direction so that they can be used to provide great strength where needed.

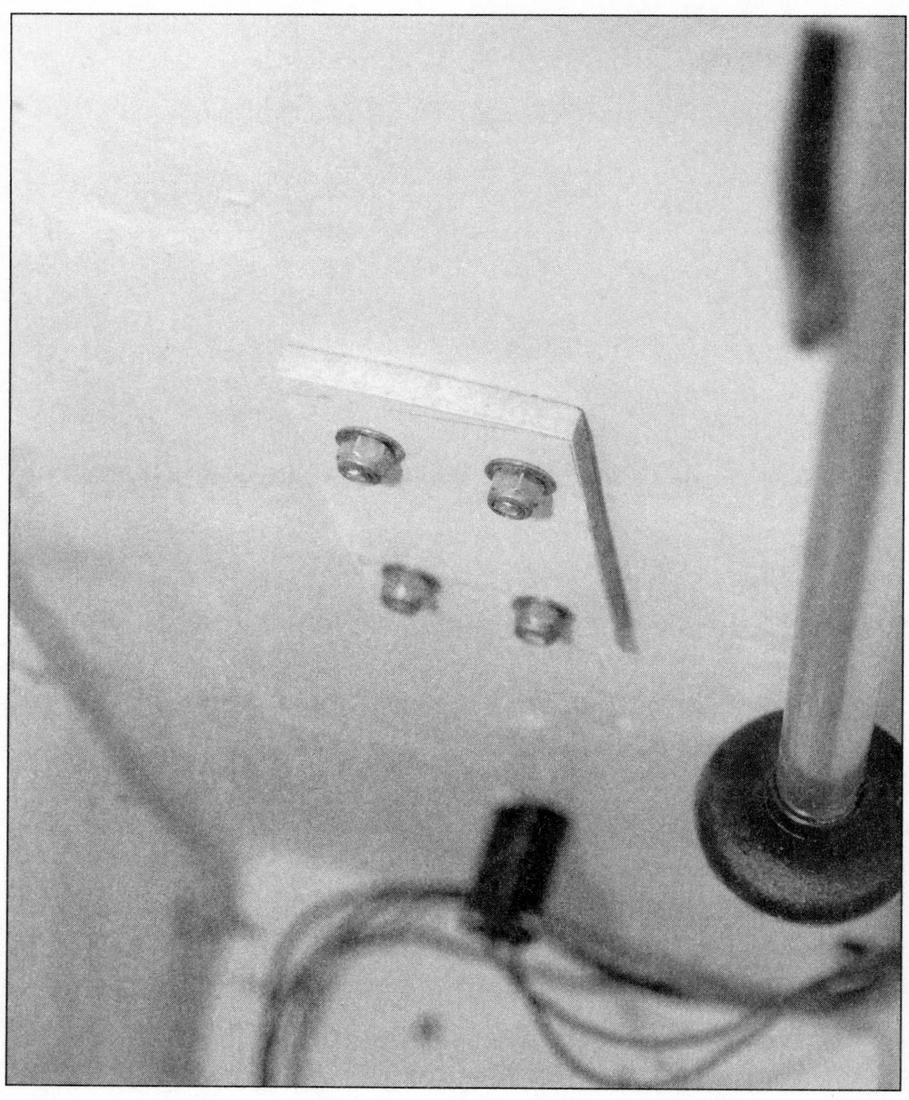

Whether a boat is built of E-glass, S-glass, carbon fiber, or Kevlar, external fittings, such as cleats, should be reinforced from behind.

S-glass is often used in conjunction with E-glass, or with high-tech Kevlar and graphite fibers.

Kevlar is the material known to most of us as the stuff with which bulletproof vests are made. Although Kevlar is much stronger and stiffer than E-glass, its big advantage is its toughness and abrasion resistance. Kevlar also resists fatigue better than fiberglass. Kevlar hulls and laminates have been around since the late 1970s. I first saw it used in flats boat hulls where weight is an important consideration.

All of us know carbon fiber, or graphite, as the material used to make our expensive fly rods, spinning rods, and plug rods. It has ten times the tensile strength of E-glass, but much more important, it also has about ten times the stiffness. It is this stiffness that makes it a hot material for boatbuilding, but for most fishing-boat hulls, is such extreme stiffness necessary?

It should not surprise you that there are only a few flats boats and bass boats on the market today made *entirely* out of S-glass,

Hal Chittum

"Vacuum-bagging" can help eliminate bubbles in the laminant and produce a tighter bond, but the process is very expensive.

Kevlar, and graphite fibers. These materials and the lighter, stronger vinylester resins used to hold them together are very expensive. Vinylester resins are also considerably more difficult to work with than polyester resins. A few builders of fishing boats have gone to even greater expense in the fabrication process by "vacuum-bagging" the whole hull, which eliminates bubbles and provides a tighter bond between resins and other materials. You are probably asking yourself, What does all of this have to do, if anything, with good fishing boats?

The vast majority of anglers with fiberglass boats should not lose any sleep over whether their hulls are stiff enough, light enough, or strong enough. I am delighted that some manufacturers are utilizing the new laminate materials in their search for better fishing boats. In the end, some of the new materials and fabrication technology will slip into strategic areas of most boats, and we will all benefit.

Aluminum

In case you haven't noticed, fiberglass and the new high-tech materials have not taken over the water completely. Aluminum has been used in canoes, johnboats, and quality fishing boats for many years. As a hull material, it is experiencing a revival on bass lakes, pike lakes, and nearshore coastal waters. Bass boats of aluminum with midsize outboards are extremely popular. On large northern lakes and rivers, where the walleyed pike is king, V-hulled aluminum boats with higher freeboard are often the choice of experienced anglers. This versatile material is also being used in a variety of other sophisticated fishing boats for both fresh and salt water. The best aluminum boats have welded hulls, although riveted hulls on smaller boats are also satisfactory. Although not as strong as steel, aluminum is much lighter and much easier to fabricate. Aluminum hulls, whether flat-bottomed or modified-V, can take a real licking in rough water and come back for more.

A Wyoming friend and fishing guide, Paul Brunn, likes aluminum for another reason. In the high-altitude reservoirs where Paul normally fishes, he wants both the protection of a boat with higher freeboard and a boat light enough to be pushed by a mid-size outboard motor. Paul points out that above 4,000 feet, horsepower and efficiency of two-cycle outboards are lower than when operated at sea level. A lighter craft, needing less horsepower, is therefore almost a necessity. For Paul, aluminum boats fit the bill.

With all materials there are some downsides, and aluminum is no exception. As with fiberglass boats, stiffness is a problem with aluminum. Most well-made flat-bottom and semi-V hulls incorporate welded stringers running lengthwise and enough

Stringers and framing are needed to give aluminum boats stiffness.

framing running across the hull to give more than adequate stiffness. Another problem is that aluminum is an excellent conductor of heat and cold. An aluminum deck can get hot in the summer. More important, winter anglers can feel the cold of a frigid lake right through the metal skin. The hot/cold problem can be remedied by placing sheets of marine plywood and/or outdoor carpet over exposed interior aluminum.

Another potential downside of an aluminum boat for many anglers is noise. Too much noise is unpleasant for anglers, and it can also scare fish. Clanging anchors, dropped rods, and moving feet on aluminum create a bigger problem than in boats built with other materials. The noise created by wave-generated hull slap is also a potential problem with aluminum boats, especially for flats anglers. Plywood or outdoor carpeting over aluminum decks and foam flotation in enclosed areas can help muffle much of the noise.

The personal boats of Lefty Kreh, Bob Clouser, and D. L. Goddard used for smallmouth bass and striper fishing are made of aluminum. Some of the best redfish guides on the North Carolina coast, including Captain Bryan Dehart, pole aluminum boats. If you choose aluminum, you're in good company.

Wood Is Still Good

For years I have had the privilege of watching strips of juniper, cypress, and other fragrant woods being twisted into beautiful hulls on Harkers Island, at the southern end of North Carolina's Outer Banks. Unfortunately, many anglers see wood as a has-been, an inferior building material. The truth, however, is that low-tech wood is terrific stuff. It is stiff and lightweight, even when compared to E-glass, S-glass, Kevlar, and aluminum. Wood's strength and stiffness, *relative to its weight,* is incredible. The bottom line is that wooden fishing boat hulls can be comparable to almost anything made with high-tech laminates and aluminum.

Nature gave wood some other built-in advantages. It is a temperature-friendly material and does not conduct excess cold and heat the way some other materials do. Then there is the issue of sound, or the lack of sound. Wood is a quiet material that helps deaden sound produced from inside and outside the boat.

For many people, however, the most alluring qualities of wood are its beauty and feel. Few would disagree that a wooden boat, whether painted or natural, is pleasing to the eye and the hand. I often think back to those old wooden rental boats with their weathered patina. Fishing from a wooden just feels right.

There are, of course, drawbacks to owning a boat made of this miracle material. By itself, wood does not offer the abrasion resistance of aluminum, or the hard finish of a fiberglass hull. Poorly maintained and unprotected wood can also expand, contract, or rot. Most of these problems, however, can now be dealt with quite easily. There are, for example, glues and alloy nails to hold wood together that are better than at any time in history. There

Relative to its weight, wood is incredibly strong and stiff.

are new coatings and paints, especially the epoxy paints, that add external toughness and help to encapsulate the wood. Wood surfaces can also be further protected by applying layers of glass cloth and polyester resin, which help with puncture and abrasion.

I am clearly not urging every angler to rush out and buy a wooden boat, but what I am suggesting is that wood should not be automatically discounted when looking for a quality fishing boat. There are still craftsmen and small boatyards in many parts of the country that can easily fashion the fishing boat of your dreams. So the next time you hear a salesman say, "Our boats contain no wood whatsoever," ask him, "Why not?"

There are no bad boat materials, but you can make a bad choice. Think carefully about the qualities of each material as they relate to your needs. And again, remember that the best materials can become a good boat only in the hands of a good builder.

Does wood last? This Simmons Sea Skiff, made of wood, has been used on the North Carolina coast since 1954!

6

Interior Designs That Make Sense

In 1973 I made the first of many trips in a small boat to the Marquesas, a magical atoll about twenty-five miles west of Key West, Florida. This area was, and still is, the best of the Florida Keys. On that first trip Captain Nat Ragland and I left Key West harbor about 8:00 A.M. and made a couple of tarpon-scouting stops along the way. The morning was "slick calm," and the ride in Captain Nat's 18-foot flats skiff was smooth and uneventful. In the Marquesas, Nat showed me his favorite playgrounds. We poled across huge interior flats with dark grass bottoms and jumped two tarpon within the first hour. On the south side of the atoll he showed me white holes where the big permit lived.

I was so mesmerized I didn't notice the stiffening breeze out of the northeast. Our return trip into a 20-mph wind was not dangerous, but sloppy. Nat's skiff had served as the perfect fishing platform all day, but I couldn't find a comfortable, dry spot during the return trip. Nat held the wheel behind a small side console on the right side of the boat. I had nothing to hang on to, so I bounced for five or six miles before crying "Uncle." Captain Ragland, the consumate professional, stopped the boat and tied one end of a dock line to the bow and the other end to a two-foot piece of wood. When we started toward Key West again, I was able to stand in the middle of the boat holding the stick on the rope like a water-skier. Nat's solution worked. By "skiing" back to Key West, I was able to absorb the pounding with my legs and not my buttocks.

That wet ride and numerous other small-boat trips made me begin to think about fishing-boat interiors. What makes an angler-friendly boat? Which interior-design features are important for my waters and style of fishing?

When you get right down to basics, two types of powerboats are used by light-tackle anglers. There are boats that we stand *in,* and boats that we stand *on.* In light-tackle angling, whether with a fly rod, plug rod, or spinning gear, most of us do battle standing up. Regardless of the type of boat, we move around to get in position to make the cast and set the hook. In some boats we move across open decks and large, elevated platforms at the bow and stern. Johnboats, flats boats, and bass boats generally have very low freeboard and little to keep anglers inside the boat; these are the types of boats we stand on. Boats with higher freeboard, such as the walleye boats used in big lakes, most V-hulled center consoles, and boats with walk-around cabins or cuddy cabins, have higher freeboard and sides to keep anglers in and water out. These are the boats we stand in.

Whether you opt for a boat to stand on or stand in, a poorly designed interior can ruin a good fishing boat. A number of years ago I read a review of a fishing boat in an outdoor magazine. The writer stated that the engineers for a particular company had "finally succeeded in removing all available fishing space" from the model in question. Unfortunately, the same thing can be said about many boats on the market today. As I have alluded to several times, the hallmark of any good fishing boat is an uncluttered, angler-friendly space.

Consoles and Seating

Most boats have seats and many have consoles, but it's surprising how uncomfortable a boat can be when seats and consoles are in the wrong place. When the seat or lean post is too close to the console, it is difficult to sit or stand. In other situations I have settled into the seat behind a console only to find that the wheel was too far away, or that the console was too high to be comfortable. Even more annoying, and dangerous, is having seats set so that you can't see over the bow at ordinary cruising speeds when properly trimmed.

No fishing boat should have cramped seating or poor visibility. Whether your boat is designed primarily for standing while under way, sitting, or both, make sure that as operator your comfort levels are met. Next, think like a passenger in your boat. Is seating for your passengers also cramped? More important, are there adequate handholds, such as small grab rails, that will give passengers a sense of security while under way? I have been the passenger on too many boating trips such as the return trip from the Marquesas, with nothing to hang on to in rough water. Small, strategically placed handrails can save a trip. Finally, whether you sit or stand while running a boat, make sure that the necessities for operating your boat safely are ergonomically placed. Are your throttle, ignition key, and kill switch in comfortable positions for safe operation? Are your compass and other necessary navigational equipment within view? Also, are important things like the throttle and compass "hidden" among numerous meaningless gadgets that are too often found on "fully equipped" boats?

Handrails and Freeboard

As mentioned above, it is important for both the operator and passengers to have something to hang on to when in a powered fishing boat. Handholds come in many flavors, such as small, individual grab rails, the grab rail around the console, or even the larger bow rail that can be seen encircling the bows of many boats in fresh and salt water. In playing with my own boats over the years, I have found that the number and location of rails in a fishing boat is a personal matter. I have long been an advocate of a *few* strategically placed grab rails, or low-profile wraparound rails. Far too many fishing boats have so much stainless steel piping, they appear to have been designed by plumbers rather than by fishermen. High bow rails and excessively large grab rails around consoles are difficult to fish around, and will grab fly lines and spinning lures. Although large bow rails, especially on boats that also serve as family boats, can add a measure of safety, many appear to have been added more for appearance than anything else.

One design issue that many people fail to consider is the shape and height of the gunnel (also known as the gunwale), which is the top edge of the side of a boat. First, remember that the amount of freeboard (the distance from the gunnel to the water) determines the profile of the boat. Boats with higher freeboard are more affected by wind than low-profile craft. In fishing boats with high freeboard the gunnels will be located from thigh-high to waist-high, depending on the type of boat and your position in the boat. In boats with low freeboard, like bass boats and flats boats, the gunnels may be only shin-high. Gunnels will normally be higher near the bow than at the stern. Do you want to be able to lean against them while fighting fish, or do you want them low and wide enough so that you can sit or walk on them? Are they wide enough to be comfortable as seats? Finally, are your gunnels wide enough to protect rods stashed

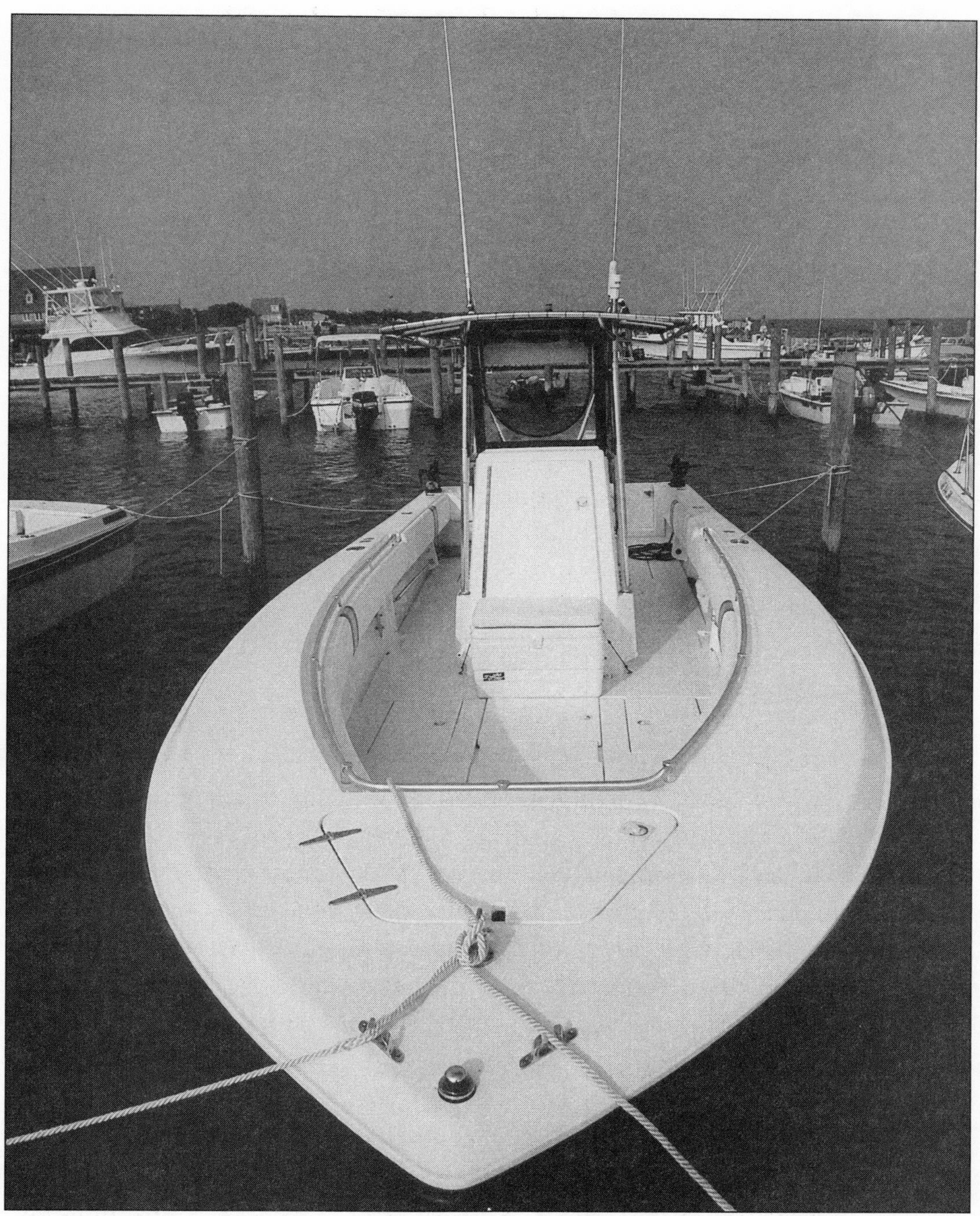

This boat has a low wraparound rail.

Some anglers prefer strategically placed handrails.

under them in rod holders? It may sound picky, but the height and width of the gunnels on your boat have much to do with its comfort and fishability.

Storage Space

Most modern powerboats used for fishing have significant storage space under consoles, seats, and hatch covers in fore and aft casting platforms. Although a boat may appear to have lots of storage spaces, make sure it is *useful* storage. Too often I have been in boats that had horizontal rod storage under the gunnels that was very difficult to access. I have also been on numerous fishing boats with lots of very small storage areas under hatch covers, which are often too small to be useful. At a shallow-water boat show I once counted sixteen hatch and storage space covers on one 18-foot boat—about ten too many.

Good rod storage is always a problem. Some boats have both horizontal and vertical rod storage racks. Horizontal rod storage is generally under the gunnels, while vertical storage is often on the sides of seats and consoles. Make sure that your horizontal storage racks have elastic tie-downs. Rods and reels that are not secured while under way can be damaged if not secured. Rigged fly rods and other long rods are best secured when their tips can be placed in tubes.

Before you buy a boat, think carefully about gear that is left on the boat, such as life jackets, a primary and secondary anchor, ropes, lines, and so on. Also think about what you normally take with you, such as a camera case, tackle bag, small duffel, rain gear, and of course your rods. Is storage space adequate so that the deck space will be uncluttered?

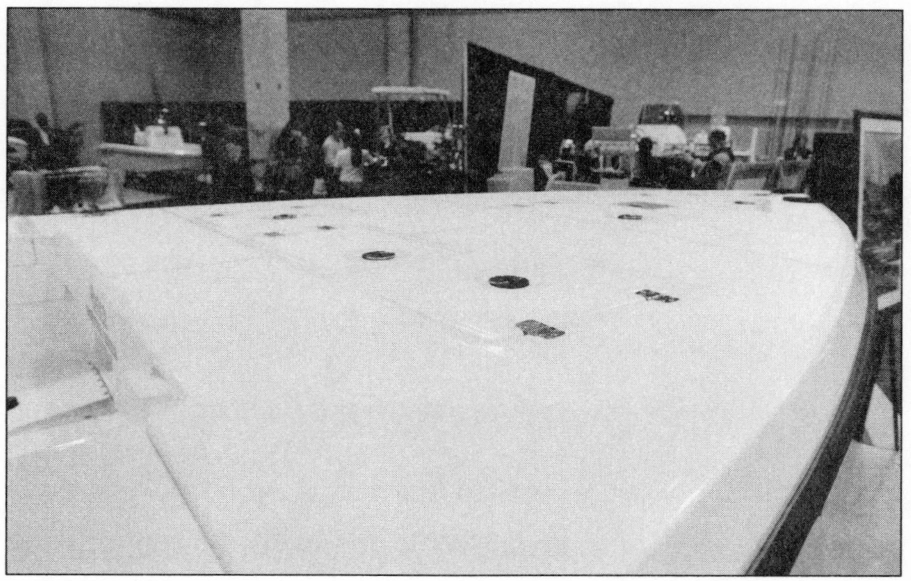

Numerous tiny hatch covers on fishing boats often mean spaces that are too small to be useful.

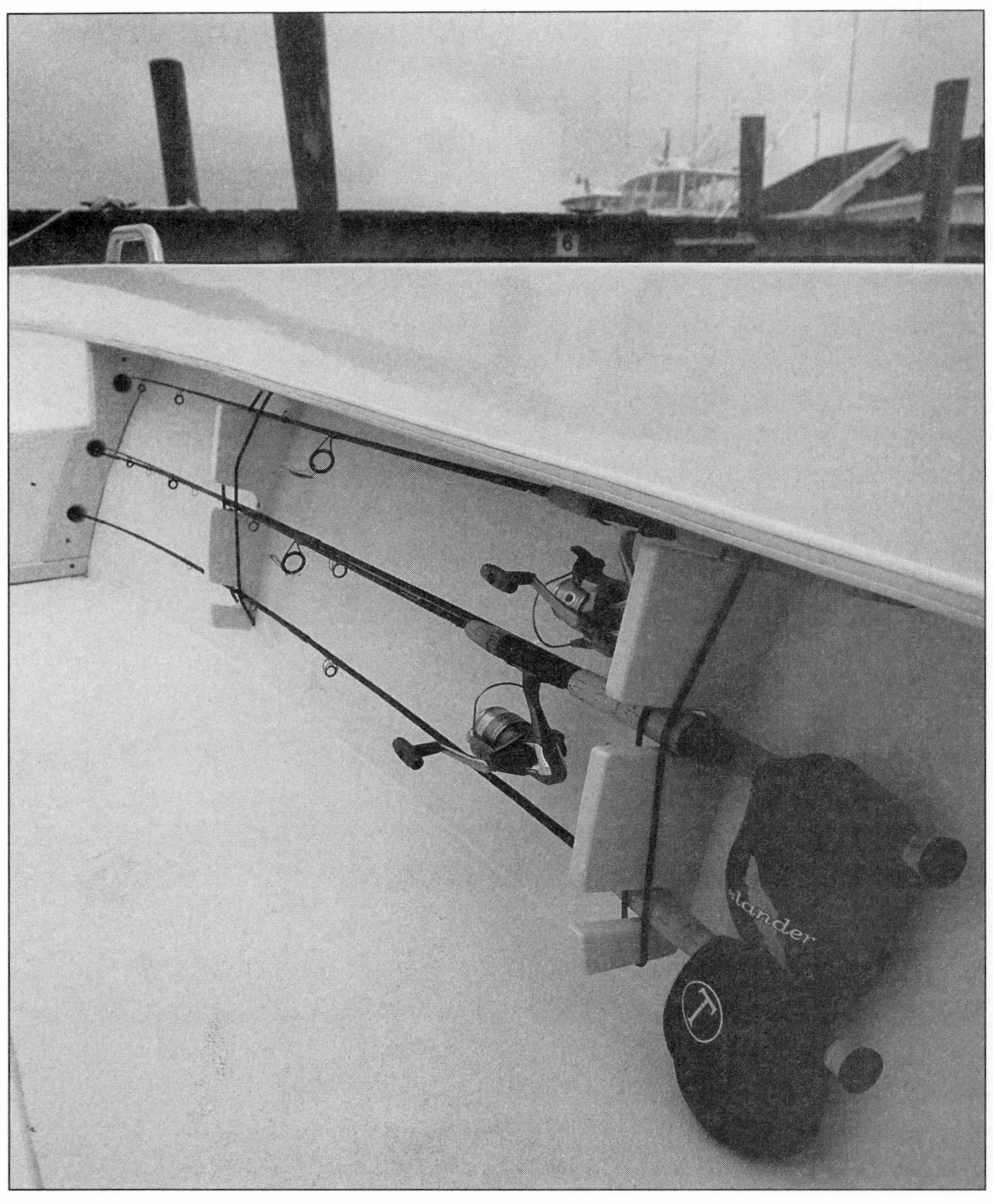

Good rod-storage systems protect delicate tips and hold rods and reels securely while the boat is moving.

Ed Jaworowski

The clean design, large hatch covers, and low-profile hardware on this aluminum johnboat make it ideal for fly fishing.

Are the hatch covers and doors on various storage areas designed so that they are secure and won't bounce when you are running in a heavy chop? Is the hardware recessed so that hinges and pulls don't become obstacles and line grabbers?

Finally, many fishing boats have at least one insulated ice chest for fish and food storage, and most have at least one livewell or baitwell. If you have a built-in insulated fish box, can it be easily cleaned? Does the box drain directly overboard or into the bilge? If your livewell or baitwell drains into the bilge, only a few rotting minnows or shrimp can make your boat stink. Livewells used to hold fish or live baitfish should generally have rounded corners or, even better, be round or circular in shape. Livewells should also have a very smooth finish since game fish or bait can be injured or killed if bounced against rough, abrading sides.

Protection from the Elements

For many years I was not a smart angler when it came to protection from the elements. When I fished in the Florida Keys and the Bahamas, the only protection from the sun was my fishing hat and what I wore on my back. I have spent countless days on rivers and reservoirs without a moment of shade over many hours. Sunscreen and clothing can do just so much.

I have started to wise up since turning fifty, and I have started carrying shade with me in the form of a Bimini top or even a large umbrella. Whether you fish in an aluminum johnboat, a center console, or a bass boat, a Bimini can be placed out of the way, and then popped up during the heat of the day to provide blessed shade. For parents who intend to fish with their kids—and I am one of those—a Bimini top is an absolute must. They usually cover one-third to one-half of all open areas in the boat. Not quite as large, but also handy, is a nice beach umbrella, which can be stored in rod racks. Although a beach umbrella doesn't cover a lot of area, it can provide needed relief from the sun for two anglers when eating lunch or just taking a break.

A very common and most useful cover for both sun and rain is a T-top. T-tops are very common on larger boats on inland reservoirs and in the ocean. They provide a permanent cover

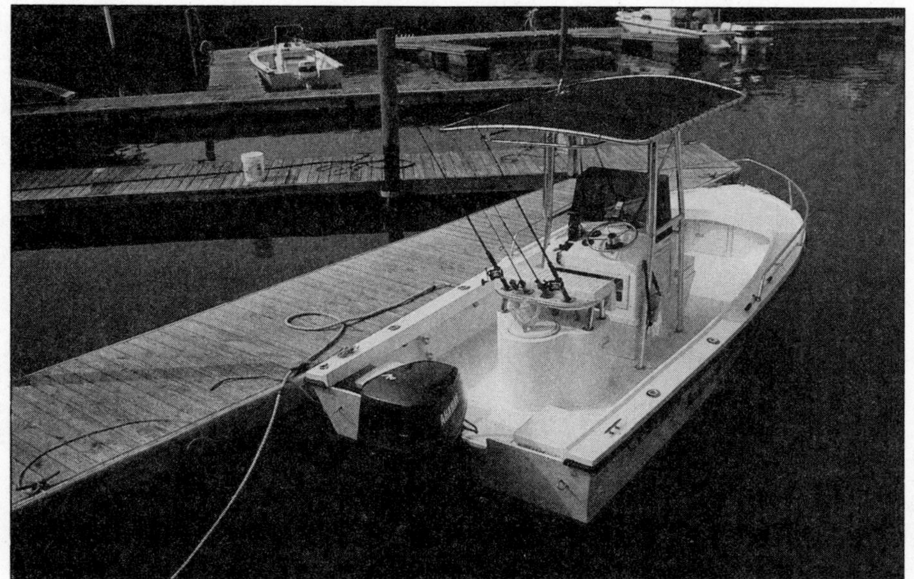

A T-top, Bimini top, or umbrella can provide blessed relief from the sun.

over the console or steering area, but are generally small enough so that they do not hinder spin or plug casting. I don't like T-tops, however, on boats primarily used for fly fishing. During heated action it is just too easy to break a fly rod tip on the metal frame.

In many parts of the country, protection from the elements does not mean protection from the sun or an occasional rainstorm. It means protection from cold, often bitter weather such as that found in the New England states, the Great Lakes, and in the Pacific Northwest. A small pilothouse, a walk-around cabin, or a cuddy cabin is not just a convenience, it's a necessity. I often fish on the North Carolina coast and on the Chesapeake Bay during the late fall and early winter when the weather is raw. Fly fishing and spin fishing both can be done easily from boats with a pilothouse or small cabin. Adaptation is easy when the reward is comfort.

Dry Feet

Many fishing boats today, except for the very smallest, have a built-up deck or floor above the waterline. These boats are described by manufacturers as "self-bailing." When a boat is self-bailing, it means that when water falls on the deck, it drains off at an angle from the bow toward the stern. The water then drains directly overboard, or into the bilge where it is pumped out. I have been in a number of self-bailing boats in which two anglers in the stern area would spend most of their time standing in a permanent puddle. I have also been in boats with drain holes so small that it took an eternity to drain only a small amount of water from a wet deck. If the boat of your dreams is of the self-bailing variety, make sure that it allows the water to get out quickly and stay out. Before you buy a self-bailing boat, test it at the dock. Wet feet make unhappy fishermen.

On the North Carolina coast there are several formidable shoals and some nasty inlets. In this marine environment I have always been partial to small boats that can get rid of water quickly. It is not at all uncommon even for an experienced captain occasionally to stick the bow into a wave or take some water over the stern. This is not a place for small drain holes. I am currently operating a 20-foot center console with a casting deck across the stern. The center of the casting deck is actually a bridge between a dry storage box on one side and a livewell on the other. On the occasions that I have taken water over the bow, it has flowed harmlessly across the deck, under the bridge, and out over the motor mounts. I hate water in my boat.

Line Containment

For fly fishermen and for anglers who have fly fishermen aboard their boats, the issue of line containment is a very important one when considering an interior design. One of the most frustrating problems I have faced over the years on many flats boats is a bow or a stern casting area from which fly lines can easily blow off into the water. Even a wind of 10 to 15 mph is enough to move a slick fly line off a deck, and it's no fun to worry constantly about your fly line when you should be concerned about your casting. Some anglers use a trash can or a stripping basket to keep line from blowing out of their boats. Others use more sophisticated line-containment accessories such as weighted line-storage buckets that can be moved around in the boat.

For me, however, nothing beats either recessed fore and aft casting decks or a 90-degree toe rail, both of which can keep line from blowing out of the boat. A recessed area of only a couple of inches or a low toe rail is all that is necessary to keep line from blowing out of a boat in normal wind conditions. I have been on too many expensive flats boats on which it was difficult to keep a

This lovely skiff has a raised casting deck, but it is recessed to keep fly lines from blowing out.

fly line in the boat even in light winds. As an avid fly fisherman, I regard poor line containment capabilities as a serious interior-design problem.

The hull of a boat determines softness of ride and stability. It is the interior design, however, that often determines whether or not the boat possesses that elusive characteristic of fishability. Few boats will possess all of the interior design features that you desire; however, the boat that you ultimately choose should have most of the features that are important for your style of fishing and for the water conditions you normally encounter. There is simply no reason to accept a poor or marginal interior design. The wrong design will adversely affect your fishing success and enjoyment on every trip. Think through your design needs before you buy.

III

MOTORS, ACCESSORIES, AND RIGGING

7

Power Options and Transom Configurations

I still have my dad's tackle box from the 1950s. The tackle box was made by Herters, and it's chock-full of wooden plugs, spinners, and spoons of the day. At least two of the lure spaces in the tackle box are filled with cotter keys, shear pins, and half-used spark plugs. For readers under forty, cotter keys and shear pins were necessary equipment for all outboard users, because they kept the propeller from falling off (cotter keys) and from damaging the lower unit after hitting a stump (shear pins).

Forty years ago, larger, faster boats were powered by conventional drive systems with the engine inside the boat, the shaft and propeller under the boat, and steering controlled by a rudder. The biggest outboards available in the 1960s were 50-horsepower smokey mammoths. Oh, how times have changed. Now fishermen have an incredible array of power systems available to them for boats of every size. There are great fishing boats available with conventional drive, stern drive, jet drive, and outboard power. We can also choose gas or diesel, and single-propeller or double-propeller rigs. In the pages that follow I will review power options available to anglers, but it should come as no surprise to anyone that over the past twenty-five years outboards have stolen the show. The vast majority of fishing boats under 30 feet are designed for use with outboards. The outboards of today are light and dependable, and when compared with those of just a few years ago, they are much more environmentally friendly and fuel efficient. However, before I sound like an ad for the outboard motor industry, let's take a look at all the power options and examine the pros and cons of each.

Conventional Drive Systems

When I think of conventional drive boats, I think of a clean transom with no outboard engine hanging off the back of the boat. I also think of the time twenty-five years ago when I had to strip to my Jockey shorts, hold a knife between my teeth like Lloyd Bridges, and dive into cold October water to cut a ball of rope off the propeller and driveshaft of a friend's inboard boat. It took about ten trips under the boat and a mild case of hypothermia to finally free the driveshaft from the phantom net rope we had picked up outside a North Carolina inlet.

For many years, one of the advantages of conventional drive systems in fishing boats was that they were powered by the same engines used to run automobiles. Ford and Chevy engines were relatively light in weight, and, most important, parts were readily available. In conventional systems the engine was usually mounted in the center of the boat with the drivetrain coming directly out of the engine and protruding through the hull. Later a gearing system called a V drive allowed engines to be placed in back of the boat near the transom, thus freeing space in the center. Whether mounted in the center of the boat or near the stern, the weight of the engine block over the centerline and partially below the waterline enhances a boat's stability.

Another advantage with the conventional systems is that automotive-style engines can produce excellent horsepower-to-weight ratios and are more fuel efficient than two-cycle outboards. Conventional drive systems can be powered either by gasoline engines or by diesel engines. Gasoline engines cost less to begin with, because they are really automotive engines adapted for use on the water. Diesel engines are more expensive, but they are extremely reliable and generally last longer than gasoline engines, an important consideration for anglers and captains who will log a lot of hours.

For fishermen, probably the biggest advantage of a conventional drive system is that the transom is clear and free of obstructions. Fish can be played right up to the back of the boat and don't have to be led around an outdrive or outboard motor. Another

Conventional drive systems are economical to run and very dependable, but they offer some problems for the small-boat angler.

advantage, pointed out to me by my son, Izaak, is that you have more room to paint the boat's name "on the rear of the boat." From my perspective, however, there are more disadvantages than advantages when it comes to using a conventional drive system on small fishing boats. First, gasoline vapor is heavier than air and can sink and collect in your bilge near the inboard motor. I simply do not like the idea of having to worry about gasoline vapors in enclosed spaces inside my boat. In a well-maintained boat, however, the chances of a gasoline vapor explosion are slim.

Second, and perhaps most important to boating anglers, is the fixed nature of the conventional system. As I discovered twenty-five years ago, if you want to look at your propeller you have to go underwater, or pull the boat up on a trailer. With a conventional system you cannot trim your motor the way you can with an outboard to change the attitude of the hull while under way. A conventional system is also much more difficult to turn and back up since the prop is fixed. With an outboard or stern-drive system the whole lower unit, including the propeller, can be turned with either the boat's wheel or a tiller, making it much easier to maneuver in tight places.

Another disadvantage of inboard power for the small-boat fisherman is that much of the boat's interior space is "eaten" by the engine block itself. I know that you can stand on it and make some use of it, but for my taste in small boats this is not a good utilization of space. Finally, if you have major engine trouble with a conventional drive system, *the whole boat* is out of commission. A replacement outboard, however, can be installed in a matter of hours, an important consideration for those who make a living on the water.

Outboards

With the arrival of the new millennium, outboards have come of age. Most outboards are still two-cycle engines, which produce a tremendous amount of horsepower for their weight. It is still possible to get the small "kicker" engines that can be carried like a suitcase, but outboards have also grown up. Outboards of 250 and 300 horsepower are now available for use in both fresh and salt water. Large outboards used alone or in pairs now push most fishing boats under 30 feet.

The new outboards, both two-cycle and four-cycle, are a far cry from the smoke pots of yesteryear. Although two-cycle engines still require a gas-oil mixture, done in the fuel tank or done automatically by the engine, they are now much more environmentally friendly and fuel efficient than at any other time in history. Manufacturers now offer direct-injected two-stroke engines. Since fuel is injected under pressure, both gasoline and oil burn more efficiently than in traditional two-cycle engines, meaning better fuel economy.

The advantages of outboards for fishermen are multifold. Since most engines are mounted outside the boat, there is more interior space for fishing and tackle storage. For anglers, however, the biggest advantage of outboards is their maneuverability. As mentioned earlier, a turn of the wheel or tiller enables the operator to direct the propeller's thrust, allowing most boats to turn more precisely in forward and reverse.

Remember also that outboards can be trimmed. Trim (the angle of the lower unit in relation to the transom) on smaller outboards is adjusted manually and cannot be changed while the motor is in operation. With most large outboards, however, the trim of the engine can be adjusted with the flick of a switch, even while under way. Also, since most midsize and large engines are equipped with an automatic trim-and-tilt feature, it is possible to raise the propeller and lower unit completely out of the water should the propeller become entangled in rope or netting. For the angler, the ability to lift an outboard completely out of the water, either automatically or manually, is a tremendous advantage over conventional drive. Boats with their engines out of the water can be poled or drifted across very shallow water. Flats and river fishing as we know it today would not be possible without modern "trimable" outboards.

Since most fishing boats today have planing hulls, it is important to have an outboard large enough to make the boat operate efficiently. I don't mean extreme power or power beyond that recommended by the manufacturer. For example, several years ago I ran a 20-foot center console weighing a little over 2,200 pounds with a 115-horsepower engine. It soon became apparent that with three people and a load of gear in the boat the engine would labor in the "hole" far too long. Even with trim tabs, 115 horsepower was not enough to get the boat on plane quickly. After I switched to a 150-horsepower engine the boat was more responsive and made me feel far safer in rough water and inlets. It is also interesting to note that with the 150-horse engine I used less fuel than with the 115. The 150-horse engine was never taxed, while the 115 always seemed overworked while running at higher rpms. Just as too much horsepower can be a "sin," not enough can also cause problems.

The lighter, higher horsepower engines available today offer anglers efficiency and reliability. They are also fast. It is not at all uncommon to see freshwater and saltwater tournament boats running at speeds in excess of 60 or 70 mph. At the risk of appearing judgmental, 40 mph on the water is fast. Seventy mph in a fishing boat borders on the absurd. No matter how tournament organizers and manufacturers try to justify it, high speeds and recreational angling are not a good mix.

For many anglers, the really important story in outboards has been the advent of four-cycle engines. In the decade before the turn of the millennium, four-cycle outboards began offering real competition to the traditional two-cycle models. Even with the latest improvement in two-cycle engines, the best four-cycle outboards are still more fuel efficient and perhaps a bit more environmentally friendly, since four-cycle engines do not require a

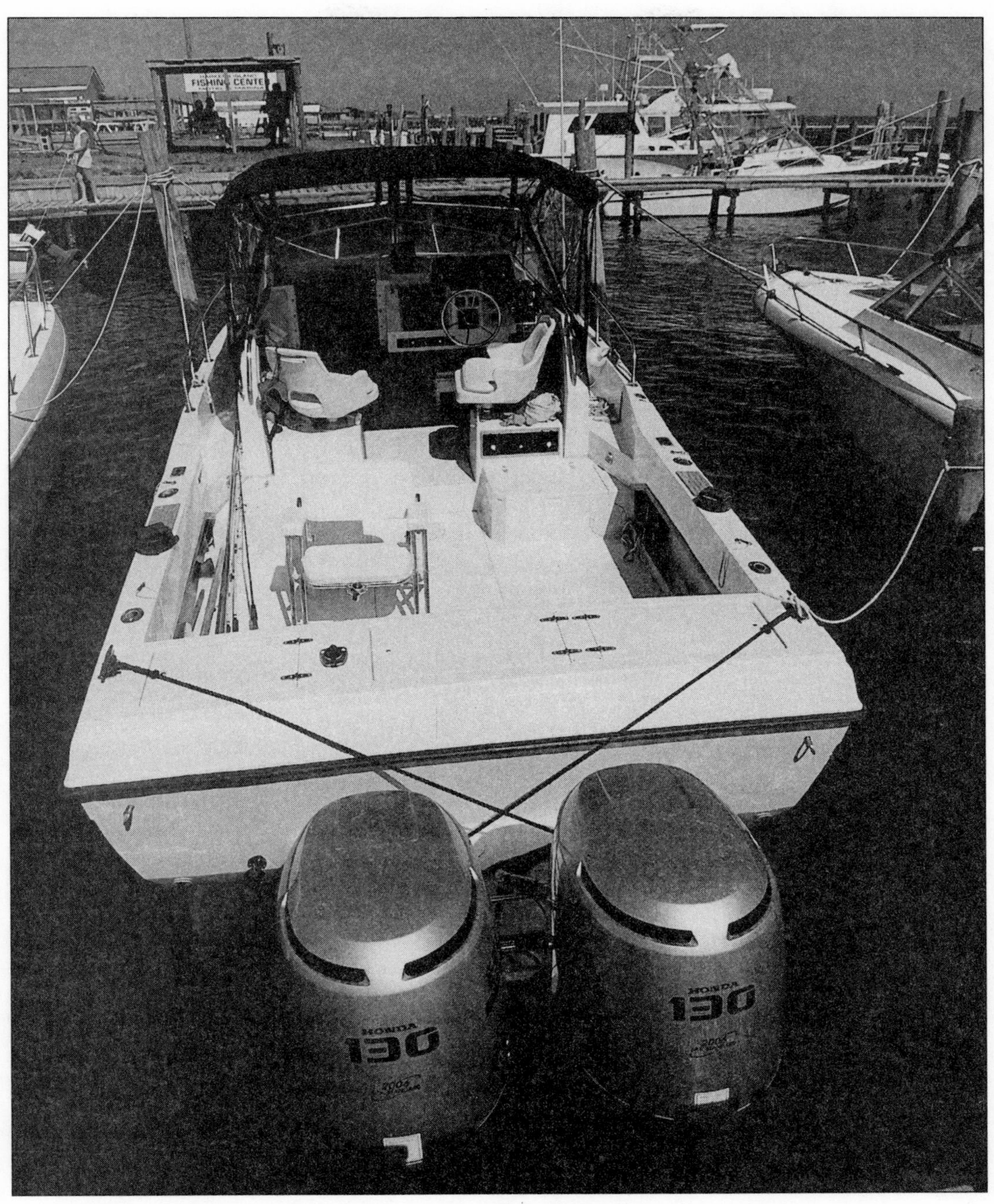

Four-cycle engines are incredibly clean and quiet. Many believe that most outboards of the future will be four-cycle engines.

gasoline/oil mix. It should be noted that four-cycle engines are most fuel efficient in the low and middle rpm range. At the high end of the rpm range they have fuel efficiency about the same as a two-stroke of equal power. Four-cycle engines are also noteworthy for another reason. The very quiet four-cycle is believed

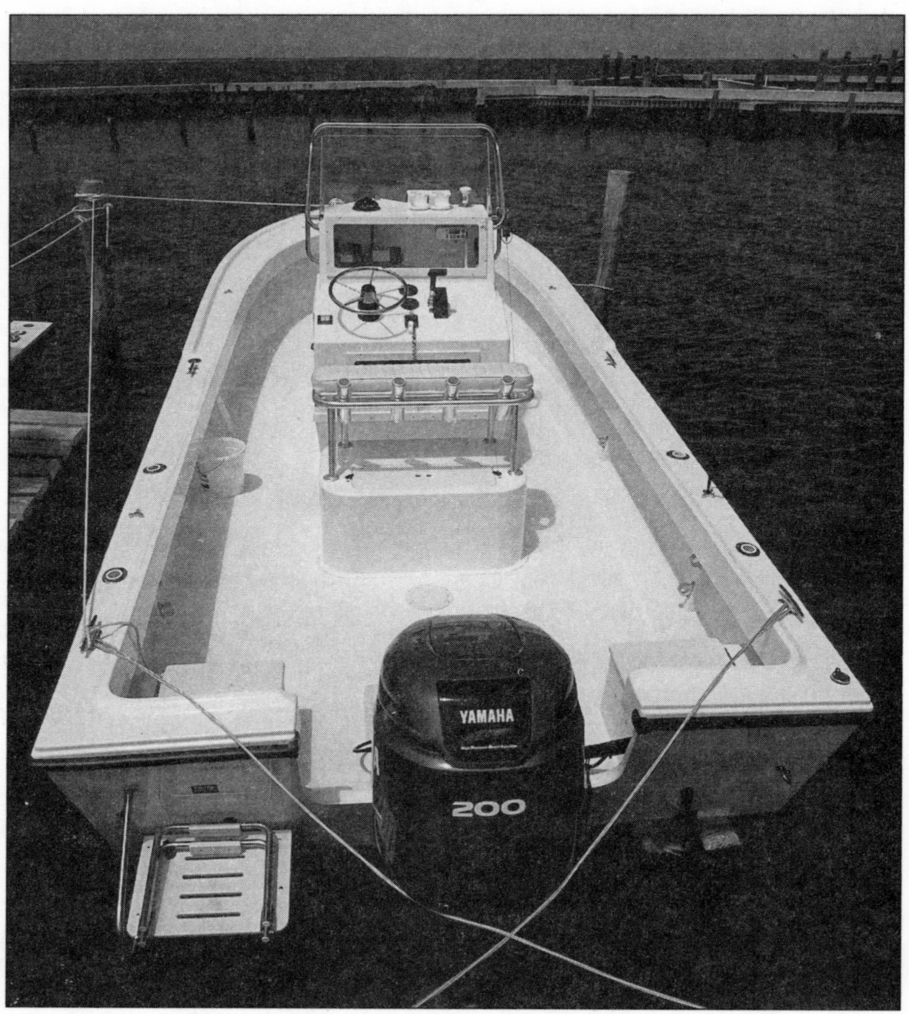

The latest two-cycle outboards are fuel-injected and cleaner than ever. They are still lighter in weight than four-cycle engines of comparable horsepower.

by many anglers to be advantageous in approaching fish, and it's also nice to finally be able to talk to your fishing buddies while the engine is running.

The only notable downside of four-cycle engines for some anglers is their weight. When compared with two-cycle engines of the same horsepower they are heavier, often by many pounds. For lightweight fishing boats, including aluminum johnboats and some flats boats, extra pounds on the transom can make a difference.

Four-cycle engines proved that outboards could be powerful, quiet, and clean; without them, we may not have developed the technologically advanced two-cycle fuel-injected engines that we enjoy today. Both types of outboards can now meet strict government emissions standards and are truly "clean machines." Although the four-stroke may well be the "engine of the future," the new two-strokes also have a bright future.

I can't leave outboards without a quick look at the relative merits of tiller steering versus boats with wheels. Most small outboards from 15 horsepower down are still used with tillers and not steering wheels. Like my father's 5-horsepower kicker of forty years ago, small outboards are light, portable, and easy to use. Some anglers and guides even prefer midsize outboards (25 to 70 horsepower) with tiller steering. The main advantage for fishermen is that using a tiller in place of a steering wheel leaves the boat completely open. With no consoles and steering cables, there is less clutter. In a small boat the stern is also the driest and most comfortable area.

Well-known anglers such as Floridian Flip Pallot and New Englander Brad Burns have long been advocates of tiller steering and "clean" boats. Anyone who uses tiller steering, however, should be cautioned that any tiller-steered outboard, especially midsize outboards, can be thrown into dangerous tight turns if the tiller is released at higher speeds. Motor torque can quickly turn an outboard. When used properly, tiller steering can reduce clutter and add enjoyment.

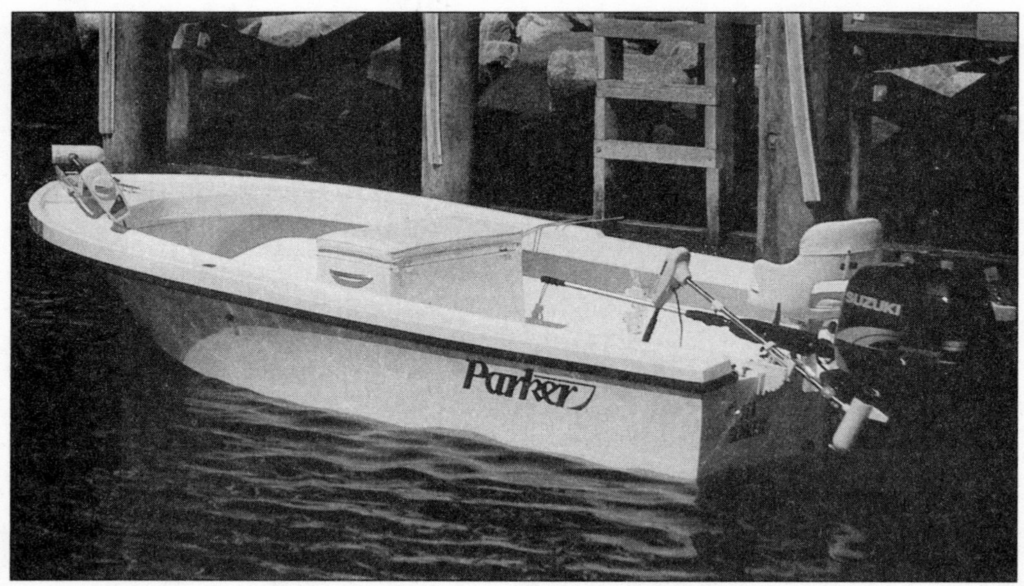

Brad Burns

Because tiller steering can mean a "cleaner" interior, many anglers prefer it.

Lefty Kreh

Stern Drives

When a conventional-drive system marries an outboard engine, the children are called stern drives. A stern drive is also known as an inboard/outboard, or I/O. This system combines the automotive-type gasoline or diesel engines used with conventional-drive systems with the lower unit of the outboard motor. Like outboards, stern drives can be trimmed and steered more easily. Inboard/outboards made a lot of sense years ago when outboard engines were still less than dependable and when it was not possible to get from outboards sufficient horsepower to push a large boat. Even though times have changed and outboards are now available for almost any size boat, stern drives, especially diesels, are still quite popular. Stern-drive systems are the one way that anglers can get the long-lasting efficiency of diesel power and the trimability of an outboard.

Stern-drive systems offer inboard economy and the "trimability" of outboards.

For the small-boat angler, stern-drive systems offer some of the same disadvantages as conventional-drive systems. In both, the engine is inside the boat, so potentially volatile vapors must be vented. The biggest problem faced by fishermen is the loss of important interior space required for the engine block.

Twin Engines

On larger boats used in big lakes and in the ocean, anglers have long had the option of twin inboards, outboards, or stern drives. Twin engines are sometimes necessary for large, heavy boats, but

Counter-rotating propellers mean no torque problems.

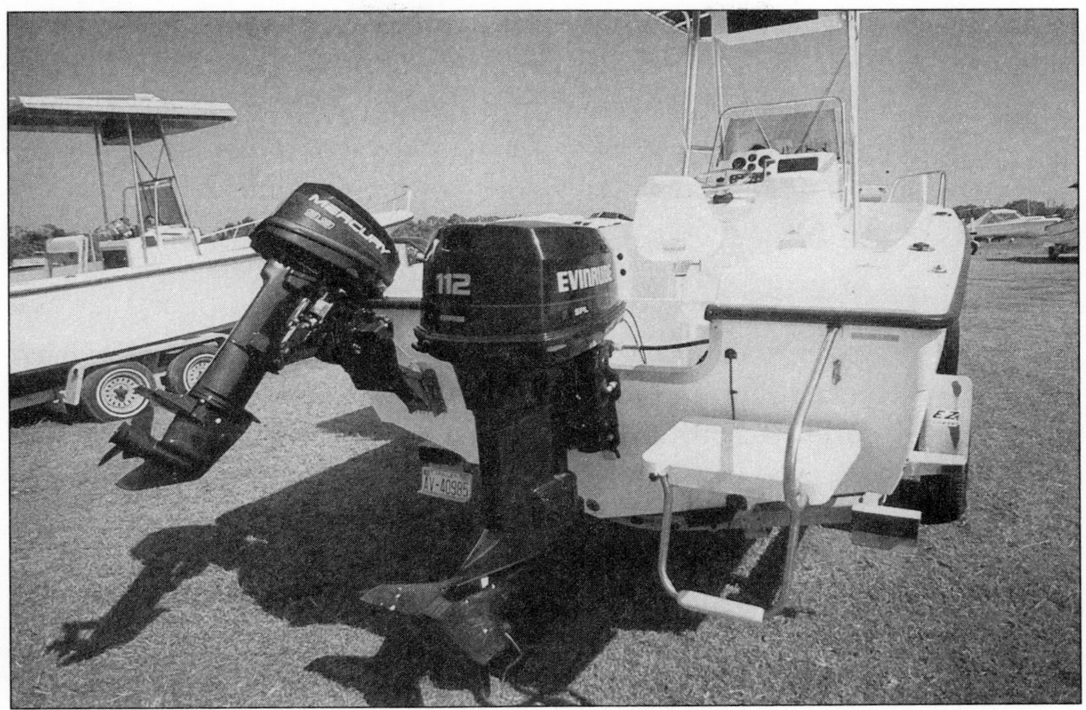

The "get home" engine can also serve as a slow-trolling motor.

they can also provide an extra margin of safety for any boat on large bodies of water. Twins also make turning and backing a breeze. For a long time there was one major disadvantage to twin outboards or stern drives. Since torque was doubled when two props were rotating in the same direction, trim and steering were sometimes made difficult. Now manufacturers are producing stern drives and outboards with counter-rotating propellers, which negate problems of torque.

In place of twin engines many anglers have long used a single large outboard and a low-horsepower "get home" engine. The smaller engine, often 5 horsepower to 30 horsepower, can also serve as a low-speed trolling motor. For anglers fishing large or remote waters, smaller, insurance motors make sense.

Brackets and Euro Transoms

Some anglers believe that a higher transom, such as those found on a conventional-drive system or stern-drive system, helps to keep the sea out in rough water and when backing down on a hooked fish. For many years some transoms on larger boats were often notched or cut out when outboards were installed. Seeing the sea on either side of their engine or engines is troubling for some anglers, especially when a little water sloshes into the cockpit.

To save us from wet feet, the bracket was invented to allow anglers to keep a high transom and still have the trimability and maneuverability of outboard power. Having the engine behind the bulkhead also helps to reduce interior noise. With the engine two to three feet away from the transom, the bracket between the boat and outboard works as a lever. Some tests have shown that bracket mounting can increase speed and fuel efficiency by 5 to 8 percent.

Brackets also brought problems. When you move the engine two or three feet away from the transom, the center of balance of the boat is changed. Gas tanks and consoles have to be repositioned to trim a boat if it was not designed for use with brackets. More important for fishermen, however, is that brackets can make playing and landing fish difficult. It is harder to maneuver a hooked fish around an outboard that is two or three feet away from the transom than when it is around an outboard bolted to the transom. For light-tackle angling, and especially fly fishing, I do not recommend boats with brackets, but I understand why many fishermen appreciate them.

Another innovation found on many larger outboard-powered boats is the so-called Euro transom. The Euro transom is another way of keeping a high bulkhead, or transom, between

A Euro transom (above) and a stern-bracket system (below) will help keep seas out, but both systems offer some downside for fishermen.

anglers and the sea. Unlike stern brackets, which are extended out from the transom, the running hull of a boat with a Euro transom extends a couple of feet beyond the bulkhead of a boat. Engines are bolted on behind the bulkhead of boats with Euro transoms. Again, Euros are different from stern-bracket systems, because the hull of the boat runs all the way to the engines.

For me, the big disadvantage to the Euro transom is that you lose a heck of a lot of clean fishing space by having a bulkhead two feet inside your boat, and you also have the problem of fishing around engines stuck out on a "platform" well beyond your transom.

Again, I know why anglers don't want their transoms cut out, and want a high barrier between themselves and the sea. For most boats, especially those with low to moderate freeboard, I prefer having outboards bolted directly to the transom where I can move around them easily. From a safety standpoint I do not mind a little water on my feet from time to time. In fact, I even like an open transom, since it allows water to escape over the motor mounts quickly. On several occasions over the years I have taken a large wave over the bow and have been delighted to see the water disappear quickly through the transom cutout around the motor. Again, I understand the problem, which is addressed by stern brackets and Euro transoms. I just happen to think that both "solutions" interfere with fishability in many boats, especially smaller ones.

Jet Propulsion

Boats with jet drives are becoming very popular on lakes, rivers, and on shallow ocean flats. Jet propulsion can be produced by inboard systems and outboard jets. When running rivers such as the Susquehanna in Pennsylvania and the Roanoke in North Carolina, outboard jets mounted on aluminum johnboats make perfect sense. With no lower unit and propellers deep in the water, boaters with jet drives can maneuver safely through obstacle-strewn waters.

Unfortunately, I still have a hard time separating the benefits of jet power for fishing boats from my visceral aversion to jet sled–type craft. Many good days on the water have been tarnished by the appearance of jet sledders, or jet bikers, which destroyed any possibility of catching a tarpon, bonefish, speckled trout, or largemouth. Even though I don't like jet sleds, more and more I see expanding possibilities for jet propulsion in fishing boats. When "good guys" such as Lefty Kreh and Bob Clouser use jet outboards with wonderful results, we should all take notice. In the coming years jet drives, especially of the outboard variety, will find more and more uses in the angling world in both fresh and salt water.

For the boating angler this is the golden age. We have available to us incredible boats and a variety of dependable power systems. You have probably noticed, however, that I have not discussed electric trolling motors in this chapter. You will find them covered in a later chapter on silent propulsion.

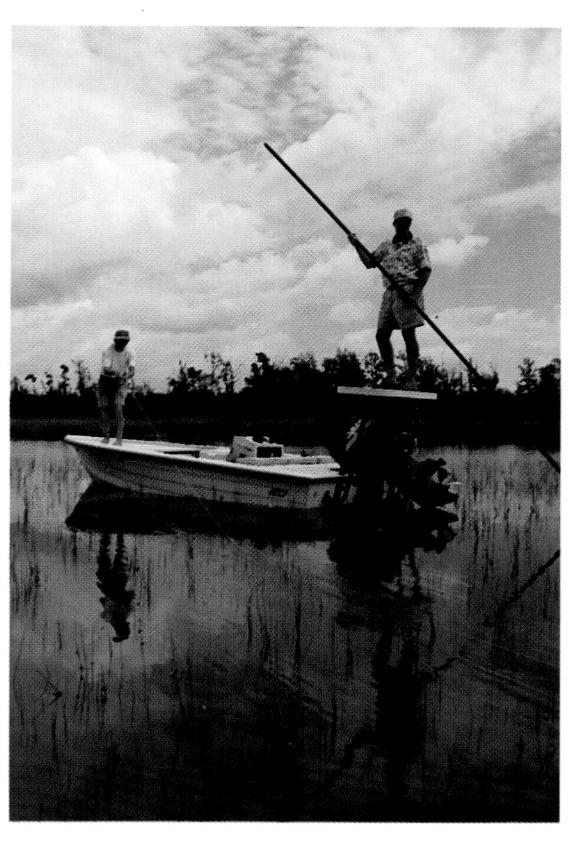

You'll need a flats boat if you fish for redfish or tarpon.

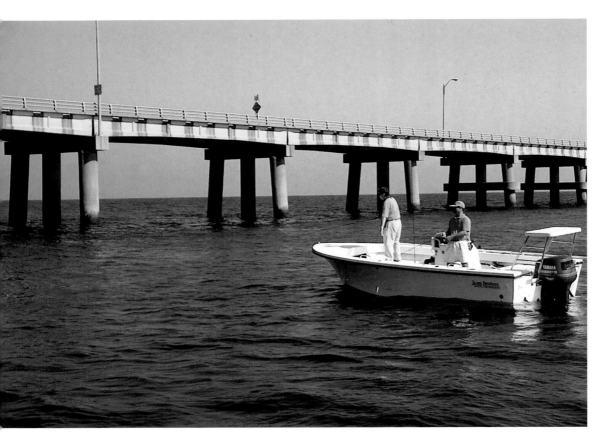

A 20-foot modified-V is ideal for bay and nearshore fishing.

If space and money were no object, every fisherman should have a "fleet."

John Kumiski

Stalking the flats

This boat has a flat bottom for stability. Another benefit to the flat bottom is that you can use a smaller motor than required for a V-hulled boat.

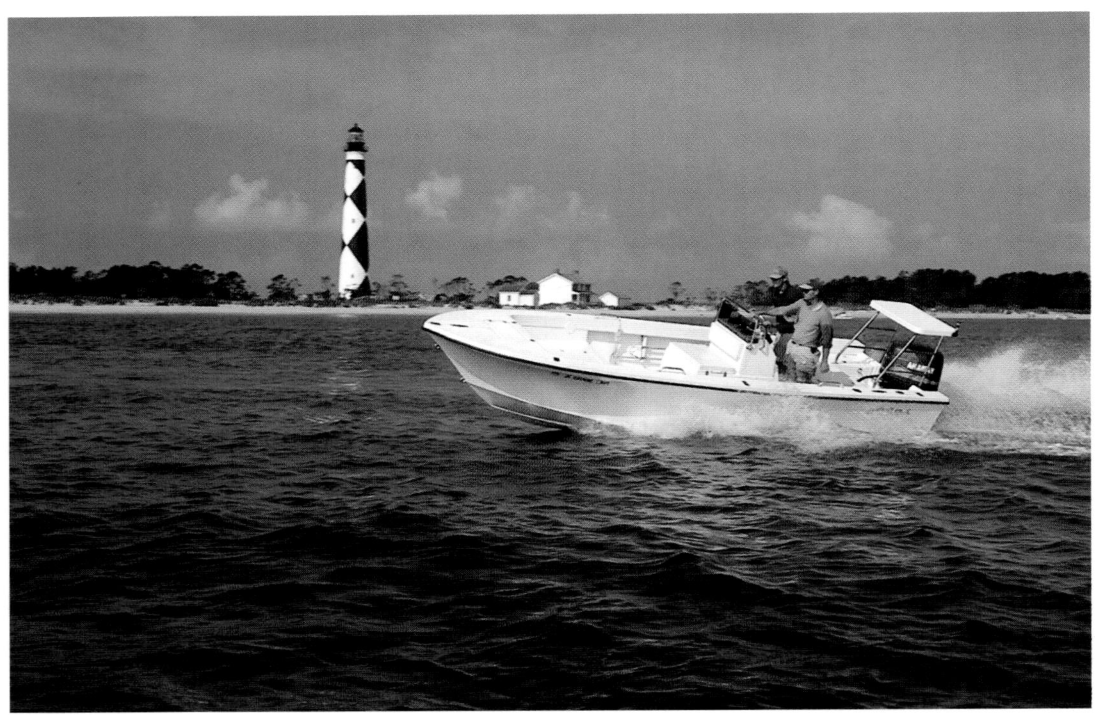

A modified-V is often the "compromise" that works, providing a soft ride and stability.

A sea kayak or stable canoe can take you quietly to remote places that are inaccessible to anglers in any other craft.

Kevin R. Du Bois

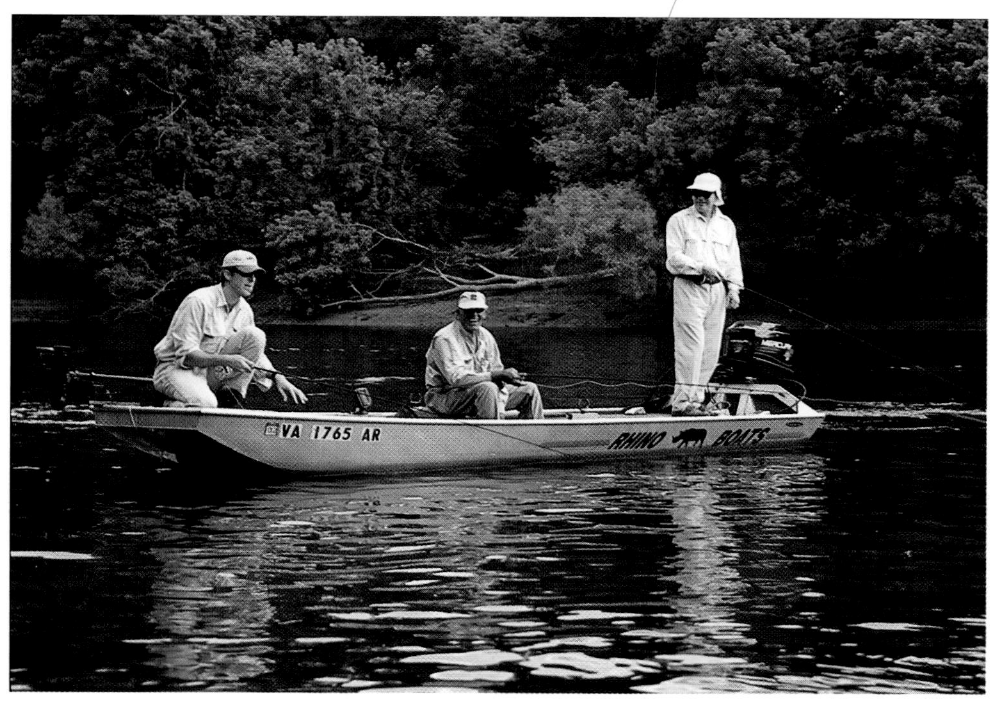

Aluminum can be fabricated into tough, lightweight fishing boats. This boat would work well in a marsh or a river.

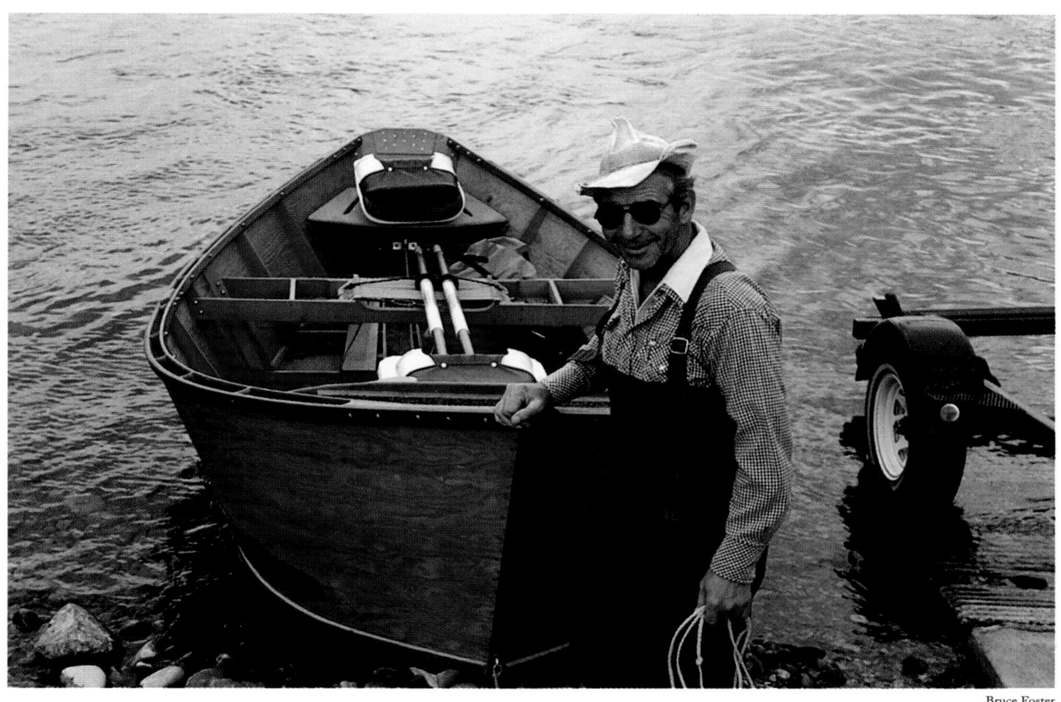

Bruce Foster

This wooden drift boat can stand up to the rigors of river fishing.

If you cover all exposed objects, such as the engine on this boat, you'll lose fewer fish to tangles.

Gerry Gibbs

Conventional drives are still found on quality custom-fishing boats, like this beautiful 25-footer.

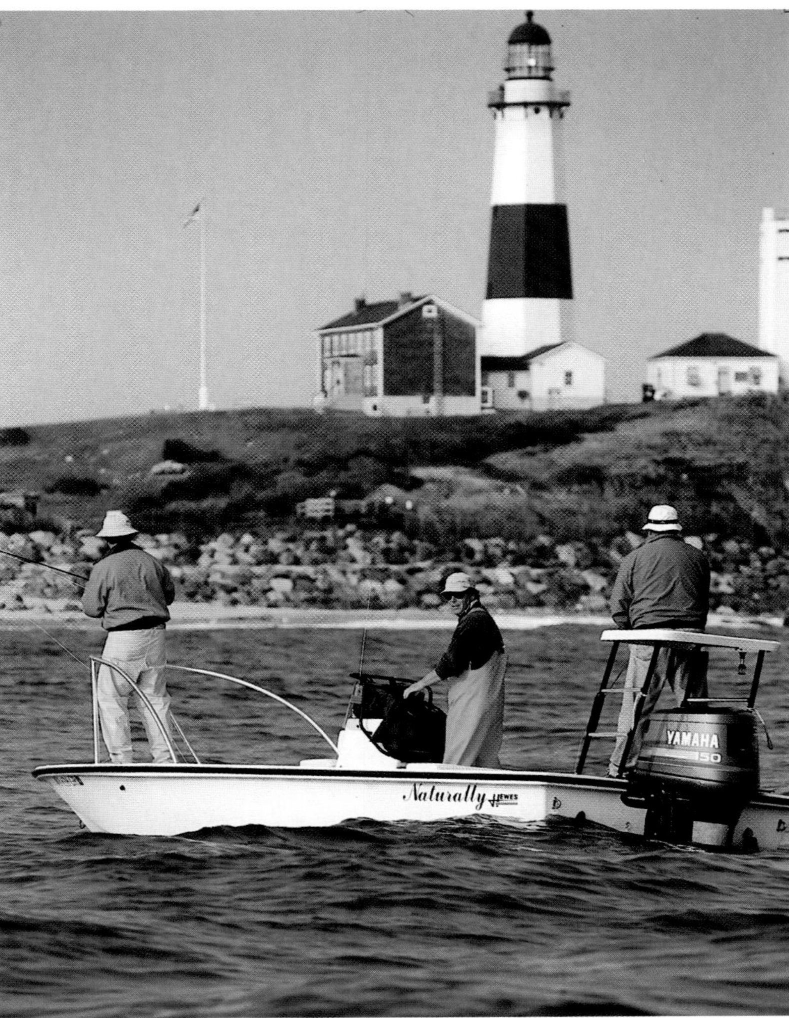

Barry Kanavy

Lean rails, or lean posts, can make standing and fishing easier and safer, especially in rough water conditions.

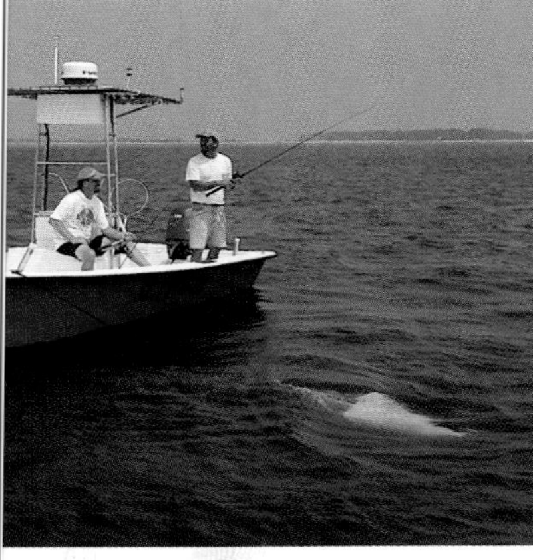

A "sea anchor" can slow drift or help position your boat.

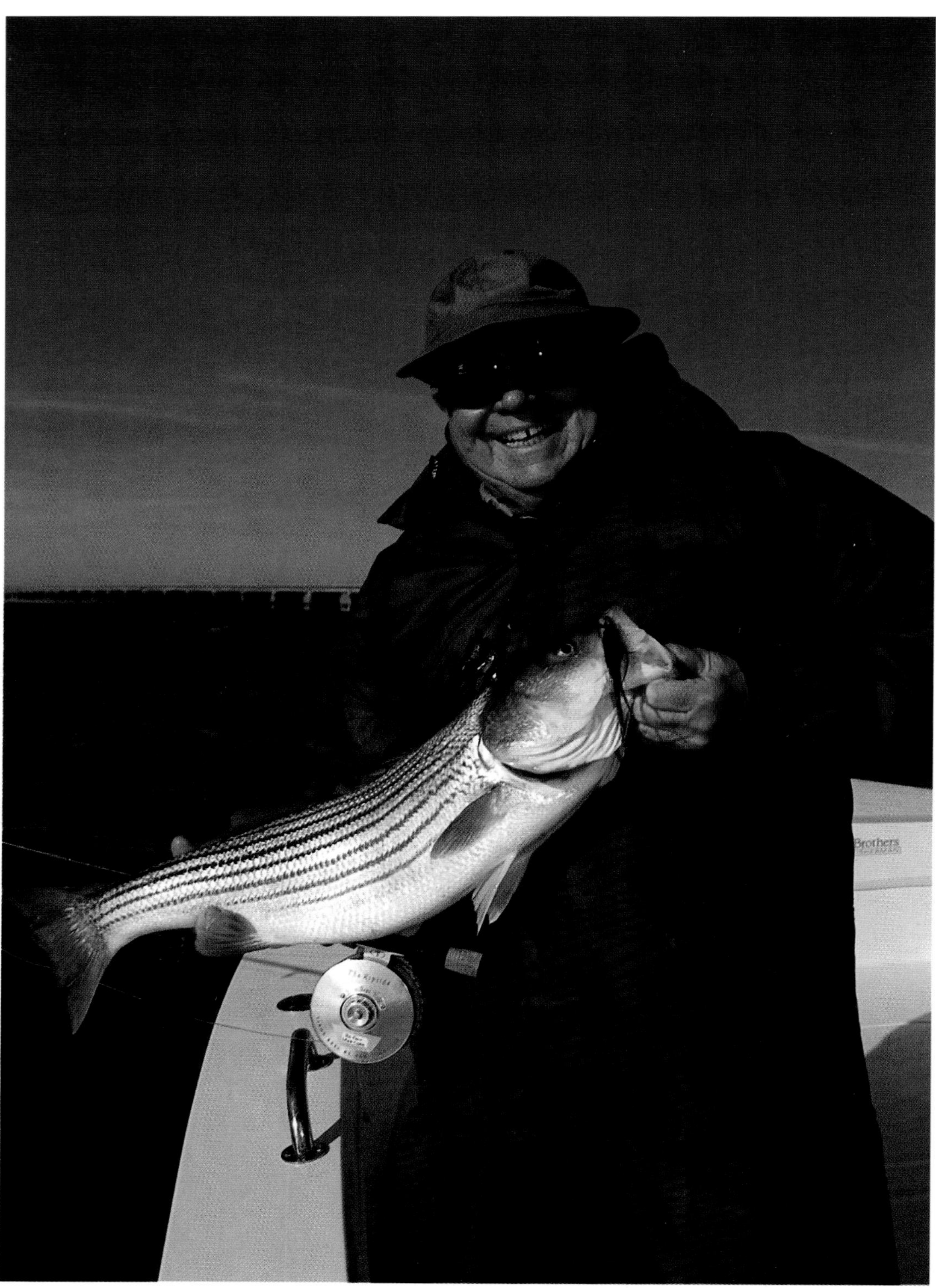

When this picture was taken the temperature hovered around freezing. Warm clothing and a nice striper kept a smile on Lefty Kreh's face.

8

ne Clutter: Choosing and ıly Necessary Accessories

ıs a chapter I would rather not write. No mathow hard I try, and no matter how pure my nglers will take offense at some of my obserpter. Criticizing the way another angler's boat y as criticizing their spouse or dog, but at the ıur wrath . . . here goes.

:auty is in the eye of the beholder. To me, the ishing boat is in its simplicity, seaworthiness, of maintenance. That's why I find it almost ıat shows and see "fishing boats" with padded ood–grain consoles, plush carpet from stem to seats, AM/FM CD/stereo systems, leatherıg wheels, and more engine instrumentation ometer, oil gauge, gas gauge, water pressure : gauge, and so on) than you would find on And then often there are enough electronic n, sonar, radar, communications, etc.) to make

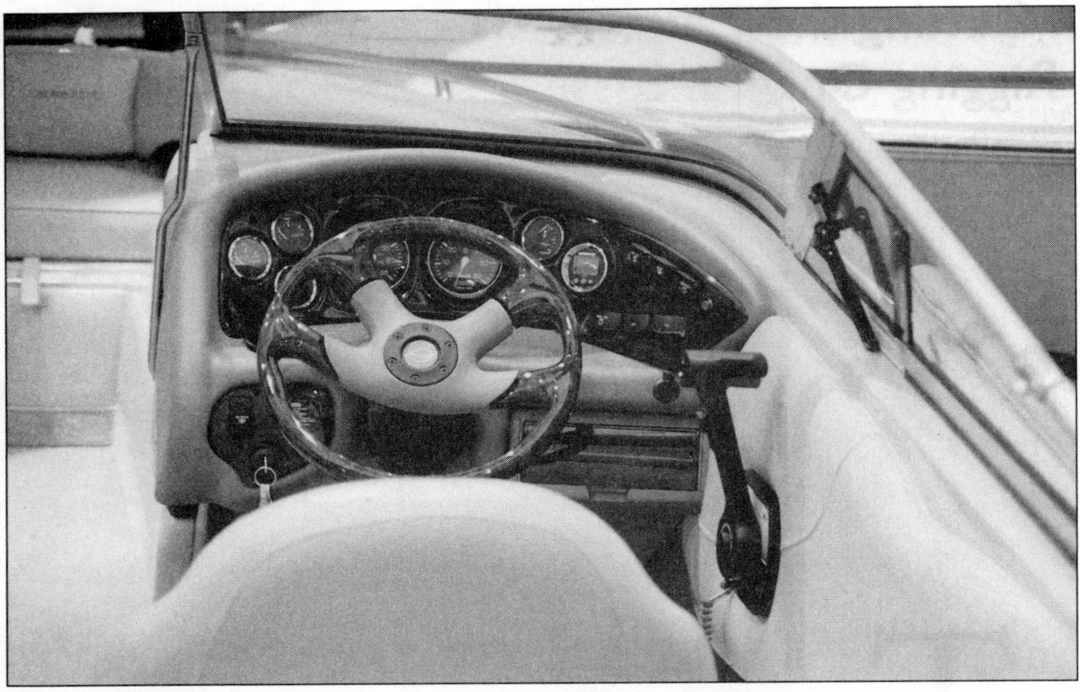

Could this be a fishing boat?

Bill Gates uncomfortable. If you want these things on a fishing boat, then by all means buy them and enjoy them. Understand, however, that most have far more to do with fishing for compliments than real fishing. In real boats, fish blood and chum are sometimes spilled on the floor, on the console, and on the seats. The last thing I want to be worrying about is cleaning the plush carpet, upholstery, and the designer dashboard on my console.

Each year I fish on many different boats in different water conditions. The best of those boats, to my way of thinking, are those rigged by or under the supervision of the angler/owner. Know your needs before you purchase a boat so that it can be rigged with only necessary equipment and accessories, and no more. Think twice before you accept a "value package" that may offer a lot of seldom-used gadgets and a lot of headaches.

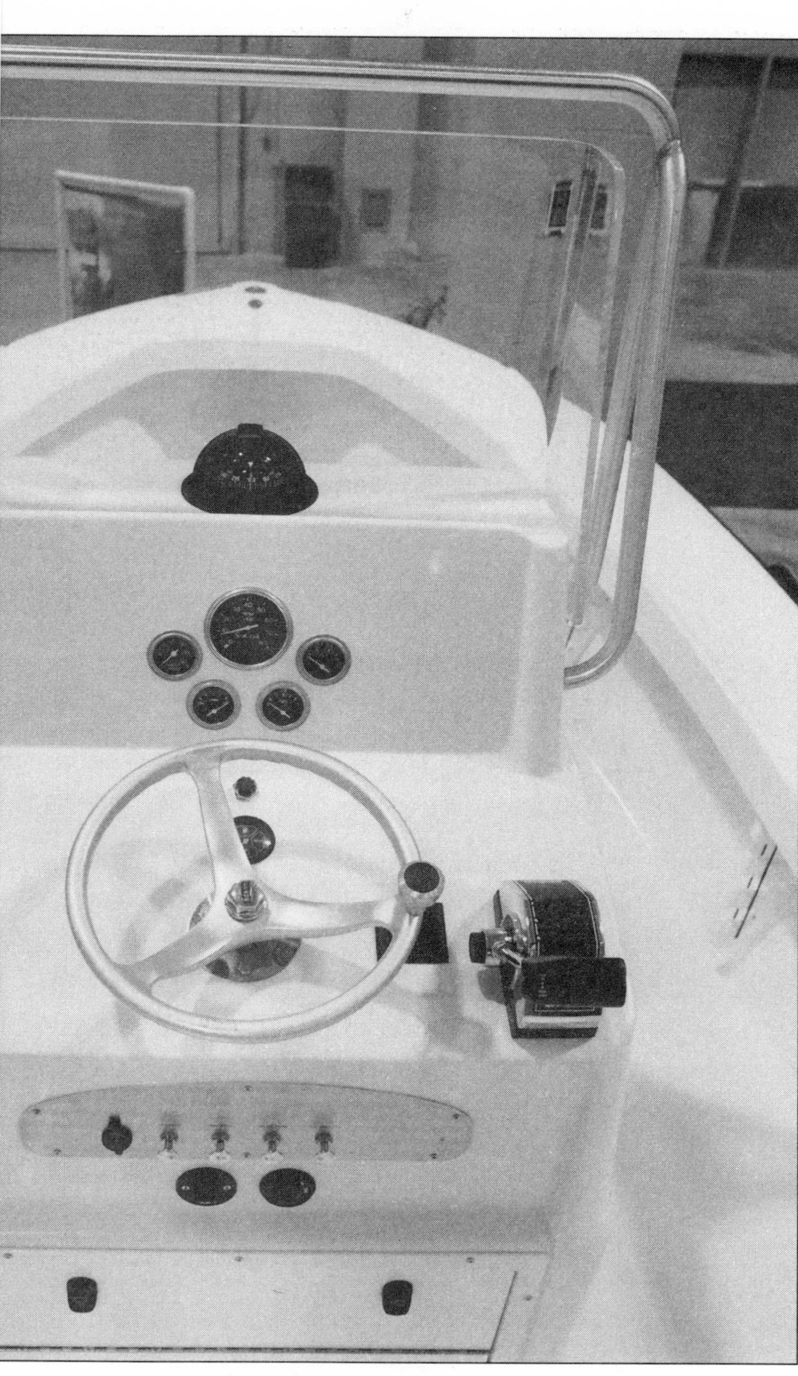

: "clean" and clean up easily.

Things That Stick Up

When considering accessories for your fishing boat, look at the things that will get in the way of movement, casting, and playing fish. Almost every boat has cleats. To cleats we attach anchor lines and dock lines. But they will also snag fly lines and grab your shoelaces. Exposed cleats on casting decks and on top of gunnels are simply not necessary in a good fishing boat. Cleats easily can be installed in more fishing-friendly locations, such as under the gunnels. For a little more money, pop-up cleats can really clean up deck surfaces.

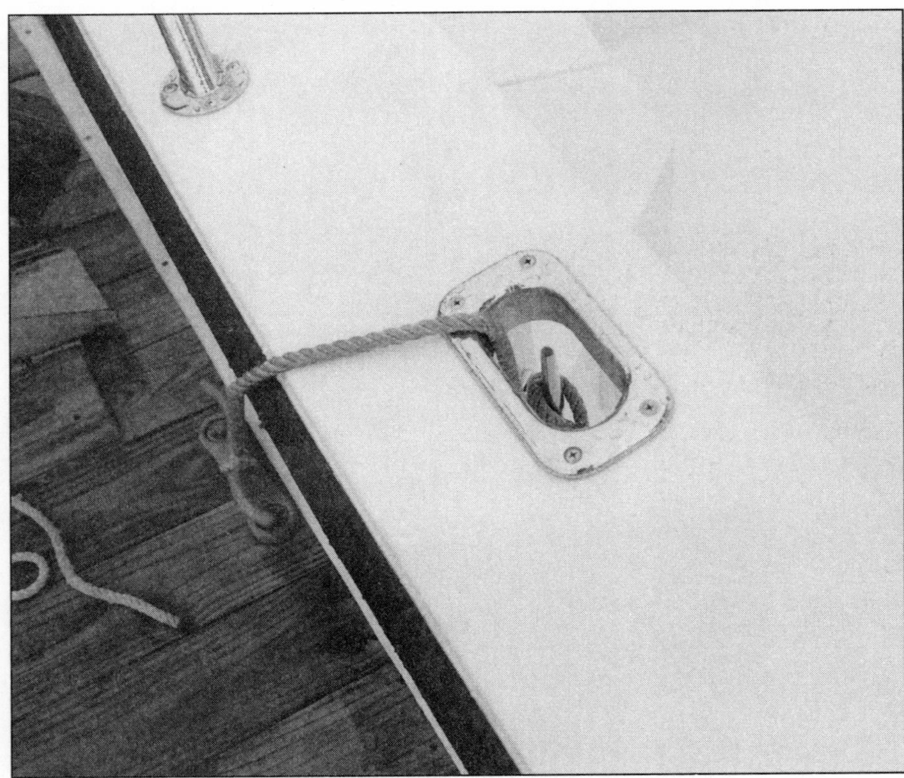

Cleats should be out of the way, not in the way. Pop-up cleats and running lights help clean up a deck.

ab rails have already been mentioned earlier
, it is important to have strategically placed
locations in the boat. What is not necessary
ts are high, decorative bow rails, which are
und with any tackle—fly, spin, or plug. Low
maller grab rails can generally provide the
ı need without major clutter. The one major
;h-bow-rail rule is the "family exception." If
ıs low freeboard and is also going to be used
:hildren on a regular basis, then by all means
ıropriate height for child safety. Just because
vever, does not mean that children should
them, especially near the bow. Whether you
ally placed rails or a more extensive rail sys-
heir purpose is the same: to help your pas-
y around the boat and to provide secure
weather or while under way.

ing lights can be pushed down out of the way.

In the early 1980s I fished at Deep Water Cay in the Bahamas where many of the skiffs had been rigged with an inverted horseshoe-shaped lean rail on the bow casting platform. The rails, or "lean posts," made of aluminum piping about an inch and a half in diameter, were just the right height to lean against with a hip or buttock. They reduced fatigue and helped me keep my balance fishing in rough water. Even though they didn't get in the way of fly lines or impede spin fishing, they could be removed easily when not in use. My 20-foot center console now has removable lean posts on the bow and stern deck to assist me and my aging angling companions.

Similar to the lean posts are the adjustable "toadstool" or bicycle seats found on the casting decks of many bass boats. These, also, are simple devices that can be sat on, leaned against, and removed when not needed. For most anglers who don't need the support of a full chair, these stools are better for fatigue and clutter reduction.

Other things that stick up and get in the way are running lights and antennae. Again, to keep your deck as clean as possible, red and green bow lights can be installed as flush-mounted pop-ups. Use them only when you need them, and the rest of the time you can keep them out of the way.

The same is true for running lights. Rather than having a tall, intrusive post sticking up near the back of your boat, running lights can be installed on top of the cowling of your motor, or on a bracket that allows you to turn it up or turn it down as needed. The same is true with antennae for a VHF radio. If you are going to be fishing only inshore waters where reception is good, a three-foot antenna on your console is often all that is necessary. My three-foot antenna is also mounted on a bracket that allows me to turn it down and out of the way when serious fishing is taking place on the boat. Needless to say, if you are fishing in more remote areas and require a longer antenna, then by all means get a six-foot, nine-foot, or longer VHF antenna. Again, however, make sure that it is installed so that it can be laid down flat on a gunnel when not needed.

There are many more things that can clutter fishing space on any boat. Trolling motors, down riggers, and push poles are all necessary items for certain types of fishing. However, it's just common sense that when the items are not going to be used, they should either be secured out of the way or removed from the boat. For example, I regularly use a push pole on johnboats and flats boats. There are numerous times each year when I do not plan to use a push pole. In the fall of the year, I fish for false albacore near the inlets and along the beaches in the same boat that I pole for redfish at other times. Having a twenty-foot push pole racked up on one side of a 17-foot boat with protruding ends makes no sense, so I leave the pole in my garage. Only

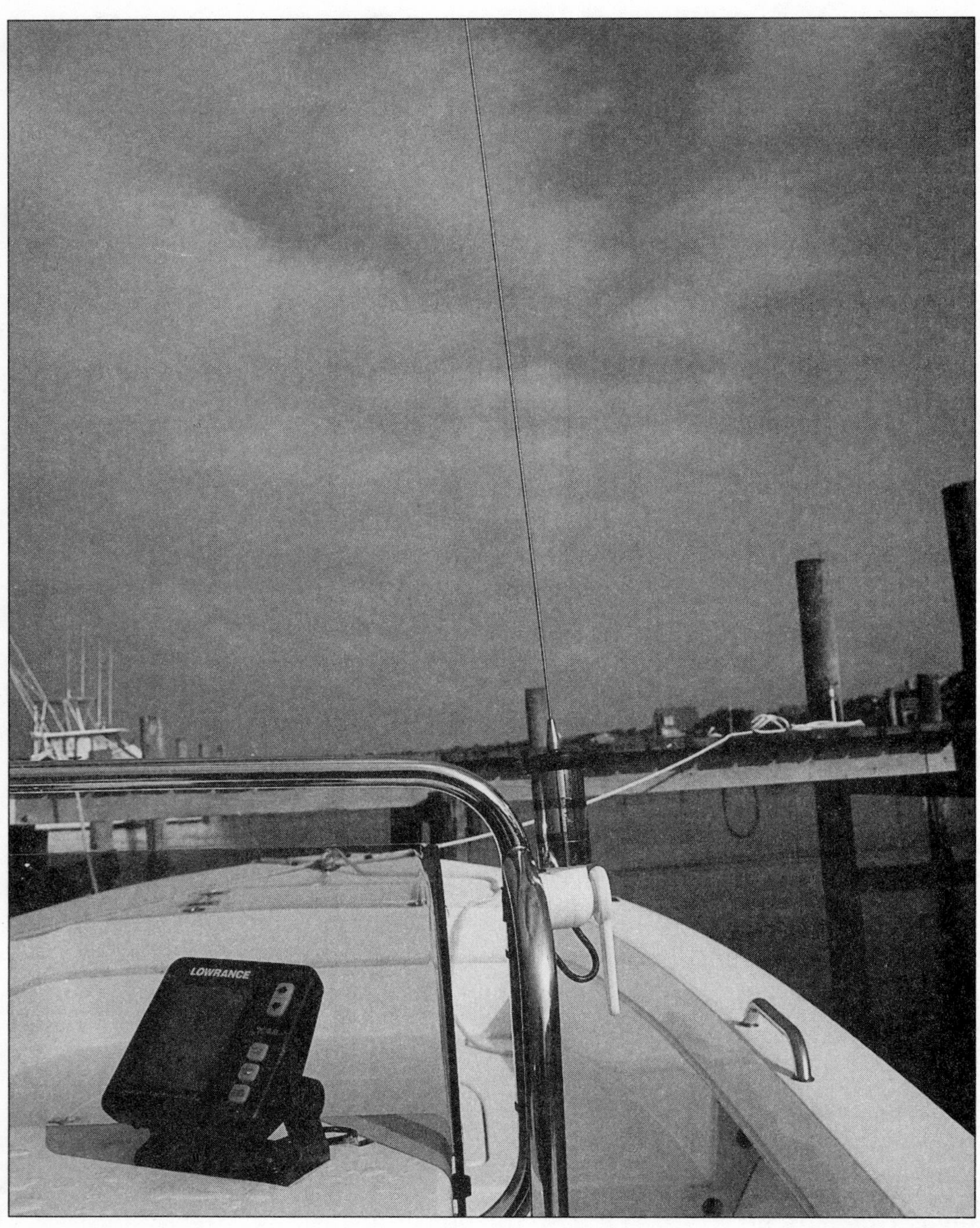

Mount your VHF antenna so that it can be turned down when not needed.

LOWRANCE
LIGHTS NAV/ANC
BILGE PUMP
LIVEWELL
WASHDOWN
ACCESSORY
ACCESSORY
Jones Brothers
MARINE

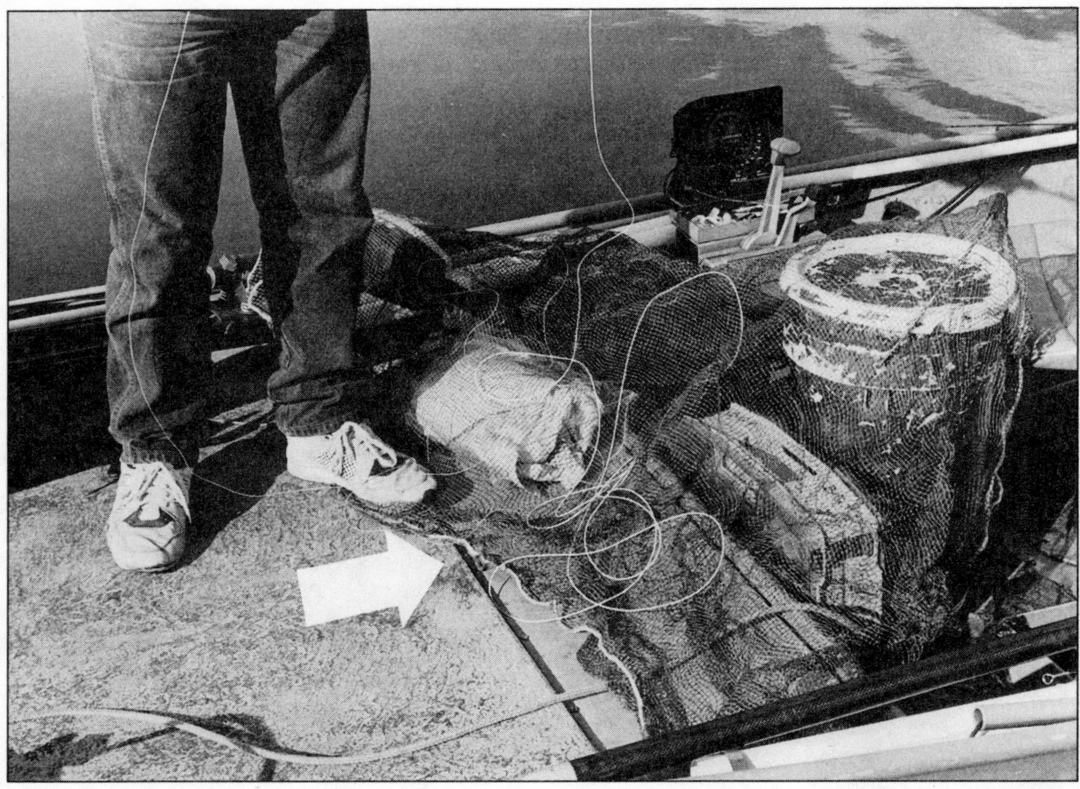

Lefty Kreh

If cluttered space or objects are in your way, cover them!

you can cut the clutter that is sticking up and protruding from your boat.

Fish Finders for Anglers

There is now a bewildering and wonderful array of electronics that can tell you about your engine, the depth of the water, the fish below, your speed, and the temperature of the water around you or beneath you. More sophisticated equipment can also provide you with pinpoint navigation assistance, and radar can give timely warning of other objects in your area. It is not at all uncommon to see boats under 20 feet equipped with navigation, communication, and sonar equipment far superior to that found on Navy ships in World War II.

The first and probably most important area where modern electronics development has aided the small-boat angler is in depth sounders or fish finders. With modern depth sounders we can now find the bottom, structure on the bottom, and fish at various levels. Some units even have the ability to look at the bottom and to scan left and right, fore and aft, with the same transducer.

My garage looks like a sonar angling museum. I have a couple of the old flashers with a neon bulb on a rotating disk. They were useful, and still are, in finding bottom and fish between the surface and the bottom. Their only drawback was that you had to look at them constantly or you would miss a school of fish. In my garage there are several cases of tightly rolled paper that were used on my paper-chart recorders in the 1970s and 1980s. Paper-chart recorders gave a recorded picture of the bottom on a moving tape that showed not only the depth, but also structure and fish. The lines on the paper chart looked very much like an electrocardiogram of the heart. A quality paper-chart recorder was a remarkable instrument, but because of the technological revolution and the computer chip, it has pretty much gone the way of the dinosaur.

Now the moving picture once provided by paper-chart recorders is available to anglers on CRTs (cathode-ray tubes, much like a television screen) and in small, inexpensive LCD (liquid crystal display) units. Because of size and expense the LCD is the small-boat angler's best choice. Waterproof LCD units can be mounted almost anywhere on your boat and provide wonderful information. Along with showing you the bottom, many also provide a "gray line" technology that helps the angler differentiate between hard bottom, soft mud, and grass. On many units, fish are displayed with their depth recorded beside

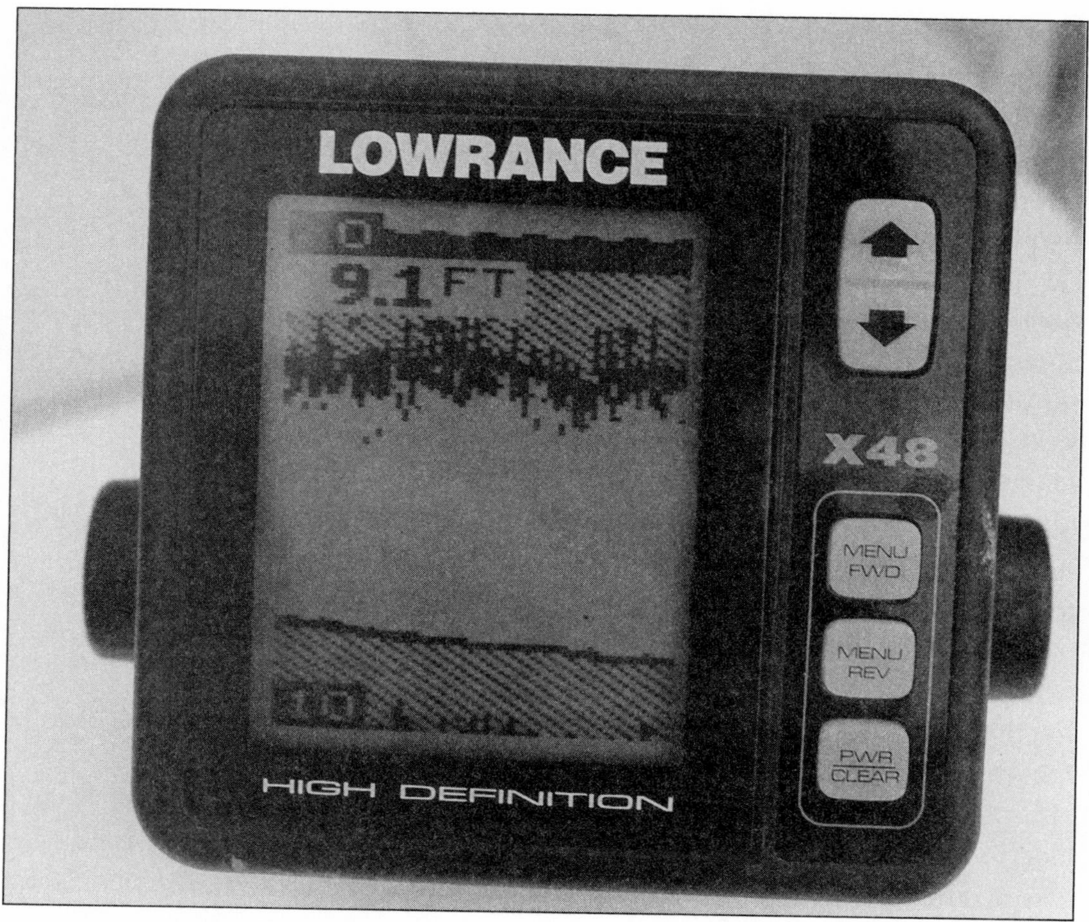

LCD fish finders are relatively small, inexpensive, and weatherproof. Depending on their cost, they can often perform many functions.

them. Even though the new LCD units by such manufacturers as Lowrance, Raytheon, Hummingbird, and Si-Tex are relatively easy to use in lakes, rivers, and coastal waters, time and experience are necessary to get the most out of these wonderful aids. Many of the LCD units currently on the market offer other information, including speed through the water, surface temperature, and a trip log. Other LCD units incorporate GPS (Global

Positioning System, which will be discussed in the next section) navigation information on the same screen. Thus, in a unit not much bigger than a portable radio, fishermen in fresh and salt water can know what's under them, where they are, and how to get home. Such integration of information into a single package helps to cut clutter.

Anglers should never forget that these miracles of sonar and navigation are just aids. In all waters anglers must still rely on their eyes and experience. Electronic information is important but addictive. Good anglers must stay in tune with nature's hints—color changes in the water, floating grass, feeding birds, insect hatches, and showering bait. Boils and rips in the water ahead can be indicators of submerged objects or a shallow bar.

Again, multifunction LCDs can be used anywhere—rivers, lakes, and ocean. No matter what type of boat you use them on, however, make sure that they are mounted where they are the most visible to the user. Whether you have a large center console or a completely open aluminum boat, mount them so that they will be an aid and not an obstacle.

Space Aids to Navigation

Navigation for small boats has forever been thrust into the world of satellites and computers. Just a couple of decades ago, boaters who had any electronic navigational equipment relied on relatively large casings to house radio direction-finders (RDFs) and the hyperbolic systems that included Loran A and Loran C. The Loran systems processed signals from two land-based transmitters. The time difference, or TD, of the receipt of signals helped define an angler's location on nautical charts. A Loran unit mounted in a boat takes the two TD numbers and converts them to latitude and longitude for display. For anglers, Loran provided, and at the time of this writing still provides, the ability to find remote fishing locations, such as wrecks and difficult-to-find bottom structure with reasonable accuracy. The big drawback: When out of range of the land-based system of Loran antennae, the information ceases.

It is almost useless now to discuss Loran or any other electronic navigation systems now that GPS has arrived. With GPS, anglers are no longer tethered to land-based transmitters; in-

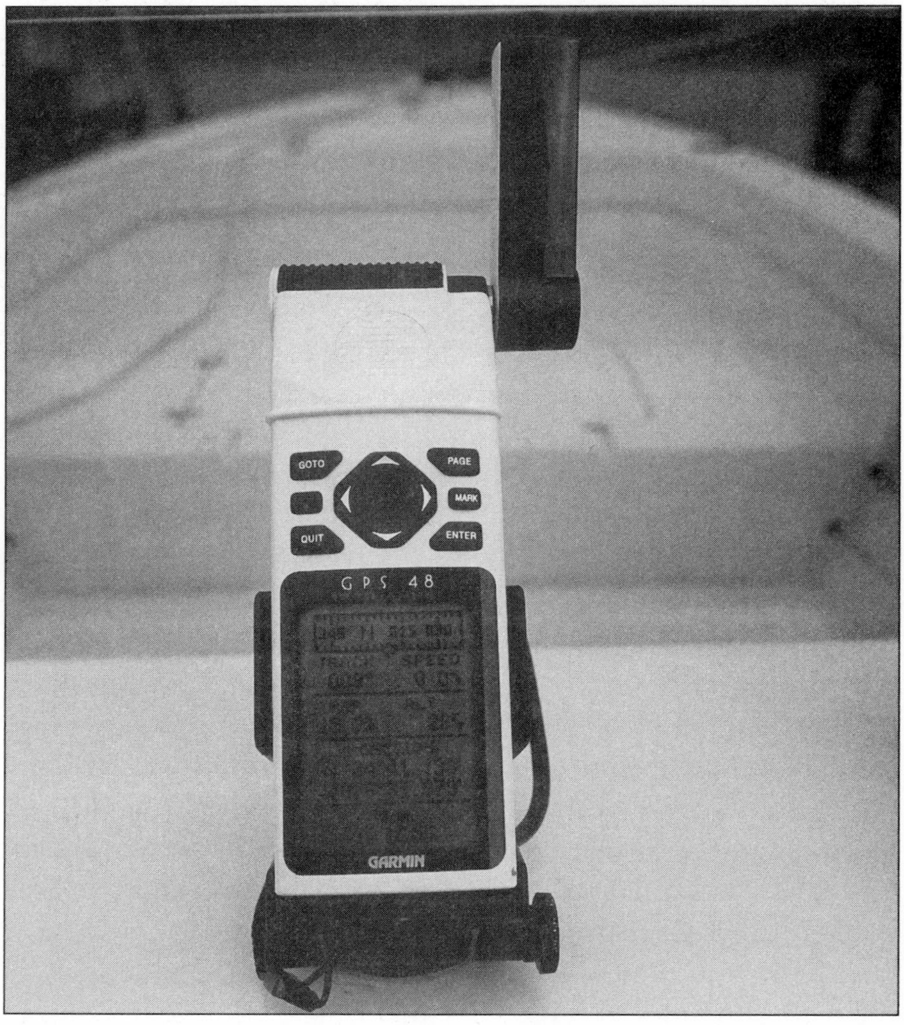

GPS is now available at modest cost to any angler. Some (as shown) are "plotter-only," and others show information superimposed over maps.

stead they receive their information almost anywhere on land, lake, or sea directly from a constellation of satellites located above the earth. Whether you opt for an inexpensive handheld unit or a permanently mounted unit that displays more information, both will calculate latitude and longitude. When you enter a way point, such as the known location of a reef, inlet, or your own dock, a GPS unit will display the distance and direction to it. Units will also provide you with your speed and the present course in which your boat is heading.

The newer cartographic GPS units, both portable and fixed, will display your position superimposed over a chart of the area. For most anglers, cartographic GPS provides superior information for locating a fish-holding location or for plotting a safe return course home. Locations and courses shown on an electronic chart provide a better frame of reference than a "plotter-only" GPS. The first time I saw course lines and numbers displayed in conjunction with a map showing the shoreline, jetties, buoys, church steeples, and shoals, I must admit that I got a warm, tingly feeling. Many units can be loaded with detailed area maps using your home computer.

GPS units can provide accurate information within 30 meters to the user. Such information gives fishermen the ability to return to exactly the same spots in featureless open waters where fish were located on earlier trips. For those demanding more detail, "Differential GPS" can provide accuracy closer to 5 meters! For this degree of accuracy, boats need a GPS unit capable of receiving information from a separate Differential Beacon Receiver (DBR). Some units come with a built-in DBR.

GPS information is available twenty-four hours a day and in all weather conditions. At the time of this writing, a handheld GPS can be purchased for less than $150 and even advanced cartographic units are less than $500. Whether you fish large lakes, winding rivers, or the open ocean, getting lost is no longer an option—unless you want to get lost.

A final thought on GPS. Until I had a cell phone I didn't realize the world needed me twenty-four hours a day. Until GPS I didn't know that I was lost. As wonderful and useful as this tool is, I use GPS only a fraction of the time when I am fishing. GPS is of little interest or use to me when I am fishing familiar waters or working the shoreline of small lakes or rivers. Your GPS unit should not replace your compass and chart. When fuses blow and batteries are dead, a compass and waterproof chart will still work just fine.

Onboard Communications

The first rule of communications for any small-boat angler is to tell somebody where you are going at your home or marina. Accidents can occur before you have a chance to communicate with anyone, and it is important that someone knows where to begin the search if necessary.

Certainly the most noticeable change in communications for the small-boat angler has been the transfer of the cell phone from the car to the boat. It is almost impossible to go to any reservoir or coastal area without hearing the sounds of cell phones. With cell phones we can communicate with our spouses, offices, and even other anglers. Cell phones, however, are definitely a mixed blessing. On the one hand, they can provide us with quick, direct communication; but they can also seriously intrude into our time on the water if we let them. A couple of years ago I fished with a gentleman who carried two cell phones and a pager clipped to his belt. He said that it was the only way he could get time away from the office. The fact is he never left the office, since both phones and the pager constantly rang and beeped throughout the day.

Where an adequate signal exists, a cellular telephone is a means for both emergency and nonemergency communications. But is a cell phone what you need in an emergency on the water? If you dial 911 in a marine environment, you are probably going to get the local sheriff or the highway patrol. If you dial 0 for the operator, you may be trying to describe a marine emergency to someone hundreds of miles away. For most on-the-water emergencies, a marine VHF radio telephone is still the best alternative.

With a marine VHF (Very High Frequency), you can count on the Coast Guard and perhaps other vessels standing by on Channel 16 in an emergency. Using a number of channels, boaters can send and receive line-of-sight signals. Using short, three- to six-foot antenna, anglers in small boats can communicate with each other over a five- to ten-mile range. Operators of the same boats might still be able to communicate with the Coast Guard or marina twenty-five miles away, which are equipped with tall base antennae.

Fixed-mount units used in fishing boats are limited to 25 watts of power, although most VHFs also have a 1-watt setting. Since VHF radios listen to only the strongest signal, boaters transmitting on the low power (1 watt) setting to another boat at close range will not interfere with other boaters tuned to the same channel miles away.

Along with the ability to reach help in a marine environment, VHF radios also provide anglers with the latest NOAA (National Oceanic and Atmospheric Administration) weather information. Some models will automatically turn to the active weather channel if a special alert is issued. Will your cell phone do that?

Handheld VHF radios have become increasingly important to the small-boat community in recent years. Because they are battery-powered, they are completely portable. Instead of 25 watts, the handheld versions are limited to 6 watts of transmit power. Although line of sight limits boat-to-boat transmission to about five miles with handheld VHF, communication between a boat operator using a handheld and the Coast Guard or a towing service, both users of tall antennae, will be much farther. Handheld VHF units are generally "water resistant" or "waterproof." Some of the new models are even submersible. The handheld VHFs are a good alternative for any boater who wants to have emergency communications and weather information at the ready. The handheld models are also ideal for the anglers who must travel "light" in kayaks, canoes, and skiffs.

One small admonition: I hear a lot of casual conversations—ship to shore, boat to boat, and sometimes duck blind to duck blind over VHF marine radios. Such conversations not only clog channels but they may be illegal under FCC (Federal Communications Commission) rules. There is a solution for those who want two-way conversations of the same quality as VHF. The new FRS (Family Radio Service) radios have only a two-mile range, but are perfectly legal for most chatter not allowed over VHF. The relatively inexpensive FRS units are ideal for relaxed personal conversations, but are not intended for emergency use like marine VHF. They are available through many marine supply houses and discount stores. I mention the FRS radio option only because I believe they may help relieve congestion on VHF channels that are important to the boating community.

Batteries and Battery Systems

It seems strange to talk about batteries as accessories, but many modern fishing boats have so many different power demands that the right battery system is also an accessory. How many times have you been to a boat ramp only to hear the sickening sound of a motor barely turning over, or worse, no sound at all? Poorly laid out or poorly understood electrical systems can cause any powerboat angler headaches.

First understand that all boat batteries are "banks." When the engine is running, a "deposit" is made when the battery is charged by the alternator. When the engine is stopped, the battery, or batteries, may be called upon to power radios, depth sounders, bilge pumps, and lights. Such items make "withdrawals" from the bank. If one accessory, such as the running lights, which draw only a few amps, is left on for an extended period of time, the bank will be drained. When needed for cranking the engine or powering a VHF radio, a depleted battery may not have enough stored power to do its job.

First, make sure that your boat is rigged with an "OFF/ON" battery switch. When you pull your boat out of the water, turn off, or isolate, your battery from unintended battery drain. When launching your boat on the next fishing trip, turn on the power and you should be ready to crank your engine. If you don't have an "OFF/ON" switch and don't want to spend the $20 to buy one, disconnect the positive, or red, cable from your battery between uses when your boat is out of the water.

Most fishing boats with large engines and a number of accessories will have two starting batteries as a safety backup. Dual systems should have a switch marked "OFF-1-BOTH-2." With the switch turned to "1" or "2" only one of the batteries will be used for cranking and only one will be charged while the engine is running. When the switch is turned to "BOTH" (on some switches shown as "ALL"), then both batteries can be charged at the same time. However, both can also be drained at the same time if a small electrical item is left on for a period of time with the battery switch set on "BOTH" or "ALL." Isolate battery "1"

When not in use, batteries should be turned off or isolated with an "ON" and "OFF" switch.

or "2" so you will always have a spare cranking battery. When you pull your boat out of the water, make sure you turn the switching unit to "OFF" to isolate both batteries from unintended drain.

Also, anglers need to know the difference between a "cranking battery" and a "deep-cycle battery." A marine cranking battery will deliver short bursts of high energy to start the engine. Even though most cranking batteries are capable of powering most accessories that have low amp requirements (VHF radio, fish finder, and GPS unit), they are not intended as a source of power for accessories that pull heavy loads, such as powerful lights and trolling motors. Since cranking batteries generally aren't used to operate power-gobbling accessories, they don't need lots of "reserve minutes," a measure of battery capacity.

Deep-cycle batteries on the other hand are designed with more reserve minutes and the ability to be recharged over and over again without damage. A starting or cranking battery can be drained, or discharged completely, only a few times before permanent damage occurs. This is why anglers who use trolling motors and other accessories that make high-power demands on their batteries over a long period of time must have batteries that can be recharged many times (two hundred or more) without damage—thus the "deep-cycle battery."

Whether you operate a 25-horsepower or a 250-horsepower motor, make sure you work with your dealer to have the right battery or batteries for the job. The choices in marine batteries are extensive. Along with cranking batteries and deep-cycle batteries, there are now dual-purpose batteries that combine the characteristics of cranking and deep-cycle batteries. With your dealer, consider such things as the weight and weight distribution of your batteries. This is especially important in such craft as light aluminum boats and flats boats. Take a close look at the cranking requirements of your engine and the expected amp drain of your accessories. Even when you are sure you have the

Get the right battery to do the job. Boating batteries come as cranking (starting), deep cycle (trolling and auxiliary power), and dual purpose.

right battery, or batteries, for your boat, know where the "OFF" switch is so that you can isolate your battery from unintended power drain when your boat is out of the water.

Additional Accessories to Consider

When I look at the boats of my saltwater heroes in the Florida Keys, North Carolina's Outer Banks, and in the New England waters, I see simple, well-laid-out boats with clean interiors and a minimum of unnecessary instrumentation. The same is true when I look at the boats of my heroes on rivers and large reservoirs. The best anglers want the right hull and the right accessories to catch fish, not impress onlookers.

As already indicated, many things that used to have their own gauges and dials are now consolidated into one unit. Again,

The console of a quality fishing boat need not be crowded. Install only the gear that you need.

many depth recorders also show speed, distance traveled, and surface water temperature. Why do you need three additional holes in your console telling you the same thing? A GPS unit will also tell you much more than your present position.

With medium-size and larger outboards, two bits of instrumentation that I regard as most important are the tachometer and the hour meter. The tachometer does a good job in telling you how hard your engine is working. And the hour meter is important in monitoring the use of the engine between routine servicing. Another thing that I like to have on all powerboats, big and small, is an accessory plug (like a cigarette-lighter plug). In this inexpensive accessory you can plug in a cell phone, a high-intensity floodlight, or other equipment that doesn't need to be permanently installed but may be needed from time to time.

Final Thoughts and "E-Boats"

With the speed, comfort, and communications gear available to anglers, many are taking their business to the water. It is not at all uncommon to hear a real estate deal, stock transaction, or a discussion with the baby-sitter taking place while waiting for the stripers to come in with the tide. Being able to mix business with one's fishing passion is not a bad thing, considering that the alternative is staying in the office in a suit. With satellites and cell phones it is now possible to get off the Internet your E-mail, stock quotations, and even the latest water temperature and weather conditions around your boat. I am sure that some clever manufacturer will, in the very near future, be advertising its bass boat, flats boat, or center console as E-boats.

My hope is that anglers will still regard their boats as sanctuaries and conduct as little business as possible in such a sacred place. For me, a fishing boat has always been a place to relax and a place to share time without interruptions (except for an occasional fish) with friends and family. If we aren't careful, the places we transact business and the places we go for renewal will become indistinguishable. Yes, we live in a "connected world." I, for one, want to maintain my fishing boat as a place where I can disconnect.

IV

PROTECTING YOUR INVESTMENT

9

Trailering, Storage, Mooring, and Maintenance of Power Boats

Boat abuse is a common problem in America. Ride down almost any road, or through any neighborhood, and sooner or later you will see a fine fishing boat parked under a tree, covered with sap, baking in the sun; or tightly wrapped in a dark plastic tarpaulin, cooking like a turkey. Mistreatment of boats has nothing to do with their price tags or the materials from which they are made. You are just as likely to see an inexpensive aluminum johnboat wasting away as you are a $30,000 bass boat or an oceangoing center console. I am convinced that for every angler who takes pride in his or her boat, there is another who does little or nothing to protect or maintain such an important investment. I am further convinced that boat neglect comes more often out of lack of knowledge rather than malice toward the machine.

Every spring I see the consequences of boat abuse and neglect manifested in a number of ways. At public boat ramps and at private marinas, I often hear silence when boat keys are turned—the sound of a dead battery. Even when batteries are charged, the sounds of motors turning over and over without cranking are a common springtime noise. With disappointed fishing buddies standing around, the owners of such boats will often mutter something like: "I can't understand it. This engine started just fine on the last trip—last year."

The problems encountered by most anglers are not associated with equipment failure but rather maintenance failure. Clogged fuel filters, gunked-up carburetors, bad gasoline, and corroded electrical connections occur because of neglect, not because of the failure of high-tech computer chips or fuel-injection systems. I am not a mechanic or an electrical engineer, but I have learned that those boat owners who adhere to a basic maintenance regimen generally have few problems. For major maintenance and repairs, or for "mothballing" your boat for a long period of time, by all means consult a dealer or qualified mechanic. However, for regular use, or sporadic seasonal use, some of the tips below can help you get more life and enjoyment out of your fishing craft.

Boat Storage and Protection out of the Water

For many anglers, boat storage is a problem. Even if you trailer your rig, finding a place to park your trailer without objection is often difficult. For example, although I have thoroughly explained to my wife why boats need protection from the elements, she still wants her car in our garage rather than a fishing boat. Why can't she understand that, even with the epoxy paints and excellent gel coats available on boats today, parking a fine boat in the sun can mean a chalky, faded finish and considerably diminished value? Parking a boat under a shade tree can do more damage than the sun. In a very short period of time, sap, acorns, needles, and leaves can stain or do permanent damage to the finish of any boat. So, for those of us without a garage, what types of boat protection should be considered?

In almost every discount store you can find large, inexpensive poly tarps. They should be used *only* for temporary or emergency boat protection. Plastic tarps do not breathe well, and a boat wrapped for protection can literally bake under intense heat in direct sun. A plastic tarp produces the ultimate greenhouse effect of heat and humidity, which can damage any fishing boat and the equipment in it. A far better alternative is a *breathable* cloth or canvas cover that can be purchased from the boat manufacturer or from a variety of boating supply houses and catalogs. A breathable cover can protect much of a boat's exterior and interior from rain, direct sunlight, and tree garbage. For anglers who spend thousands of dollars on a fishing boat and accessories, it makes little sense to skimp on a good cover that will significantly prolong a boat's life and appearance.

As already indicated, the best protection for a boat is to store it out of the elements entirely. Although modern fishing boats can temporarily withstand harsh weather conditions, they were

Boat covers should be made of breathable cloth or canvas.

Dry-stack storage may be expensive, but so was your boat.

never intended to be parked in the cold or direct sunlight for long periods, or wrapped like a taco. For many anglers the storage problem is solved by dry-stack storage available on many lakes and at coastal marinas. At such facilities, giant forklifts are used to lift boats out of the water and place them on cradles stacked four or five high in giant metal barns. Dry-stack storage will protect your boat from the elements, but for many anglers the cost can prove prohibitive. In some areas the cost of storing a 20-foot outboard can run a couple of hundred dollars a month. This is a lot of money, but it may still be reasonable when one considers the deterioration and consequent loss of resale value that occurs when a boat is unprotected. For my own boat-storage needs, I have settled on a lockup storage facility where

If you keep your boat on its trailer, a garage or shed is the best protection.

my boat can be stored on its trailer. This situation is best for me since the boat is always accessible and ready to travel. Although expensive, my park-it-yourself covered bay costs much less than most dry-stack-storage operations, which must pay for forklifts and the employees who run them.

Keeping Boats Clean in and out of the Water

Many large (over 30 foot) fishing boats with hulls of wood, fiberglass, or aluminum, remain in the water. They are too long and heavy to trailer or store out of the water, and without anti-fouling bottom paints, their hulls would soon be covered with plant and animal growth. For some fishing guides, anglers who live on the water, and others who work on the water every day, keeping a small boat in the water may be unavoidable. For most recreational anglers with small boats, myself included, the use of antifouling paints is not necessary. Even though there are a number of excellent bottom paints containing copper compounds and biocides that will inhibit underwater plant and animal growth, the best option is the "three-day rule." If you trailer your boat or keep it at a dry-stack facility, simply pull it out of the water every three days so that the hull can be washed and dried. By adhering to the three-day rule, especially in salt water, damage and discoloration to any boat's hull by algae, barnacles, or other aquatic growth can be virtually eliminated. I follow this rule religiously even during the best weather and fishing conditions. Again, pull the boat out, wash the hull with mild soap and water, and let it dry before sticking it in the water for another

After three or four days in water, plant and animal growth can begin to get a foothold. Clean hulls with dishwashing detergent or low-abrasive cleaners. Avoid the harsher abrasives, such as the Comet shown in the picture.

three-day stint. I am aware that at certain times of the year water temperatures and other conditions would allow me to leave my rig floating longer than three days. However, by adhering to my three-day rule, I never have to worry.

Although care of your boat's hull is important, please don't forget the care and cleaning of the boat's interior and hardware, especially after use in salt water. After a day in salt water, the minimum care required is a quick scrub with a deck brush using soap and water, followed by a freshwater rinse. Salt water is a real villain and can pit or discolor even the finest grade of stainless steel. Without soap and water you will not get the salt off your boat! For most interior cleaning I use biodegradable liquid dishwashing detergents.

When used with a brush they will clean anything on your boat while causing little or no environmental damage. Once a fishing trip has ended, I am a big fan of the high-pressure carwash systems available in most areas. For a couple of dollars you can blast your boat and trailer with high-pressure soapy water followed by a high-pressure rinse.

Unlike barnacles and heavy algae that can affect a boat's performance, stained hulls or interiors not only look bad, they can diminish resale value if not dealt with. There are times when stains caused by algae, dirty water, and rust cannot be removed by soap and water alone. Although I have seen scrub-free "toilet bowl cleaners" used with great success on problem stains, these can be *dangerous* solutions that can burn both skin and eyes. Many boating houses supply heavy-duty stain removers both in liquid and gel forms that can get the job done. Before using any of these extraordinary cleaning solutions, consult with your boat's manufacturer about their effects on gel coats, especially colored gel coats. One commonly available cleaning solution that I have found useful in dealing with problem stains is the low-abrasive cleanser Soft Scrub. I keep it in my boat for light-duty stain removal. Although I frequently see them used in boat-cleaning operations, *powdered abrasive cleansers* (Ajax, Comet, etc.) *should be avoided* for use on gel coats and paints. These abrasive cleansers are just a step away from using very fine sandpaper.

Motor Maintenance

I know a number of guides who run their outboards more than two hundred days a year. Many will run the same engine for several years without any significant problems. Such long life and endurance is a tribute to both the manufacturers who build the engines and the fishing guides who maintain them. Since these "working engines" will be run more hours in a year than many recreational anglers will log over several years, why do so many engines with low hours break down? It is generally agreed that without proper maintenance, it is more damaging for engines to sit for weeks and months than to be run every day. Engines that aren't used are more likely to develop problems related to their fuel systems, electrical systems, and even corrosion.

I have always considered myself a year-round angler and try not to let long periods of time pass without exploring the opportunities. Even with the best of intentions, however, there are periods of weeks and perhaps even a month when my boats are not used. Since I do not "winterize" any of my boats with fogging solutions and long-term storage lubricants, I have developed some other habits that help protect my rigs and keep them ready to go. Most are little things, but when taken together they will extend the useful life of any engine. One of the first things I try to do is take care of the fuel in my boat. By keeping fuel tanks filled there is little room for condensation. Even a little water in the fuel system can be damaging. Also, if there is any chance I will not be using the boat for an extended period of time (over a month), I add a fuel stabilizer. Fuel stabilizers, which are available at any good marina and boating-supply store, help keep gasoline fresh and help prevent gunk and varnish from getting a foothold on fuel-system components. After you have added the suggested amount of fuel stabilizer to your tanks, make sure that you run your engines long enough so that the stabilized fuel has gone through your fuel lines and into the engine itself. Another fuel additive that I use when I am not running my engines on a regular basis is one that inhibits carbon buildup on piston rings. Unless piston rings are "free," power head damage can occur. Again, please note that the addition of fuel stabilizers and additives that inhibit carbon buildup are not intended to take the place of "winterization." Such additives do, however, protect fuel and engines that are run on a less-than-regular basis.

Of all the things I can think of to do for an outboard, nothing is easier than spraying the power head with a liquid corrosion inhibitor. At least every couple of months, remove the cowling from your engine and liberally spray everything—the wires, spark plugs, hoses, and all metal surfaces—with a coating of a lubricant such as CRC 6–56 or WD-40. These lubricants, and others on the market like them, will help force moisture out of all electrical connections, keep hoses pliable, protect gaskets, and prevent corrosion. Since these liquids can be flammable, they should be used when the *engine is off and cool* and where there is adequate ventilation.

The average angler/boater can do much to lengthen the life of an outboard engine by giving the lower unit regular tender loving care. It is easy to change the lubricant in most lower units simply by removing a couple of screws. High-quality lubricants for the lower unit can be purchased at virtually any marina and boating-supply house. The lubricant should be changed at least twice a year (I prefer spring and fall) to keep water and corrosion from damaging sensitive parts. As simple a procedure as it is, there will always be a few boat owners who will never change the lower unit lubricant until the motor seizes and the damage is irreparable. Also, at the same time you change the lower unit

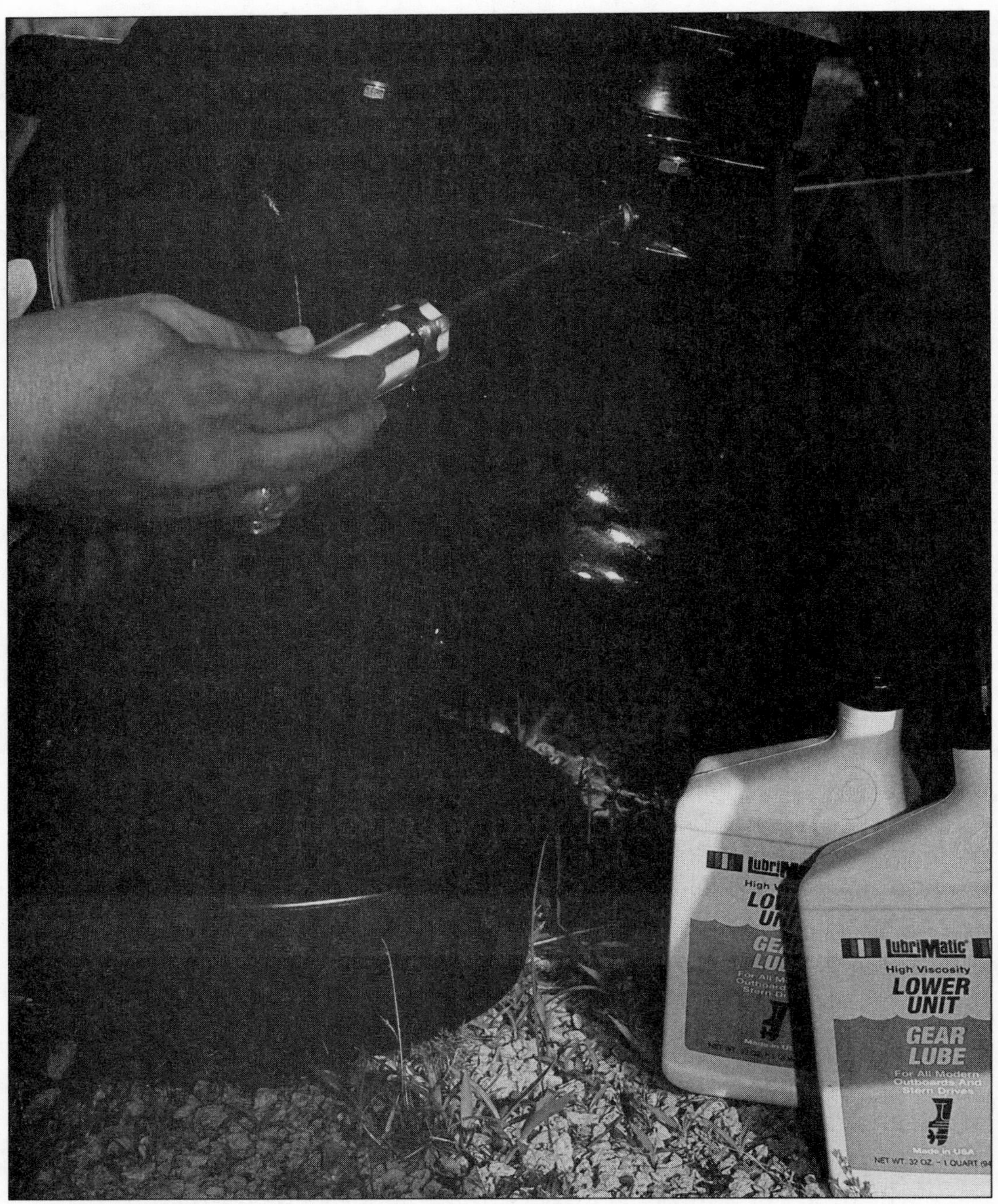

Changing the lubricant in the lower unit is an easy job that should be done twice a year.

lubricant, use a grease gun and top off the grease supply at each grease port on your engine.

If you use your boat in salt water, there is another very important step that must be taken to ensure the health of your lower unit. Whenever you pull your rig out of salt water to store it, flush out the lower unit of your outboard or stern drive with

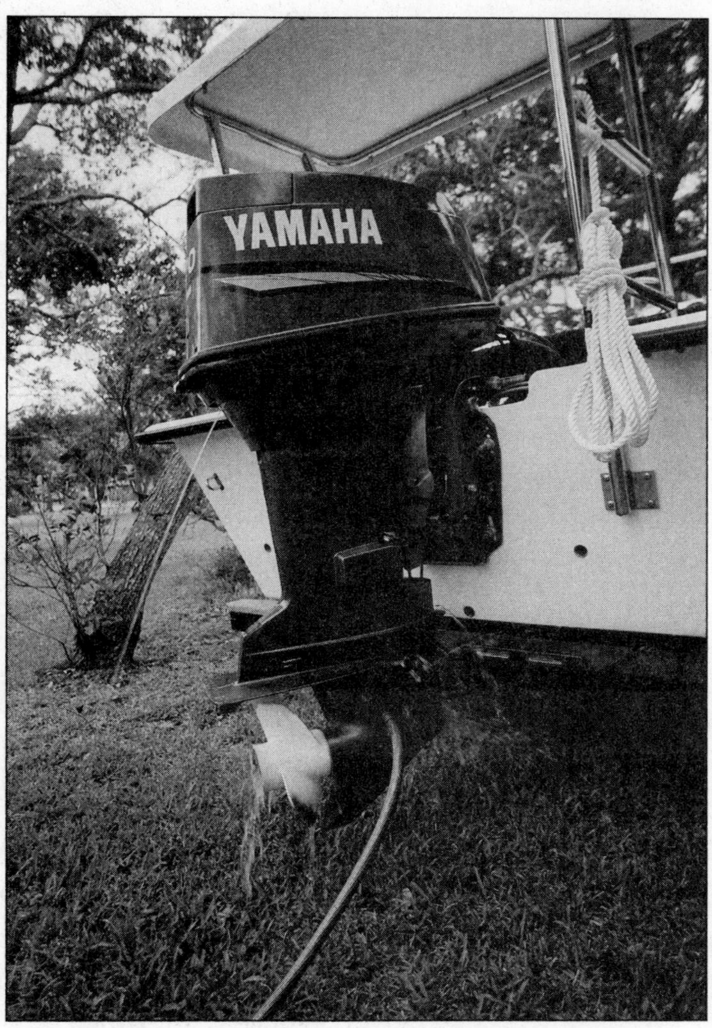

Flush your engine after use in salt water even if you plan to keep it out of the water only a few days.

fresh water. Whether I have used an engine in salt water for a few hours or several days, I try to make it a habit to run the engine for a few minutes using a flushing unit and garden hose. By circulating fresh water through the lower unit, corrosion-causing salt water can be purged from the interior. This is especially important if you know your boat will be out of the water for several days or weeks. Finally, whenever you plan to store your boat after use in fresh or salt water, make sure that your lower unit is in the *vertical* position so that no standing water can stay in the lower unit or around the cylinder head.

Galvanic Corrosion

One of the most potentially damaging problems that can affect every outboard, stern drive, and conventional drive is galvanic corrosion. This is the chemical reaction that can cause serious damage when dissimilar metals found in every power system are joined together electrically. With salt water as the electrolyte (the conductive fluid) engine metals that are less "noble" will corrode, while more noble metals will not be damaged. The least noble metals are referred to as anodes, while the more noble metals are referred to as cathodes. When two dissimilar metals are joined together to form a galvanic cell, the anode will corrode.

This is why virtually every engine on the market today will have attached "sacrificial" metal plates or attachments to protect all of the other metals found in the engine from galvanic corrosion. The most common sacrificial anodes are usually made of zinc alloys, which are less noble than any metals used on important engine parts. The most common sacrificial anodes found on outboards are the mini rudders. These finlike attachments will become pitted and marred over a period of time, but not to worry, since this is what they are designed to do. Once corrosion becomes noticeable on an outboard's mini rudder or any other

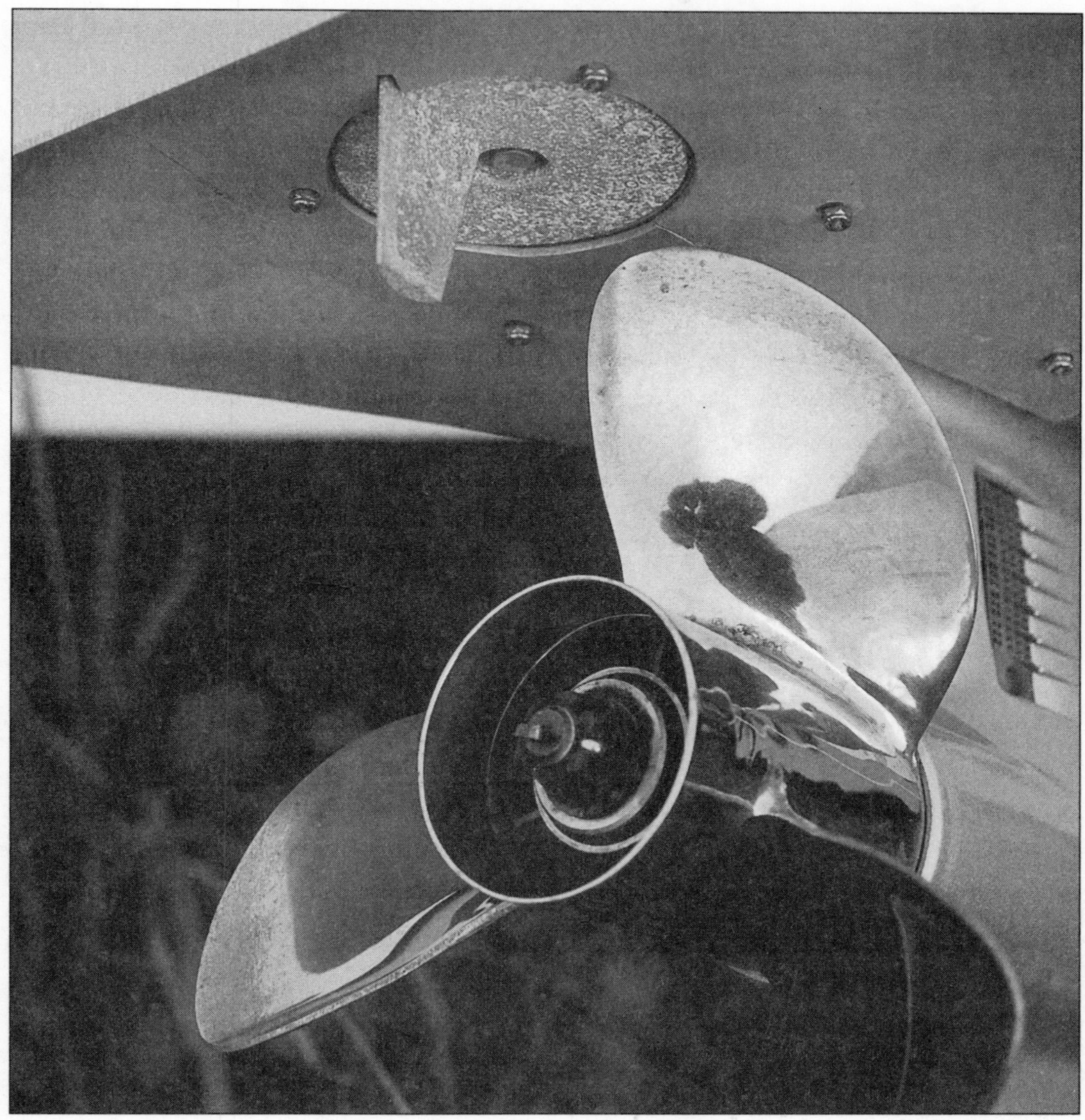

Galvanic corrosion should first show up on the zinc "mini rudder," or other sacrificial anodes.

sacrificial metal plate, they should be replaced immediately. The costs of these protective parts and the skill necessary to replace them is minimal. Remember that without these sacrificial attachments, the damage to the power plant on your fishing boat from galvanic corrosion can be expensive or irreparable.

Even though freshwater is not nearly as conductive as salt water, galvanic corrosion can still occur in inland lakes. Although sacrificial anodes made of zinc alloy are still the most commonly used, some freshwater anglers use anodes made of magnesium alloy. Magnesium is even less noble than zinc and may provide the best protection in freshwater. The bottom line is that whether you fish in fresh or salt water you must be aware of and protect your engine from galvanic corrosion by replacing manufacturer-recommended anodes on a regular basis.

Trailer Protection

You can't go fishing if you neglect your trailer. Compared to a modern fishing boat and outboard motor, a trailer is a simple piece of equipment, with only a few things that can go wrong. The trailer parts that have ruined more fishing trips than any others are probably the wheel bearings. If wheel bearings aren't properly packed with grease and checked regularly, water and other contaminants can get in the bearings and allow them to overheat. Failed wheel bearings will leave you and your angry fishing buddies stranded on the interstate. Most trailers now come equipped with spring-loaded devices that allow axle grease to be kept under pressure around the bearings. By regularly adding grease through these devices, you can protect your wheel bearings and your fishing trips.

Boats, motors, and trailers are often bought as a package, and herein lies the problem. To save money, many trailers are equipped with smaller, inexpensive tires and wheels. They are fine for short trips and light-duty work, but if you intend to trailer your boat on a regular basis and take long trips, buy the largest tires for which your trailer is designed. Small tires turn much faster than a larger tire at the same speed, and can be another factor causing wheel bearings to overheat and fail. Also, if you regularly trailer over long distances, consider getting radial tires for your trailer instead of the traditional bias-ply tires that are standard. Finally, make sure that you have a spare tire of the same diameter as those on your trailer. A spare tire is inexpensive trip insurance, yet it is amazing how many anglers travel without one.

Somewhere along the line of the evolution of fishing boats, "designer" trailers evolved. It is now possible to buy steel trailers painted or enameled the same color as your car or your boat. All anglers would do well to consider galvanized trailers and galvanized wheels in place of painted ones. A galvanized frame (also acceptable are the newer all-aluminum trailers) is an absolute must for use in salt water and brackish water, and in my opinion equally important for freshwater anglers. Even though the corrosion potential for those using their boats only in freshwater is not as high, there are still plenty of road salts and other corrosive contaminants that can get into nooks and crannies and shorten the life of nongalvanized trailers. No matter what kind of trailer to which you entrust your boat, make sure that all of its components, frame, rollers, springs, and wheels get a thorough washing and rinse whenever you wash your boat.

Ah, yes, about those trailer springs . . . Just like the wheel bearings mentioned earlier, which need protection from highway contaminants and the ravages of salt, trailer springs also need a little care. Over the years I have heard literally dozens of concoctions used by anglers to coat their trailer springs in an effort to protect them from corrosion. I have seen springs coated with axle grease, painted with heavy oils such as STP, slathered with used motor oil, and sprayed with moisture-displacing lubricants such as WD-40. The spring protector that I now use was shown to me by Steve Coward, an extraordinary mechanic on Harkers Island. Steve suggests that you baste your trailer springs with used vegetable shortening or even Crisco right out of the can. Steve cautions that you should be careful not to select used vegetable shortening containing salt, which comes from hush puppy mix or seafood batters. There are two advantages to Steve's salt-free vegetable shortening: Springs are well protected against corrosion, and any grease that does happen to enter the water while launching your trailer is biodegradable.

When you have your boat off its trailer, take the opportunity to lubricate your trailer's rollers or carpeted skid pads at least twice a season. The best lubricant I have found for trailer rollers is white lithium grease, available at all boating-supply houses. Whether you have a few or a lot of rollers on your trailer, each must be working properly for easy launch and retrieval of your craft. For flat-bottom boats and even V-hulled boats resting on trailers with carpeted skid pads, there is a way to dramatically improve your trailer's performance. If you liberally apply liquid silicone spray to all exposed carpeted areas you will swear that your boat is moving over ball bearings. Liquid silicone will not harm your trailer or boat finish. No matter what kind of boat you own, liquid silicone on your trailer's carpeted supports will make your life at the boat ramp much more enjoyable.

Finally, there are many excellent trailers on the market today. Some are designed as "float on" trailers and are intended to be almost fully submerged. Many trailers, however, are designed to allow you to launch and retrieve your boat without being submerged. Even if your trailer is galvanized, your springs are coated, and your axles are greased, a trailer will last longer if it doesn't need to be submerged at the boat ramp. Also, regardless of whether you are an old hand at launching and retrieving fishing boats, check with your boat and trailer dealer about the correct launch techniques for your rig. You may find that you've been dunking when you didn't need to.

There are a number of other things that I could say about fishing boat trailers, such as: Get a good trailer lock, spray all electrical connections with a moisture-displacing lubricant, and always chock the wheels of your car when launching your boat at a ramp. If you are new to boat trailering, however, the most important thing you can do is practice backing techniques. Nothing is more frustrating or embarrassing than being unable to back your boat quickly at a narrow, crowded boat ramp. If backing a trailer does not come naturally, take your boat and trailer to a deserted parking lot and practice backing until you get it right. Years ago I frequented a marina where the crusty owner was regularly heard hollering at patrons with less-than-perfect trailering skills: "If you can't back it, park it!"

Electronics

None of us would intentionally leave a personal computer, portable radio, or cellular telephone outside, unprotected from the elements. Yet many of us park our fishing boats in open fields or marina slips with VHF radios, GPS systems, and fish finders with LCD screens exposed to the sun and elements. Even though the electronics available to boaters today are remarkably weather-resistant, it makes no sense to leave them unprotected for extended periods of time. In years past I have had only myself to blame for fogged screens on my depth recorders and GPS systems. A breathable cloth console cover can help, but better yet, take the time to remove your expensive fishing and navigational electronics so that their useful life can be extended to years instead of just a couple of seasons.

Also take the time to protect the electrical connections on your boat from corrosion. Although a regular application of a moisture-displacing lubricant is good, nothing does a better job than petroleum jelly to plug the holes of electrical connections and keep the moisture out. At the suggestion of my master mechanic friend Steve Coward, I now keep a jar of Vaseline in my boat, with which I regularly dab exposed electrical connections, and also chapped lips and hands on a cold day.

* * *

It should now be abundantly clear that complicated fishing boats have more complicated maintenance problems. Multiple radios, redundant navigation equipment, electric motors, different livewells for bait and fish, and even a cool stereo system may seem desirable, but prudent anglers should choose only those items they really need, and then maintain them properly. A good fishing boat should be one of the joys of your life, not a cause of headaches and frustration. Once you have committed to the boat best suited to your needs, also commit to a regular maintenance program for the hull, interior, engine, trailer, and electrical equipment.

10

Ropes, Knots, and Anchors

Most anglers I know have a pretty good repertoire of knots for tying on hooks, building leaders, and making loops. Although we try to get the most use out of line used with spinning, conventional, or fly tackle, we don't skimp on line. It is not at all uncommon to pay $50 or more for a new fly line, or to pay $20 to fill the spool of your spinning reel. Without good lines and good knots, our high-priced tackle would be worthless.

After years of observation I am sad to say that the same anglers who demand and use the best fishing lines often skimp on rope when it comes to their boats. This chapter could have been entitled "Tom's Pet Peeves," because nothing makes less sense to me than paying thousands of dollars for a fishing boat and then trying to secure it at the marina with $5 worth of ski rope. Further, even if it's not cheap rope, I often see frayed ropes, badly knotted ropes, and short ropes used for mooring lines and anchor lines.

Several years ago I arrived at my local marina after a strong thunderstorm had blown through in the early-morning hours. Most boats had held up well to the wind and rain. Two boats, however, were badly damaged. One 20-footer had broken loose and battered an adjoining boat so violently that its grab rail and gunnel near the port (left) bow were all but destroyed. The owner of the 20-footer, which had also been damaged, explained to other boaters that it was not his fault. "The weather service never indicated that the thunderstorms were going to be so severe," said the clueless owner.

The truth, however, was in plain view of everyone. The boat that had been broken loose had been secured with tiny, cheap lines that could not have held a canoe. Good ropes for mooring and anchoring are not a luxury but a necessity. Fortunately, the right dock lines and anchor lines are not that difficult to choose, and you do not have to be an expert on "marlinespike seamanship" to tie decent knots. In fact, five or six knots and splices are all that the average angler/boater needs to secure a boat in most conditions.

Choice and Maintenance of Rope

Throughout this book I have talked about keeping fishing space clean and uncluttered. This means keeping unnecessary ropes and lines neatly stored when not in use. Untidy ropes make footing unsafe and can snarl fishing line and lures. The choice of material for dock lines and anchor lines is simple. They should be either of nylon (polyamide fiber) or Dacron (polyester fiber). I know that there are plenty of other ropes on the market, but nylon and Dacron are the only ones that truly fit the bill. Cotton ropes, for example, are not nearly as strong, and they abrade easily. Manila ropes were the best available prior to World War II. Even though Manila ropes are still available, they rot easily and are rough on your hands. Ropes of polypropylene fiber are low in cost and light in weight. Because they float, they are fine for attaching to life buoys, but they're a poor choice for mooring and anchoring.

Both nylon and Dacron ropes are similar in strength at the same diameter. Dacron ropes are often seen as braided ropes. They are very popular among sailors because they do not stretch much, are resistant to abrasion, and are easy to work with. Even though Dacron is good, nylon ropes are the best choice for the average boater/angler. They are strong, abrasion resistant, hold knots well, and stretch, meaning that they absorb shock better than any other material. Although I prefer twisted rope on fishing boats, braided ropes are also an excellent choice.

Although there is no hard-and-fast rule, for lighter boats 18 feet and under, I find that nylon stock 3/8 inch in diameter works well for both anchoring and mooring. Three-eighths inch is also the smallest rope I use for those purposes since anything smaller is rough on the hands. For heavier boats, and any boat 19 feet or larger, I prefer 7/16- or 1/2-inch diameter nylon. Rope of this size will be adequate for anchoring, mooring, and towing.

Although situations change from dock to dock and marina to marina, five lines are standard equipment in any powerboat. I carry four lines twenty feet in length, or if the boat is larger than 20 feet, at least the length of the boat. These are used to secure my boat in a slip or between pilings. My fifth line is used both as a launch line and as a "spring line," an extra line often necessary to keep a boat from moving forward or backward when tied in its slip. My fifth line will normally be thirty feet in length or, for boats over 20 feet, one and a half times the boat length. A longer launch line is often helpful on and off a trailer. With four good dock lines and one longer launch/spring line, you should be able to secure your boat between pilings or in most marina slips. Later in this chapter I will show you how to make a sea-gasket coil to properly store your dock lines.

For anchor line I always choose nylon because of the shock-absorbing properties of this material. Nylon is also fairly easy on the hands when retrieving an anchor. The amount of anchor rope you carry is largely dependent on the types of water you fish. There are situations where a short rope and a heavy anchor will hold you in place while you fish protected waters. For anchoring in normal conditions, however, you should have at least four times more rope than the depth of water below you. This is called scope—the ratio of the anchor line length to the depth of the water. Thus, if you intend to anchor in twenty-five feet of water, the shortest anchor rope you should carry should be one hundred feet. For rough weather and for guaranteed security, the scope should increase to six to one, seven to one, or even more. As a rule of thumb, I carry an anchor rope in both fresh and salt water of 150 feet in length. In most freshwater lakes and nearshore coastal waters, an anchor rope of this length is usually adequate. You can tell, however, that for deepwater anchoring (50 feet or more) 150 feet is not nearly enough. As extra security I also carry another one hundred feet of rope that can be used to lengthen the anchor rope or serve as a towrope.

I should also add that when operating a powerboat I *always* carry an extra anchor, though not necessarily of the same style or with the same length of rope. Both should be capable of holding the boat in place under normal conditions. It is easy to lose an anchor by getting it stuck on the bottom or failing to secure an anchor line, so it is foolish not to have a spare. The second anchor can also be invaluable in helping to position your boat, when wind or tides conspire to move you away from that perfect fishing location.

Although a good set of dock lines and anchor ropes should last a long time, they are not a permanent investment. Just as you are willing to change fly lines or spool up your conventional reels with new monofilament, you must also be prepared to replace dock lines and anchor lines as needed. A badly frayed dock line or anchor line may mean a loss of 50 percent or more of the rope's strength. Also, know that unwanted knots in your dock lines or anchor line can also reduce the strength of the line by half or more. Knots should always be removed, but if they can't be untied the line should be replaced or the line cut and spliced.

Simple Knots Every Boating Angler Should Know

In my fishing and boating library I have a substantial number of books dealing only with knots. One book, *The Ashley Book of Knots* by Clifford Ashley (Doubleday, 1993), boasts coverage of 3,900 knots, so consider yourself lucky that I'm going to force you to learn only a half dozen. Before we get to the knots, however, it is important that you secure the ends of your ropes to keep them from fraying and unraveling, also known as unlaying. Probably the most common way of securing line endings is by "whipping." Whipping is just a method of tightly wrapping nylon twine around the ends of your rope to keep them from unraveling. Another method closely related to whipping is the use of electrical tape. By tightly wrapping the end of a rope with electrical tape for about one inch, you can temporarily keep the rope from unwrapping. However, neither whipping nor electrical tape can match the artistry and permanence of the back splice. The back splice is a simple but elegant way to finish off the ends of any rope on your boat (see illustration). Not only does a back splice permanently keep any twisted rope from unraveling, but it will also tell other anglers and boaters that you know what you're doing!

Every bit as important as a properly secured rope ending is the loop. A loop in the end of your launch line and dock lines is almost a necessity. A loop can be placed quickly over a cleat in your boat or on a pier. Although there are many ways to make a loop in a rope, the only one worthy of mention is the eye splice. The eye splice is a simple, seamanlike method of putting a loop into a rope, which also has the added benefit of preventing further unraveling. The eye splice (see illustration) may look

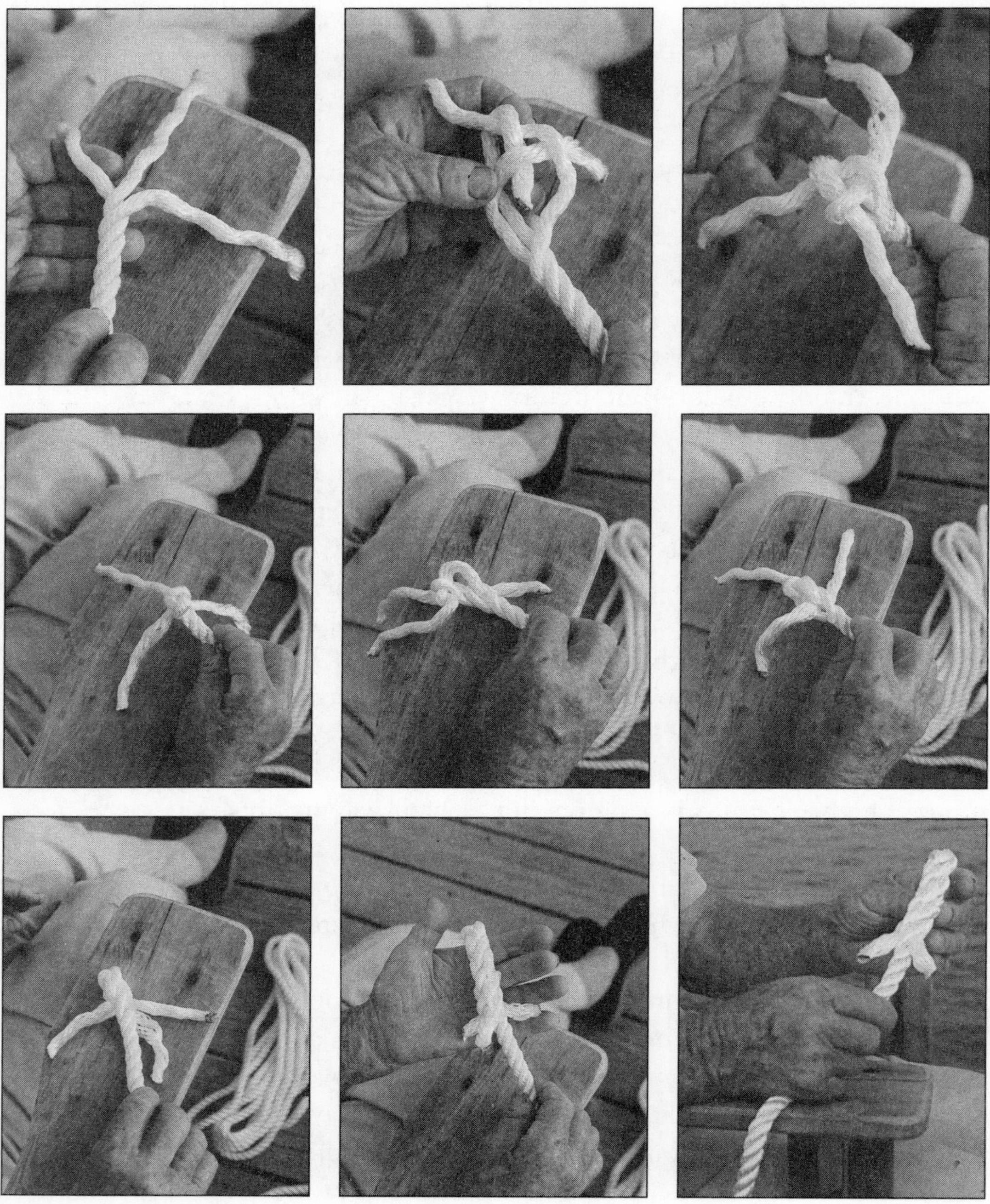

The back splice is elegant and simple. Ropes finished with a back splice have a professional look.

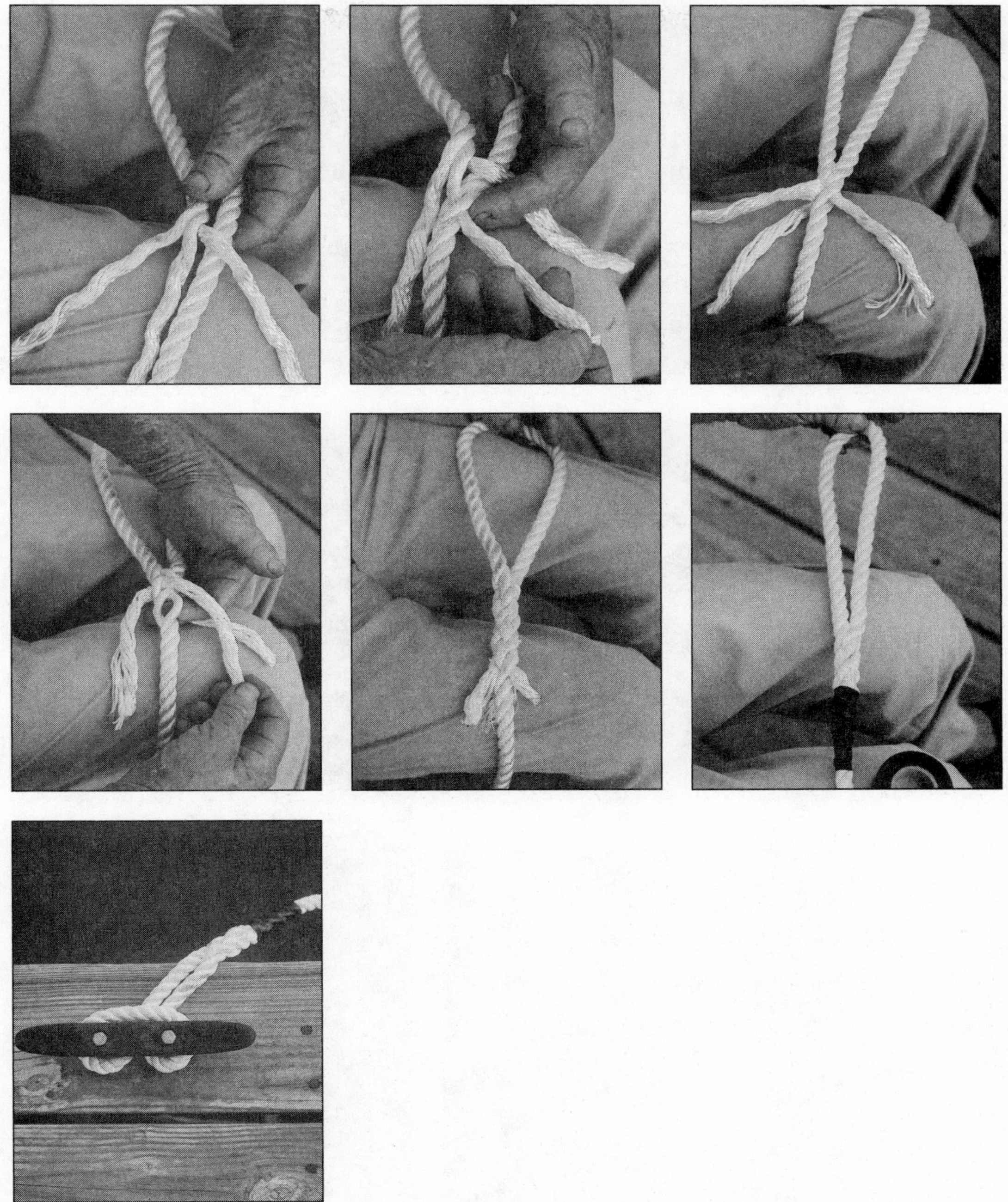

The eye splice is the only permanent loop worthy of mention. The hands belong to Captain Donald Willis.

complicated, but if you study the diagrams carefully, you will soon be able to do a perfect eye splice, making you the envy of every fisherman in your neighborhood. Over the years I have periodically gone into "splicing binges" in which I produce over the course of several evenings a number of dock lines with an eye-splice loop on one end and a back-splice finish on the other. I never run out of dock lines, and like fly tying, splicing rope is great therapy.

Once you have dock lines of the proper size and length, secured and looped at the ends, you are ready to tie, hitch, and

The clove hitch can be tied quickly to a piling or tree limb.

loop. Among the first knots in your repertoire should be the clove hitch (see illustration). The clove hitch is commonly used to quickly tie your boat to a piling or tree limb. It is safe for most short-term docking, and, most important, it is easy to untie. It can be a stand-alone knot or it can be stabilized to make a secure overnight mooring knot by adding two half hitches.

Another frequently used, but often incorrectly tied hitch is the cleat hitch (see illustration). The cleat hitch is used to attach lines to your boat or to a dock. It is the procedure most

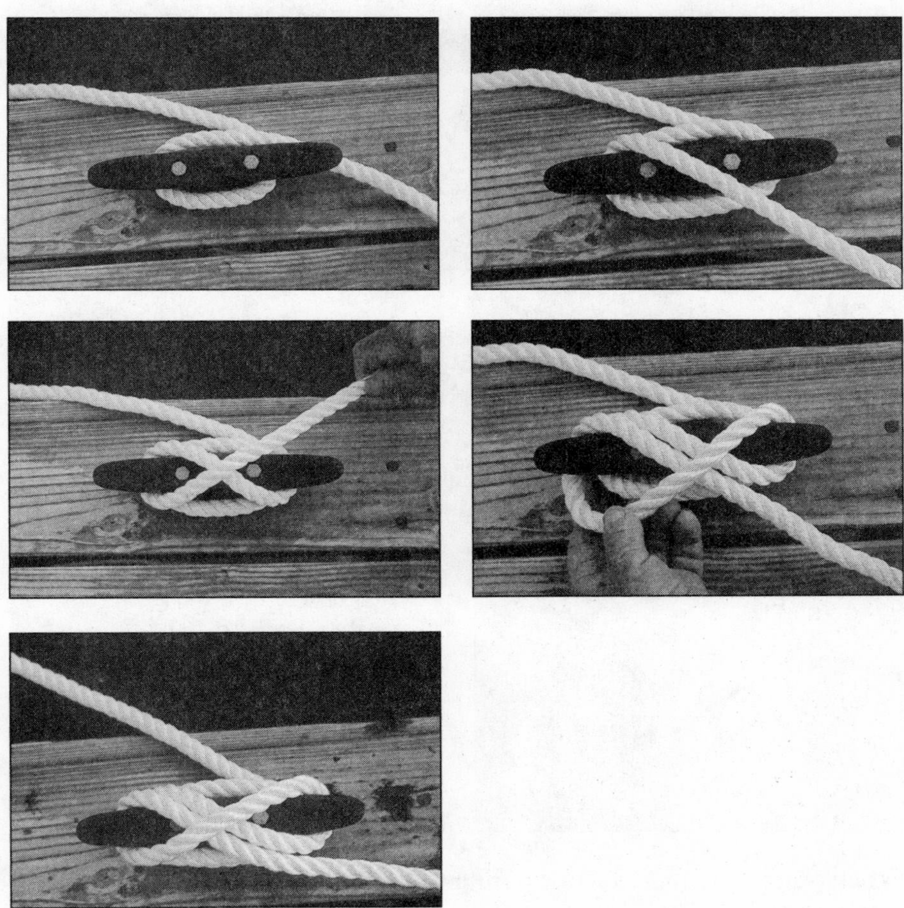

The cleat hitch when properly done is not bulky and is easy to untie.

used to fasten your anchor line to the bow cleat. Although it looks very simple in the diagram, it is often incorrectly done because anglers mistakenly think that by making many crossing turns they will make it stronger. When properly tied, a cleat hitch is not bulky and, more important, is easy to remove quickly if necessary.

Another extremely basic knot for anglers and boaters is the round turn with two half hitches (see illustration). This is

When tying to a piling for an overnight stay, nothing beats a round turn with two half hitches.

another very simple knot that has many applications. It can be used for tying a line to a piling or a ring. It can even be used to attach the rope to your anchor, although for that job it should not be your first choice.

A close relative of the round turn with two half hitches is the anchor bend (see illustration). This is an excellent knot to tie to the ring holding your anchor. Because the line through ring opening is doubled, the anchor bend has excellent breaking strength.

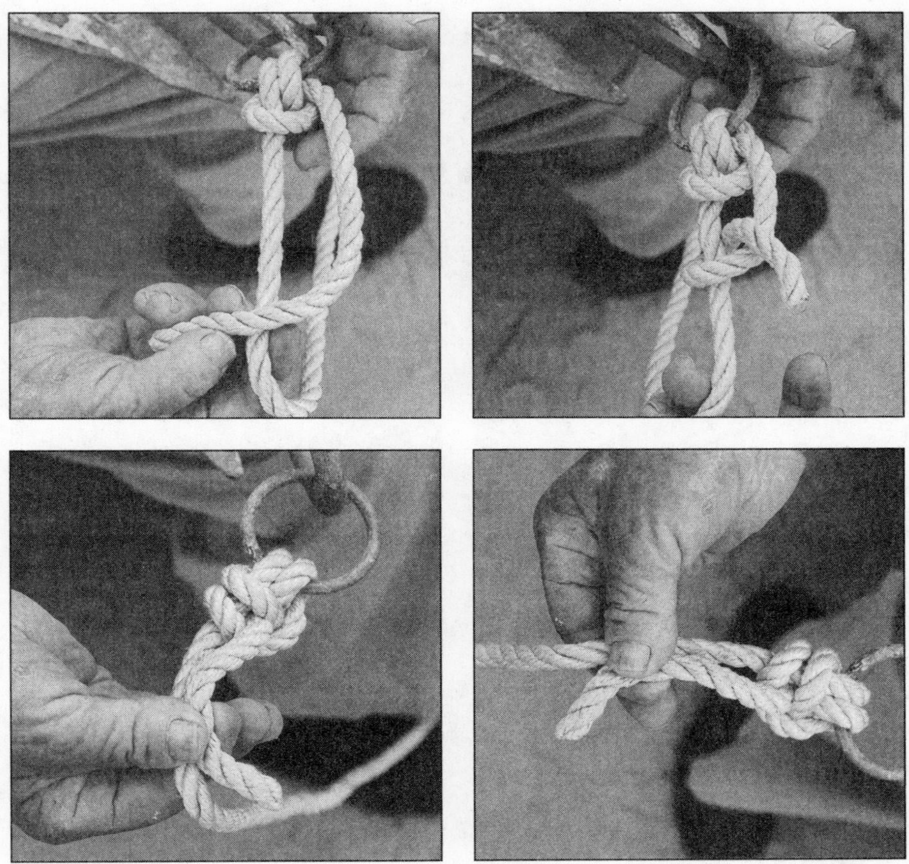

If you don't use an eye splice, the anchor bend is a safe knot for tying your rope to the anchor ring or chain.

I told you that I was going to keep this knot lesson simple, and in doing so I have saved the best for last. The bowline (see illustration) is probably the most basic and important knot available to the boating angler. The bowline is used to form a loop that will not slip when the rope is under tension. It is the knot of choice for towing another boat or in other situations when heavy loads will be placed on the line. As with many other knots, the bowline is strong and does not slip, but its real beauty is that it is easy to untie. On a number of occasions I have towed other

The bowline does not slip and is easy to untie. To work properly it should be under strain.

Nothing looks better on the boat than properly stored rope.

boats or been towed myself. In almost every instance a bowline was tied through the bow eye of the boat being towed. After the trips were completed, the loop was easily untied and the boats freed from each other. No knot is easier to tie and untie, or has more uses, than the bowline.

Again, the hitches and knots above are among the most useful, but are merely representative of hundreds of other knots used by boaters since before recorded time. Like a great fishing boat, a great knot is also simple and uncomplicated.

Finally, in the section on ropes I promised to show a method for properly stowing dock lines and anchor lines in coils ready for immediate use. The best way to stow line is with a sea-gasket coil (see illustration). The sea-gasket coil, which in some areas is also referred to as a "rabbit" because of their speed of use, is simply a way of securing coiled line so that it can be stored and quickly used without tangling. Once you learn this neat method of securing your lines, you will never have a messy pile of rope in your boat again.

An Anchor for Every Purpose

Whether you fish in farm ponds, large reservoirs, slow-moving rivers, or the open sea, the only way to stop your boat is with an anchor. The right anchor and enough rope are arguably the most important items carried in your boat. Even though my main purpose in this section is to evaluate various anchors as fishing tools, never forget that the anchor or anchors on your boat are critical in an emergency. The right anchor can help you maintain your position when your engine fails. Over the years I have been the operator or passenger on many boats when the engine has failed because of a blown power head, overheating, a dead battery, a fouled propeller, or, most embarrassing, no fuel. When the engine fails in open water, getting the anchor out is generally the first priority of a boater while the situation is being assessed. Several years ago I was fishing a half mile off a beach where fairly heavy surf was piling up. Things were fine until our propeller fouled on a line from an unseen crab pot. With the wind blowing toward the beach, it was critical that our anchor be deployed immediately and that it hold. When the anchor held, we were able to raise the motor and cut off the offending line. Always carry the best anchor you can afford for the types of water and bottom conditions you are likely to encounter. An anchor can save your boat, or your life.

If you were able to tour my garage, you would find an array of anchors for almost any boating and fishing condition. There are anchors that can dig into hard, sandy bottom in coastal waters. There are grapnels, or rock anchors, that will hold on a rough, rocky bottom or shell-strewn bottom. There are also heavy, mushroom-shaped anchors that will hold reasonably well in soft mud. I also have "anchors" that will not stop a boat. These are drift anchors and sea anchors, whose main purpose is to help slow down and control a boat's drift. For anglers who fish different water conditions, a collection of the right anchors is an integral part of your fishing tackle and will often play an important part in your success.

The most commonly used anchor by small-boat fishermen is the Danforth. These anchors are ideal for holding in sand, mud, clay, or other hard-packed bottom. These relatively lightweight anchors have flukes that dig into the bottom (see illustration) and grab it until pressure of the anchor rope is released or reversed. In addition to the terrific holding power of a Danforth anchor, a very appealing feature of this anchor is that it can be laid flat, which makes storage and handling easy. Although I have shied away from endorsing brands in all areas of this book, it should be noted that there are many Danforth imitators that may not hold as well.

In coastal waters, where the Danforth is king, I usually carry two of the proper size in my boat. One Danforth, with a six-foot galvanized chain, is tied to my 150-foot-long primary anchor rope. My second Danforth and anchor chain are secured to a shorter 75-foot rope. This is the "stern anchor" that I use along with the primary anchor to put the boat in the best fishing position. On the end of the short anchor line there is an eye-splice loop to which I can quickly attach additional anchor line when needed in an emergency.

Another easily stored anchor that is good for shallow-water anchoring is the folding anchor (see illustration). The folding

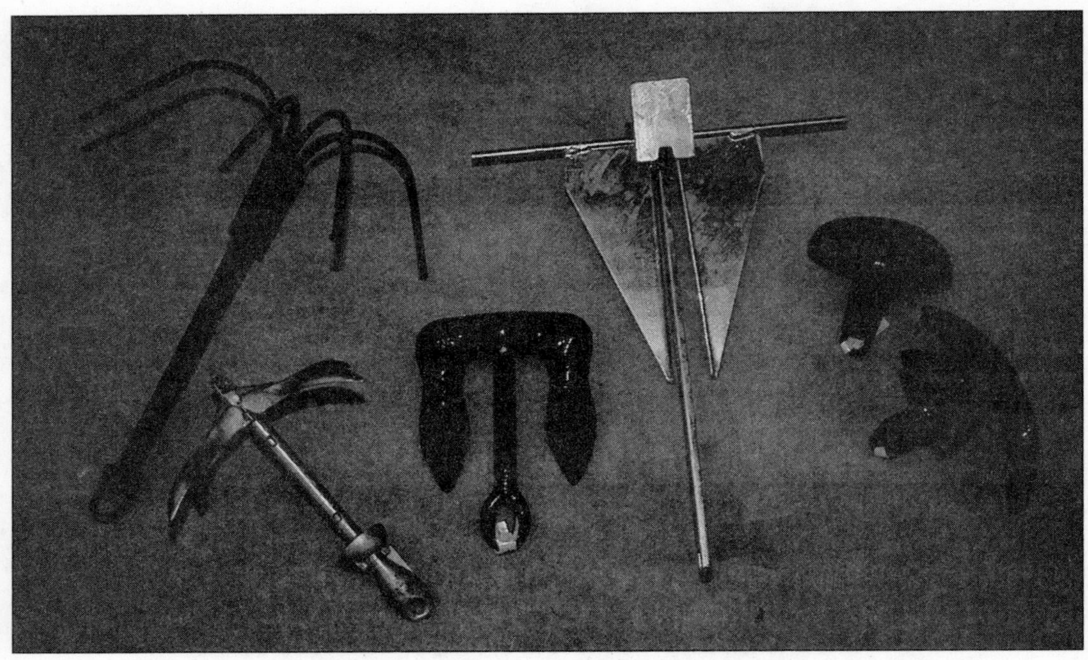

The anchors shown are as follows (left to right): grapnel, light-duty folding, Navy anchor, Danforth, and mushroom anchors.

anchor can be used in smaller, lighter boats and will hold reasonably well in shallow water, in mud, and on grass bottoms. It is a good light-duty anchor, but should not be your primary anchor. Another commonly used anchor that comes in a variety of weights and sizes is the mushroom anchor. The mushroom is designed primarily for soft mud and sand. When pulled across the bottom, its weight, usually ten pounds or more, will help dig into the mud. It is an excellent anchor for mud bottoms in reservoirs and slow-moving rivers. During the spring striper run on the Roanoke River in eastern North Carolina, the mushroom is the anchor most commonly used by johnboat operators to hold in soft mud sediment.

Another heavy anchor that works well for anglers fishing over soft mud bottoms is the Navy anchor. The Navy anchor for small boats will also weigh ten pounds or more. Like the mushroom anchor, its weight helps it to dig into soft bottoms. Even though the Navy anchor is not high on the list for most anglers, I own a couple in different weights, which I regularly use over muddy river bottoms. Another type of anchor mentioned earlier is the grapnel, or rock anchor (see illustration). The grapnel is relatively lightweight and made of steel bars bent into four to six hooks. Rock anchors can be used to hold in riprap around bridges or over other rocky, jagged bottoms.

There are a number of anchors used by fishermen that are not anchors in the traditional sense. These are the drift anchors,

Bob Clouser

A heavy chain can help slow a boat's drift.

which are generally heavy weights suspended on short ropes that drag across the bottom and slow the drift of your boat caused by current or wind. They are not intended to bite or hold the bottom. An ideal drift anchor is an old window weight or even a dumbbell. Several years ago I bought a used twenty-pound dumbbell at a yard sale. Since then it has served admirably as a drift weight in both river and ocean settings. Another excellent drift anchor is a piece of heavy plastic-coated chain, which can also help slow the speed of a boat. The mushroom anchor mentioned earlier will also serve well as a drift anchor when used on a short rope.

Another type of drift anchor that is not a deadweight anchor at all is the "sea anchor," which is nothing more than a canvas bag or a heavy plastic bag pulled through the water. These "bag anchors" can often be as effective as deadweight anchors in slowing drift. They can also be effective if you loose power in a storm and need to keep your bow facing oncoming waves.

There are numerous other anchor types available to the boating angler. The ones discussed above, however, are probably the most useful to the small-boat angler. Even though I use almost all the anchor types listed above several times during the course of a year, 80 percent of my anchoring needs can probably be covered with a Danforth and a mushroom anchor. Both hold reasonably well in specific bottom types, and the mushroom anchor can also serve as a drift anchor.

Before leaving the subject of anchors, do not forget that an anchor can do its job well only if there is adequate anchor line to provide the proper scope. Having a good anchor but not enough anchor rope is surely the equivalent of being up a creek without a paddle. Since I know you buy the best available tackle that you can afford for your fishing needs, please consider an anchor and quality rope as part of your tackle.

V

HUMAN-POWERED BOATS

11

Great Rowboats . . . Skiffs, Dinghies, Prams, and Drift Boats

As I finish writing these final chapters I am looking forward to a project with my eight-year-old son, Izaak, five-year-old daughter, Rachel, and our eighty-five-year-old neighbor, Captain Donald Willis. At those ages it seems that the stars are lined up just right. For many years I have wanted to build a great rowing skiff, and I have wanted to work with Captain Willis. With my crew standing ready, now is the time for this very special project.

The skiff will be built in my backyard on Harkers Island, utilizing the construction technique of plank-on-frame. The primary material used in building her will be white cedar, also known as juniper, the traditional boatbuilding material on the North Carolina Outer Banks. When completed, she will be a family fishing boat and powered only with oars. Although she was planned at 13½ to 14 feet in length, with an overall beam of just over 5 feet, nothing is ever measured or drawn to scale on Harkers Island. As a nonmotorized rowing skiff there will

This beautiful skiff, made with juniper strips, was built in a day-long demonstration on Harkers Island, NC. Note the "rocker," or lift, at the stern.

be just enough rocker, also known as "tuck," so that the transom will clear the water, thus reducing drag while being rowed. She will be built so that the bow, or stem, will stay submerged, which will help reduce pounding and noise. Her freeboard will be relatively low, approximately twelve inches, high enough for safety but low enough to cheat the wind. From this skiff I will fly fish for seatrout and redfish, and the children will catch spots and croakers on shrimp from several nearby "sweet holes." This will be a fine fishing boat, but even more significant, it will be a boat bearing the fingerprints and hammer marks of Izaak, Rachel, and Captain Willis.

Boats with oars, especially boats made of wood, can still be among the most quiet and seaworthy available to anglers. There is an array of oar-powered craft for use on ponds, rivers, lakes, and nearshore waters: General categories include skiffs, prams, dories, and drift boats. In each category there are great regional variations in design and intended use. Many small boats with oars make fine fishing boats since they are generally stable, uncluttered, and simple in design. From a great rowboat you can fish standing or sitting, hear yourself think, and enjoy conversations with companions without motorized interference.

This little rowing skiff has wide gunnels.

Although I have clearly indicated my preference for rowboats made of wood, extraordinary rowing/fishing craft can be found made of solid fiberglass, aluminum, and laminated materials with light cores of foam or balsa. A few rowboats, especially prams, are small enough to cartop or slip into the back of a pickup truck; others, including the extremely popular drift boats used on eastern and western rivers, need to be trailered.

The rowboats in this chapter are craft you really can consider building yourself. Even if you aren't blessed with a neighborhood filled with boatbuilders as on Harkers Island, you can find magazines and books offering patterns and plans for dinghies, dories, skiffs, and drift boats. I have several friends who have built boats from mail order patterns using marine plywood and construction techniques such a "glue-and-screw" and "stitch-and-glue." Finished boats can be varnished, painted, or given much more permanent protection with epoxy and fiberglass. For the more advanced and technically inclined builder, boat kits and plans are available for do-it-yourselfers able to weld aluminum, work with fiberglass, or do more intricate work with wood.

Skiffs

By heritage and design, skiffs are simple, stable, hardworking, mostly flat-bottomed boats that can be powered with oars, small outboards, or sail. Skiffs are in a way like striped bass; they come in all sizes and seem equally at home in coastal waters, inland reservoirs, and slow-moving rivers. Since the term is so loosely used and is applied to so many boats, it is not possible to give meaningful dimensions and design features. As already indicated in discussion of my planned "skiff," there are a few features that are pretty common.

Skiffs have a pointed bow and a squared stern. Those with a little rocker in the stern work better as rowboats, since there is

This little rowing skiff has high freeboard and a small skeg.

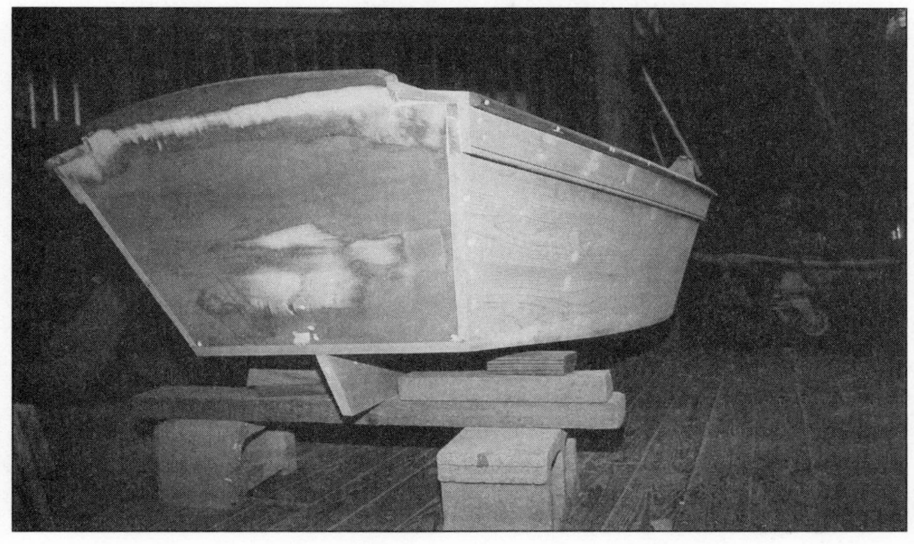

less drag. Skiffs intended to wear a small outboard motor should have a flat bottom and a notched, reinforced transom. Finally, most skiffs with which I have been acquainted have had a small skeg, a fixed, finlike protrusion attached to the bottom of the boat at the stern. No matter how the skiff is powered, a skeg will help it to track straight.

Dinghies

Dinghies are to skiffs as prams are to drift boats, since both are essentially smaller, scaled-back versions of their larger siblings. Although the term dinghy is often used to describe any small rowboat between 7 and 10 feet in length, with a pointed bow for fine entry, there are important differences between small, rowed fishing craft. Although some boats called dinghies have flat bottoms, many of the "true" dinghies often have more rounded bottoms and chines than do most skiffs. The rounded bottoms and sides of these small boats give them additional "reserve stability," which was discussed earlier in this book. You will remember that boats with flat bottoms have great initial stability, but often lack the reserve stability of boats with more flared sides or more rounded hulls. Since dinghies are, by their very nature short, small, and relatively lightweight, the higher, rounded sides found on many dinghies allow them to heel over without flipping (more reserve stability). Like rowing skiffs, dinghies that are rowed generally have enough rocker to keep the stern out of the water and a skeg to help them track straight.

Another group of small boats often categorized as dinghies are the "peapods." Peapods are beautiful boats 8 to 12 feet in length, and shaped like a peapod. They have rounded bottoms with a pointed bow and stern. This is why they are also referred to as "double-enders." Although peapods are rowed with oars instead of paddled like a canoe, to the uninformed they might look like a round, fat canoe. Again, because of the rounded sides and bottoms, and wide beams of four to five feet, peapod-type dinghies make fine stable fishing craft for one or two anglers.

If you thought skiffs were just for commercial fishermen, and dinghies were just tenders for yachts and other large boats, think again. Skiffs and dinghies are safe, track well, and can provide anglers with a totally different experience from that available in our high-speed world of metal-flecked boats.

Drift Boats and Prams

In the 1970s I took a wild ride in a drift boat through a stretch of class-3 white water down the New River in West Virginia. I was not on a thrill ride, but a serious fly-rodding trip for smallmouth bass. The western-style drift boat, also known as a McKenzie riverboat, enabled us to travel safely through rapids and unproductive fast water and then hold over pockets and seams to fish in places unavailable to any other angler. Some of the best fly fishing I have enjoyed has taken place from the comfort and security of a drift boat, on such rivers as the Bow River in Canada and Montana's Yellowstone and Bighorn Rivers. One trip with guide George Kelly on the Bighorn stands out most vividly, since air temperatures that day rose to over 100 degrees. With the high temperatures, however, came afternoon winds that blew clouds of grasshoppers into the river from the bluffs above. Over and over again George moved me into position with his drift boat to present my grasshopper imitations to cruising, gulping brown trout. The size of the fish and the perfect casting opportunities made me an eternal fan of these craft.

Like a dory, drift boats are stable, flat-bottomed rowboats with high, flaring sides, but unlike a dory, most have extreme rocker and from the side look like a floating banana. With exaggerated curve from bow to stern, they have great longitudinal stability, enabling them to dip and rock like a hobby horse in fast-moving water. Also, like a dory, drift boats draw very little

Bruce Foster

Drift boats, like their dory cousins, have high flared sides.

water. Thus, with its flat bottom and extreme rocker, a drift boat in the hands of a good oarsman can be maneuvered easily cross-current and through holes and seams in boulder-strewn rivers.

Most drift boats in the 14- to 16-foot range have a bottom width of just over four feet, but can have an overall beam of six to seven feet. Unlike other rowing craft such as the skiffs and dinghies mentioned above, drift boats were built for the light-tackle angler. Anglers can fish out of the bow or stern, and most come with kneelocks for bracing while standing. Just as the flats boats of the Florida Keys have migrated and populated the flats of the world, the same has happened with western drift boats. For example, they are now very popular on many of the great trout rivers in South America. Also, although drift boats are not designed to track in a straight line like a good skiff, they have begun to show up in coastal estuaries in the hands of anglers seeking stripers and other saltwater prizes. They are safe in light surf and can be maneuvered in rips. Drift boats are great platforms from which to cast.

As noted earlier, drift boats also have a small relative, the pram. Rowing prams are flat-bottomed boats with squared sterns, bows coming in lengths from eight to twelve feet, and beams between four and a half and five and a half feet. Many of the smaller models fit neatly into the back of a pickup truck or through the doors of an SUV. Though not designed for white water, prams are regularly used on slow-moving rivers, reservoirs, and protected coastal waters. For many trout anglers, especially on western lakes, prams are beginning to take the place of float tubes and other "belly boats." With a pram, anglers can not only cover more water, but they also provide a much better vantage point for spotting fish than float tubes. Prams, like drift boats, are exceptionally stable platforms on which to sit or stand while fishing. They also have some rocker, but not as extreme as the rocker found on drift boats. These stubby little craft with wide sterns and a blunt bow are agile on the water and fun to row. Although I instinctively think of prams as one-man boats, models 10 feet and longer are ideal for two anglers.

Like other boat forms reviewed in this book, drift boats and prams are available in a variety of materials. Most commercially made drift boats are built with fiberglass or aluminum. Custom wooden drift boats are also available. Excellent drift-boat plans and kits are also available for the hobbyist and those wanting to save money. Prams are also available in wood, fiberglass, or aluminum. Finally, since few fishing boats are as simple in design as prams, even the most ham-handed among us can build one.

In recent years fly fishing has surged in popularity across North America and around the world. Whether on coastal flats, reservoirs, or streams, fly fishing has become known as "the quiet sport." In fly fishing there is more direct contact with the line than in any other form of fishing. The line is cast and hooks are set while in the hands of the angler. The "direct" contact between fisherman and fish in fly fishing is in a way very similar to the direct contact that anglers in skiffs, drift boats, and prams have with the water. Not only because they are quiet, but also because they can take you to fish in shallows and rivers often inaccessible by other craft, human-powered boats are making a comeback. Although the simplicity and uncluttered space of most rowed craft make them ideal for fly fishing, they are equally suited for those who enjoy spinning and conventional tackle.

Although I have no intention of giving up the comfort, speed, and technical advances of modern powerboats in fresh and salt water, I know for a certainty that I will be spending more time in my own human-powered craft and in those of others in the years to come. Because it's already happening now, it doesn't take a prophet to predict that the second boat of many powerboat anglers will be a good skiff, drift boat, or one of their quiet relatives. Rowboats are in.

12

Kayaks and Canoes for Anglers

By 1960 I considered myself an old hand in salt water, brackish water, lakes, and rivers. Fly fishing was my passion, a passion that was indulged by my parents. As I indicated in an earlier chapter, we were boatless, but we were mobile since we owned a 5-horsepower Johnson and knew the boat-rental liveries in our region.

With all the real fishing opportunities afforded to me, I still enjoyed a highly developed fishing fantasy world. In several of the outdoor magazines, advertisements appeared every month for a folding kayak. Although I had never seen a kayak, I soon convinced myself that with a folding kayak I could fish any river, reservoir, and even the surf. In my fantasy world I could also see great schools of fish just beyond the breaker line and my kayak knifing through the breakers to reach quarry available to no one else. In the summer and fall of 1960, my fantasy became a need when I decided I was missing out on the majority of good fishing water in some of the four- and five-acre farm ponds near my North Carolina home. By late fall of that year, my need had become an obsession. I would rake leaves, mow yards, and work as a soda jerk—anything to earn money to buy that folding kayak.

On Christmas morning, 1960, Mom and Dad pulled off my greatest Christmas surprise. At the very end of family festivities, my parents signaled my two older nonfishing brothers, who produced a box big enough to carry a golf bag and set of clubs. In the box were numbered wooden poles with metal ferrules on each end and a smelly, vinyl-coated canvas skin. It was the folding kayak, my magic carpet to the waters of the world. I had never seen or used a kayak and had never held a double-bladed paddle in my hand. By late Christmas afternoon, however, I had already flipped it twice in the cold, waist-deep water of a nearby farm pond.

Although I did catch hundreds of bluegill from my kayak in the spring of 1961, my magic boat was pitifully underused. I never conquered any great rivers, or paddled through heavy surf to reach giant bluefish and stripers. What I did learn, however, was that a lightweight portable boat could take me to previously unreachable waters in ponds, reservoirs, and slow-moving rivers. I caught bass, several species of sunfish, and a few trout, but never came close to reaching my full potential in that most wonderful Christmas surprise.

Today, however, I see anglers living my Christmas dream in almost every type of water that I fish. Along with great canoes, which have always been available to anglers, kayaks are now becoming incredibly popular in both fresh and salt water. Just like the explosion of saltwater fly fishing in the 1990s, the availability of good kayaks also exploded during the same period.

In many angling situations, canoes and kayaks make perfect sense. They are lightweight, portable, and can take you quietly into the domain of almost any fish. Just as with a good rowboat, both canoes and kayaks allow anglers to operate with great stealth, but unlike most rowboats, canoes and kayaks are generally light enough to be carried or dragged to isolated ponds, inaccessible stretches of river, and remote coastal-marsh "holes" where only redfish can hide.

Currently, along with several other fishing craft, my wife and I own a 16-foot canoe and a 17½-foot tandem sea kayak. Our boats are used primarily for fishing reservoirs, slow-moving rivers, and protected coastal waters; so it is only about canoes and kayaks with good fishing qualities that I offer advice. Any canoe or kayak, including white-water models with extreme rocker, and long, slim, fast-cruising models can be fishing boats. But it is safe to say that neither those built for white water nor those designed for cruising/touring are the most desirable for the ordinary angler. In the pages that follow I have, therefore, laid out the various types of canoes and kayaks on the market today. I have then tried to isolate from the available craft only those most suitable for the paddler/angler.

Canoes for Anglers

You may recall from the discussion of powerboat and rowboat hulls in earlier chapters that I make a distinction between initial stability and reserve, or final, stability. When looking at the available canoe shapes and hulls, we must again visit the issues of stability. Just as with powerboats and rowboats, canoes can be built with flat bottoms, rounded bottoms, and shallow-V hulls (see illustrations). Also, like the angler who first steps into a flat-bottomed johnboat, those who step into a flat-bottom canoe will have a feeling of security and stability. Canoes with completely flat bottoms turn well and actually feel very safe in flat water, light rapids, and rips. Again, however, appearances are deceiving, because a flat-bottom canoe, which possesses tremendous initial stability, has almost no reserve, or final, stability. This simply means that if an angler leans too far to one side while

Canoes and kayaks come in many shapes and sizes. Some have "rocker" for quick turning (see above), while others have straight bottoms for better tracking.

casting or landing a fish, a flat-bottom canoe is more likely to capsize quickly than a round-bottom canoe or one with a shallow-V hull.

Neither a round-bottom canoe nor a canoe with a shallow V has that instant "stable feeling," but both of these hull shapes possess much more reserve, or final, stability. For the angler this simply means that although flat-bottom canoes are fun to paddle and feel safe in light-water conditions, they might not be the best choice for an all-around fishing canoe. A boat with a *slightly* rounded bottom or a slight V will give you a better combination of initial stability and reserve stability. Also, remember that a shallow-V hull generally tracks better, while a canoe with a rounded bottom generally maneuvers better. Finally, if you already own a canoe with a flat bottom, just be aware of its limitations and enjoy it.

Just as with the powerboat hulls, other factors come into play in determining the fishing characteristics of a canoe hull. Other important considerations in choosing a canoe are length, beam (width), and rocker. Generally speaking, wider canoes, those with more beam, are more stable. Canoes with more longitudinal curve, or rocker, can be maneuvered or pivoted easily. Banana-shaped canoes are said to have extreme rocker. If you are choosing a boat for use in a lake or coastal sounds where paddling in a straight line is important, then a canoe with no rocker will probably be your best choice. For coastal rivers and other slow-moving rivers, a boat with a *little* rocker works well. Simply stated, the more rocker, the more difficult it is to make a canoe track well.

In choosing a fishing canoe, length and beam need be considered together. For example, an 18-foot canoe with a thirty-two-inch beam and a slight V is considered a "cruising" canoe, with speed as the number one priority. Take the same 18-foot canoe but give it a beam of thirty-six or thirty-eight inches and

Although more slender canoes are faster and cover more water, a canoe with more beam is a better choice for most anglers.

it becomes slower and more stable. It would also be classified as a "tripping" canoe because of its ability to carry a significant volume of gear.

For all-around stability and handling for fishing in lakes, ponds, and slow-moving rivers, I prefer a canoe 16 to 17 feet in length with a beam of thirty-six inches. Such a canoe is manageable by one or two anglers and can carry enough tackle and gear for a day's fishing. As indicated earlier, I would stay away from a canoe with a completely flat bottom and go with one with a very shallow V or a slightly rounded bottom to give more overall stability. Although canoes of 13 and 14 feet with a wide beam, say thirty-eight inches, are very stable, they are also slow and lack the overall storage and cargo capacity of a 16-foot boat. The shorter, wider canoes may make a fine boat for the individual angler, but they do not offer the versatility of the longer canoe.

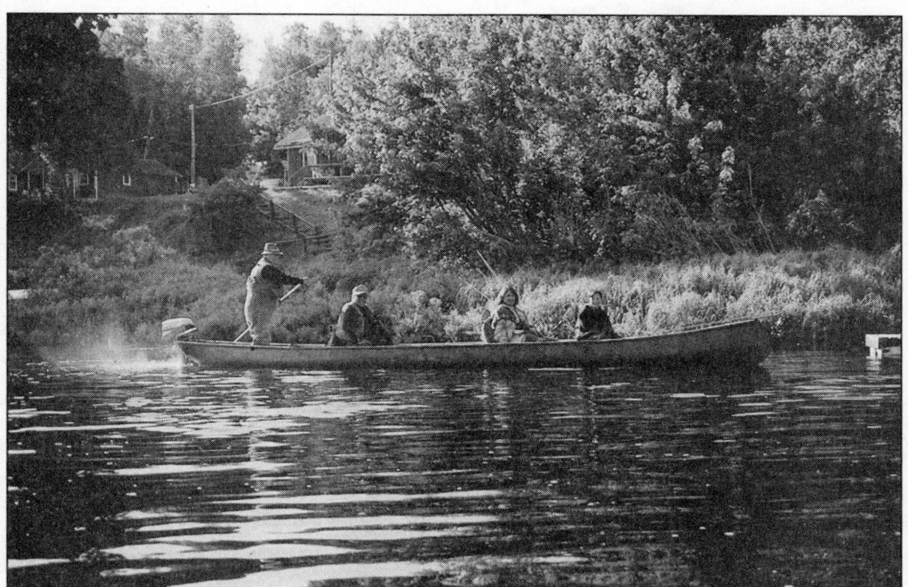

Bruce Foster

Canoes come in all sizes for every kind of fishing, like these large outboard assisted canoes used on Canadian salmon rivers.

For most anglers I know, and certainly for me, small- and medium-length canoes are "sit-down" fishing craft. I know some fishermen who can stand and cast in almost any canoe, but they are the exception. Whether the operator is kneeling, sitting, or standing, canoes provide a superb platform for fly fishing or other light-tackle angling. The one modification that I have made in several canoes is something I learned from Lefty Kreh years ago. Because moving around in a canoe can be an awkward

Lefty Kreh

No matter what type of canoe you choose, rod protection is important. You may have to install your own racks like these installed by Lefty Kreh.

Lefty Kreh

endeavor for most of us, it is important to protect your valuable rods. Lefty showed me how to install a couple of PVC tubes to protect rigged fishing rods (see illustration) when not in use. Although your canoe may not be as pretty with the PVC tubes installed, you won't have to worry about the sickening crunch of a foot landing on your favorite rod.

Just as with powerboat owners, you can often hear lively discussions among canoe owners about the best materials for canoe construction. Depending on the type of fishing you plan to do, there are a variety of materials from which to choose. Recently I accompanied my son to a day camp in coastal North Carolina and noticed a dozen Grumman aluminum canoes stacked up ready for use. Although at least twenty years old and covered with the marks of many summers of abuse, those canoes were just as seaworthy as the day they were built. Aluminum canoes are tough, but they have one minor drawback as fishing boats; they are noisy. Unfortunately, the manufacture of aluminum canoes is almost a thing of the past because of many excellent alternative materials. However, if you should find an old Grumman, buy it, take it fishing, forget about the noise, and put it in your will for your great-great-grandchildren.

Although it is still possible to find strong, light, and beautiful custom-made wooden boats, the best choice for a fishing canoe is probably one made of fiberglass, Kevlar, ABS (acrylonitrile butadiene styrene) plastic, or polyethylene. Just as with powerboats, the best fiberglass canoes are "hand laid." Fiberglass canoes are tough, but if damaged they can be repaired easily with fiberglass cloth and the proper resins.

Canoes made of Kevlar follow essentially the same lay-up process. The resulting canoe, however, is much stronger and at least a third lighter than a comparable fiberglass canoe. Although Kevlar canoes are more expensive than a fiberglass boat of the same design, anglers who have to make a long portage across an open field or around a marsh to reach fishable water may think that the price differential is well worth it. Other strong, stiff materials, such as graphite, bound together by vinylester resins, make it possible to fabricate canoes even lighter than those made of Kevlar.

Probably the most widely used canoes rented by outfitters and liveries are those made of either ABS plastic or polyethylene. ABS canoes are actually canoes made of multiple layers of foam and ABS plastic. This "sandwich" construction allows canoes to be built that are tough and even lighter than fiberglass. Equally tough are those made of polyethylene. Canoes made of ABS and polyethylene both have a number of advantages for anglers. Both will return to their original shape after a collision with a rock or stump. They also tend to slide over obstacles rather than hang up, a problem with aluminum. Most important for anglers, however, is that both types of plastic canoes are quiet and are relatively good insulators against cold water.

Even though kayaks have now passed canoes in sales and popularity, for most anglers a stable canoe is still a better choice for many fishing situations. No angling craft is simpler or easier to transport. Other than essential safety equipment, angling gear, and your paddles, nothing else is needed unless you are going on an extended outing. Whether you are dragging your canoe only a few yards up a bank to your car, or carrying it a couple of hundred yards across an open field, you will learn to "think light." For example, instead of carrying a mushroom anchor, carry a nylon mesh bag, which can be filled with rocks or pebbles

Eddie Nickens

A monster largemouth bass would be a thrill in any boat. Writer Eddie Nickens caught this prize from a canoe while fishing for sunfish.

to make an ideal anchor for shallow ponds and slow-moving streams.

Canoes should never be considered the poor man's fishing boat; rather, they should be considered the craft of choice where access is limited and stealth is a requirement. The exceptional fishing qualities of a canoe are always driven home to me when I visit a fellow outdoor writer, Eddie Nickens. On display in his house is a picture of Eddie with a grin as wide as the beam of his canoe, holding a twelve-pound largemouth bass in one hand and a fly rod in the other. He released the huge bass after he and his angling partner swore an oath not to reveal the location of the catch.

Kayaks

On Christmas Day, 1960, I saw myself as an Eskimo in a seal-skin-covered craft of ancient design. I never imagined at the time that kayaks would ever gain popularity or that they would be available in an infinite number of styles, sizes, and materials. Now kayaks of various designs can be seen from swift mountain rivers to the oceans. Just as with canoes, it is critically important that you choose a design suited for your fishing needs. Like canoes, many kayaks are designed for speed, white water, and even rough ocean waters. The most important factor to an angler who intends to use a kayak as a fishing platform is stability. Many touring kayaks do not work well as an angling craft when paddles are exchanged for rods.

It should be remembered that, for many anglers, kayaks are used as a means to get you to your fishing destination and not as a platform from which to fish. For example, kayaks that are used in white water can take you to inaccessible stretches of water for trout or smallmouth, and sea kayaks can take you to coastal marshes or rock outcroppings where no other boat can go. Once at the destination, however, many anglers wade or fish on foot

Kevin DuBois

For many anglers kayaks are used as "get there" boats and not as fishing platforms.

Kevin DuBois

Kayaks can get you to locations inaccessible to anglers in other boats.

before packing the kayak for the trip home. If you are new to kayaking, the first thing to remember is that, as fishing craft, kayaks do not have the same interior space as a canoe for storage or movement. Most are designed with a cockpit for one person, so any tackle and gear must be stored under bungee cords over the stern and bow deck or in small dry hatches under the forward or aft bulkheads. I have often heard it said that you sit in a canoe but *wear* a kayak. In most kayaks you sit in your cockpit at or below the waterline. This can give you excellent stability but a low vantage point from which to cast.

If you plan on fishing in your single-person kayak, expect to experience a few problems. Kevin DuBois, an avid kayak user in both marsh and open water in the lower Chesapeake Bay, once shared with me his three most common kayak fishing concerns, ones that are certainly shared by other kayak anglers. First, when an angler in a single kayak paddles to the area holding fish, the paddle must be put down and the rod picked up to make a cast. In open water, wind or current can quickly move the angler out of position, making it necessary to put the rod down and paddle back into position. Second, Kevin noted a problem that I have also experienced on a number of occasions. If you hook a large fish such as a cobia, false albacore, or big striper, it is hard to get leverage because you are sitting at water level and because kayaks are so light that they can be pulled by the fish. These modern "Nantucket sleigh rides" may be exciting, but they also underscore the potentially serious "leverage" problem. Third, and finally, Kevin believes that serious safety problems can arise when a kayaker tries to fish among larger powerboats. Because of their low profile in the water, kayaks can be hard to see among waves and boat wakes. For safety reasons, anglers in kayaks should avoid high-traffic fishing areas. There are plenty out-of-the-way locations better suited to kayak use.

I again emphasize that the world of kayaks is a world of specialty boats. If you plan on purchasing a kayak as a vehicle from

Like canoes kayaks come in a tremendous variety of sizes and shapes.

which to fish, talk with other recreational and angling kayak users who frequent the same waters. You may decide on a short, compact kayak 10 to 13 feet in length. Those with beams above thirty inches can provide a stable platform for anglers in small lakes and more protected waters. These are not good boats for covering lots of distance, because short kayaks tend to be slow and not as seaworthy as longer touring kayaks. Short, wide kayaks and open-deck kayaks can be great fun for anglers in protected warm waters. For most anglers an open-deck kayak should not be the boat of choice in open or cold waters.

For anglers who intend to cross and fish larger bodies of water, a touring kayak with adequate beam would be the best choice. Kayaks with moderate beam from 14 to 18 feet in length can take well-equipped anglers across larger unprotected bodies of water and still provide a platform stable enough for fishing. Again, remember that many anglers use kayaks as a "get there" boat and seldom fish sitting in their kayaks. The kayak Kevin DuBois uses on the Chesapeake Bay is 14 feet in length, has a twenty-seven-inch beam, and has a built-in keel. Kayaks of the same length, with beams from twenty to twenty-three inches, are fast but are less user-friendly for inexperienced paddlers and most anglers.

Up to now I have discussed kayaks as only single-occupant craft. Many good kayaks—both open-deck and touring models—are designed for two people. My wife and I have a 17-foot touring kayak with a beam of twenty-nine inches. For us, the beauty of dual-cockpit kayaks is that one person can devote his or her entire attention to casting and playing fish while the other can concentrate on maneuvering into and holding the right position.

Materials used to build kayaks are essentially the same as those used to build canoes. Kayaks of fiberglass or Kevlar are ex-

In a dual cockpit boat one person paddles, while the other can concentrate on fish.

cellent performers because of their stiff, lightweight hulls. As with canoes, Kevlar and other high-tech fibers can reduce weight by as much as one-third. Wood kayaks are light in weight and absolutely beautiful, but can be extremely expensive unless you build your own. "Skin" models with both fixed and folding frames are also available. Needless to say, skins are not those of real sea mammals, but rather skins of coated nylon or other tough fabrics. The real news in kayak construction in the past twenty years has been the continued development of polyethylene in all segments of the kayak market. Polyethylene kayaks are easier to build, less expensive to buy, and can absorb more abuse than a similar-size fiberglass boat. Anglers new to kayaking, especially those looking for a shorter, wider craft or a kayak with an open deck, will appreciate the stability, versatility, and wallet-friendly characteristics of polyethylene.

With the advent of polyethylene and other lightweight high-tech materials, the distinction between canoes and kayaks, row-boats and canoes, and kayaks and surfboards has become blurred. "Canoes" with oars, not paddles, are now available. Wide, square-stern canoes, long used in Canada, are now available through catalogs and canoe shops across the country for anglers who want to mount a small outboard or an electric motor for primary propulsion. Some manufacturers have crossed kayaks with catamarans and produced kayaks with outriggers that are almost impossible to turn over. Because of their extreme stability, they can serve as platforms for both casting and playing fish. Wide canoes with poling platforms can also be seen in coastal marshes.

No matter what they are called, however, canoes and kayak-type boats can be a great addition to any angler's fleet. Canoe trails for anglers and campers are available in some parts of the United States and Canada. Not only can they travel where powerboats are never seen, but some waters are actually set aside

Lefty Kreh

Canoes, whether paddles or poled, can take you to special places in fresh and salt water. Here Ted Juracsik holds a nice snook caught while fishing with Flip Pallot.

for no-motor craft. For example, some of the best fishing near the Kennedy Space Center is in a no-motor zone primarily poled and paddled by anglers in canoes and kayaks.

As already indicated, kayaks and canoes are used by anglers seeking almost every type of fish, from sunfish to tarpon and from smallmouth to false albacore. Once the hook is set it is often difficult to tell whether the angler or the fish is in control. Hooking a large game fish with a fly rod or spin tackle from a canoe or kayak in a remote area away from the crowd was the type of excitement that I envisioned in 1960 when I so desperately wanted a folding kayak. Now that I am in my fifties, I am less supple and not quite as strong, but I still intend to fulfill some of my teenage angling ambitions.

13

Quiet Propulsion: Push Poles, Oars, Paddles, and Electric Motors

In my son's bedroom is a large framed photograph of the Izaak Walton stained-glass window from England's Winchester Cathedral. When my wife and I chose the name "Izaak" for our firstborn son, we did so simply because we liked the sound of the name when spoken and the way it is spelled. It didn't hurt, however, that there was great admiration in our household for Izaak Walton, the author of *The Compleat Angler* (Modern Library, 1998), first published in 1652. The Walton window shows the image of a man at peace with the world, reading under a tree with his rod and creel nearby. At the bottom of the window in bold letters is the phrase "Study to Be Quiet."

Although I am sure that, for Walton, the phrase at the bottom of his window had layers of meaning, for me it has always meant that, in angling at least, quiet does not come easy. Before we can see and hear the world around us, we must work and study to create the necessary silence. Most of us never have a clue as to how many fish we scare away while on foot or in a boat. The simple fact is that stealth is an art often talked about, but seldom practiced, except by a handful of anglers. When you see one of the great ones wading a trout stream or poling a tropical flat, it is like watching a great blue heron or an egret working its quarry. Today's light-tackle angler has an arsenal of "quiet tools," both ancient and modern, to help with the stalk.

Although the house of every fish should be approached with quiet and reverence, some fish are more sensitive than others. They are sensitive not only to noise and shock waves generated from inside a boat and from waves slapping against the hull, but they are also sensitive to shadows and movement at great distances. Large trout in still water, largemouth bass along a shallow shore, bonefish and redfish in ankle-deep water, and stripers over a light sand bottom are just a few of the characters with which we must play the stealth game.

In this chapter on silent propulsion of boats with hard hulls, I will offer an overview of equipment and technique. Most important, however, I hope to stimulate your desire to "study to be quiet."

Push Poles

The push pole was probably man's first instrument of propulsion on the water. Since before recorded time human beings have been pushing dugouts, baskets, and other craft in coastal shallows and rivers in both tropical and cooler climates. Although modern push poles are made from fiberglass or graphite materials similar to those found in our rods, most boats are still poled with wood. My first exposure to poling was on the Currituck Sound in the mid-1950s. Guides used the same skiffs to take "sports" bass fishing in the summer and duck hunting in the winter. Although these boats were equipped with small outboards to get across open stretches, guides would pole anglers with ash push poles, called "shoving poles," twelve to fourteen

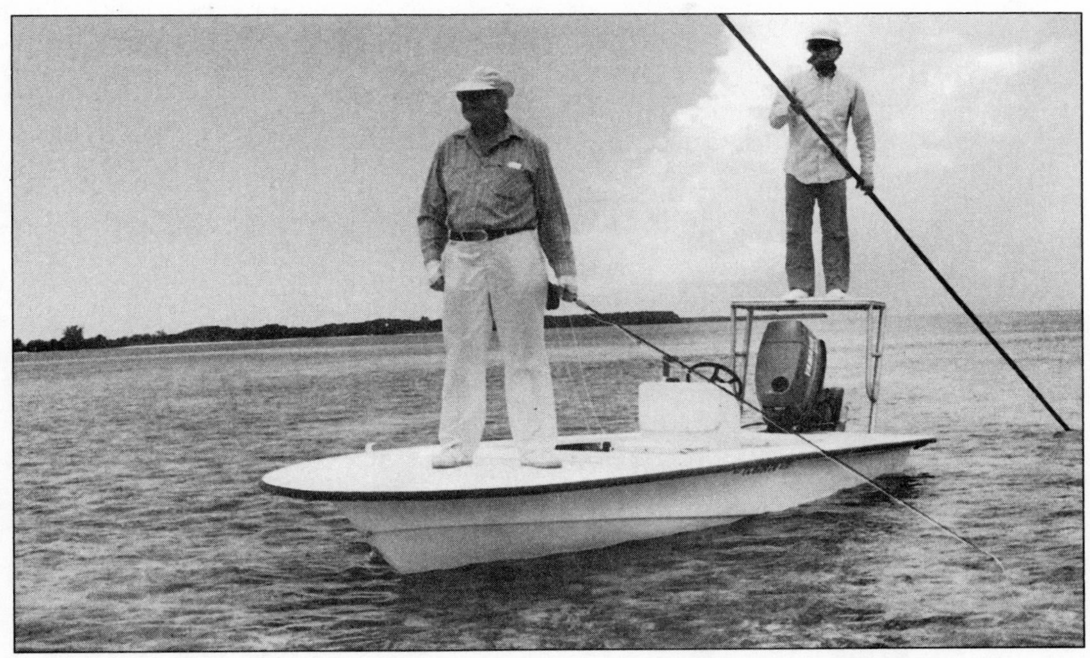

Lefty Kreh

The push pole was not invented in the Florida Keys, but many shallow water light-tackle techniques were developed there. Here, Capt. Steve Huff and Del Brown are searching for permit.

feet in length. With an ash pole, a guide poling from the stern could cover a tremendous amount of water quickly, thoroughly, and silently. Only with a shoving pole and the outboard motor tilted out of the water could guides cover some of the weed-filled waters preferred by brackish-water largemouth. It was only after I had fished several times in the Florida Keys in the late 1960s and early 1970s that I realized that the poling technique used by Keys guides was the same as that employed by the Currituck bass guides.

Perhaps because of my early association with push poles, I enjoy poling boats when in search of a tremendous variety of fish. I regularly pole coastal flats for redfish and seatrout. I also love poling shallow edges of reservoirs and ponds in search of bass, sunfish, and large carp, which I consider to be an exciting and widely misunderstood game fish. If you are new to poling, the first thing you must understand is that almost *any* light, stable boat can be poled. You do not need a specially designed flats skiff to play the game. Depending on the type of boat, the poler can stand on a stern poling platform several feet above the boat, on a stern casting deck, on the bow, on the gunnel, or even standing on the boat's floor at water level. It is true that many boats can be poled just as easily from the bow as from the stern.

Poling is really quite simple. To go straight place the end of the push pole parallel to the centerline of the boat and push. To go to the left, place the pole and push to the left of centerline. To go to the right, place the pole and push to the right of centerline. Photos by Paul Bates.

When I first began fishing in the Florida Keys for bonefish and tarpon, there were no poling platforms. Guides typically poled from the bow of the boat while anglers fished from a raised casting area at the stern. Whether you have a custom-designed flats boat, a wooden rowing skiff, a bass boat under 17 feet, or an aluminum johnboat, you can be part of the quiet world of poling.

First, let's take a quick look at push poles. In a johnboat, skiff, or small bass boat without a raised poling platform, you will need a push pole fourteen to seventeen feet in length. For those with poling platforms, push poles of eighteen to twenty-one feet are more desirable. It is now possible to pay considerably more for a stiff, custom-made graphite push pole than you would pay for a high-end electric trolling motor complete with batteries. There are, however, excellent push poles available in fiberglass or a combination of fiberglass and graphite, costing about as much as a fine fishing rod. Many people still make their own push poles using wooden dowels or a length of aluminum or PVC pipe. Although I like to save money, would-be polers should exercise care in using homemade wooden or plastic poles because they are exposed to great stresses while in use and can shatter or splinter. In the Bahamas and in Central America, many of the native guides do just fine with push poles made from dried "debarked" pine saplings. Again, however, if you can afford a good rod, then by all means invest the same amount in an adequate push pole.

Even though most anglers just learning to pole a boat will invariably pole in circles, the technique used to pole almost every kind of boat is essentially the same. Right-handers usually begin by holding the push pole on their left side with their right hand above the left hand. The end of the push pole is then placed in the water at a slight angle away from the transom, *parallel to the centerline of the boat.* Only if the boat is pushed with the push pole parallel to the boat's centerline will it go straight. The boat should track straight whether you are standing in the center of the boat or off to one side as long as the force exerted by the push pole is parallel to the boat's centerline.

When the pole is placed firmly on the bottom, at a slight angle away from the boat, the poler exerts forward pressure by "walking" hand over hand for at least three arm reaches. The pole is then quietly pulled out of the water with the hands returning to "the starting position," while again placing the pole at a slight angle to the boat parallel to the centerline. With a little practice the pole can be pushed and retrieved with such a nice rhythm that the boat will develop momentum, making the poling process even easier.

Turning the boat is actually easier than making it go straight. To turn right, plant the push pole to the right of the boat's centerline and exert the same forward pressure discussed earlier. If the pole is placed and pushed so that pressure is exerted only slightly to the right of the boat's centerline, then the turn will not be extreme. If, however, the pole is placed and pushed at sharp angle to the boat's centerline, then the right turn will be sharp.

To make a left turn, simply plant the pole and exert pressure to the left side of the boat's centerline. Again, the sharper the angle, the sharper the turn. When trying to keep a boat on a straight course, a slight turn to the left or right is often necessary to compensate for a shift of weight in the boat or the effects of wind and current.

A properly poled boat can be the most quiet and effective means of approaching any game fish if the water is shallow enough. Generally, when water under the boat gets five or six feet in depth, placing the pole and getting two or three good hand-over-hand pushes gets more and more difficult. For shallow coastal flats, marshes, and freshwater shorelines, no other means for stalking is more pleasurable to me. Not only do you get to move quietly toward fish, but with a push pole you can also effectively position your angler in the best angle to cast. For example, once you get within casting range of a fish or group of fish, you may want to turn the boat left or right to give your angler a better look at the fish, or in a better position to take ad-

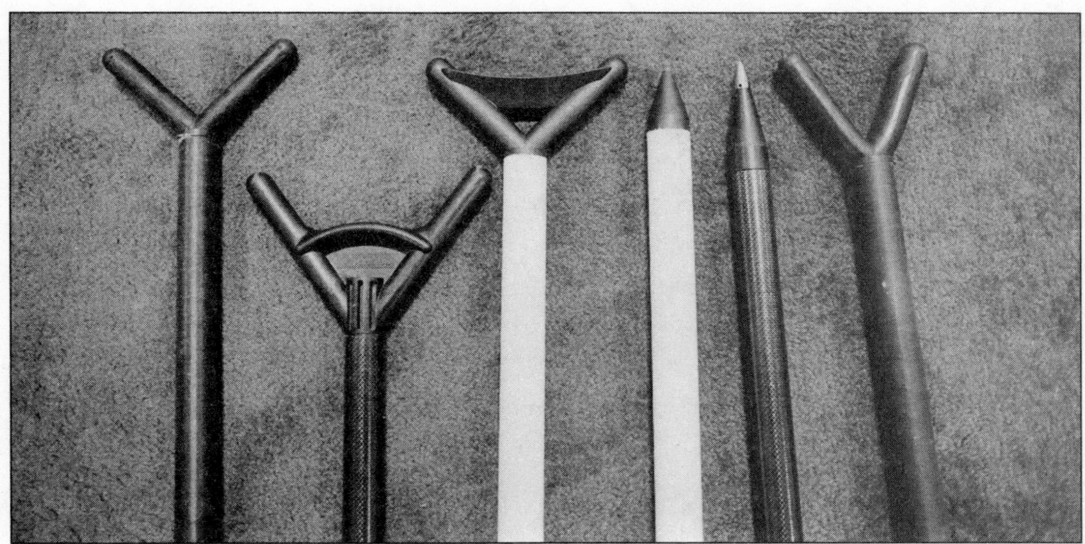

Push poles have pointed ends for working over hard bottoms and forked or flat ends for working over grass and mud.

vantage of the wind direction. Finally, most push poles come with one end pointed and the other end forked. When working over hard sand, shells, or a rocky bottom, the pointed end should be placed in the water. However, if the bottom is of gooey mud or grass, the forked end will allow you to propel the boat without burying the end of the push pole in goo.

Although push poles are generally used to propel a boat, steer a boat while drifting, or to better position an angler when approaching fish, they can also be used to secure a boat. With the pointed end down, a push pole can be forced into sand or mud at an angle, leaving the forked end of the push pole no higher than the top of your outboard or poling platform. Anglers who tie up to a push pole are said to be "staked out." When poles are used to stake out, make sure that the pole is not thrust into the bottom anywhere near vertical. If your boat is tied to a push pole not forced into the bottom at the proper angle (45

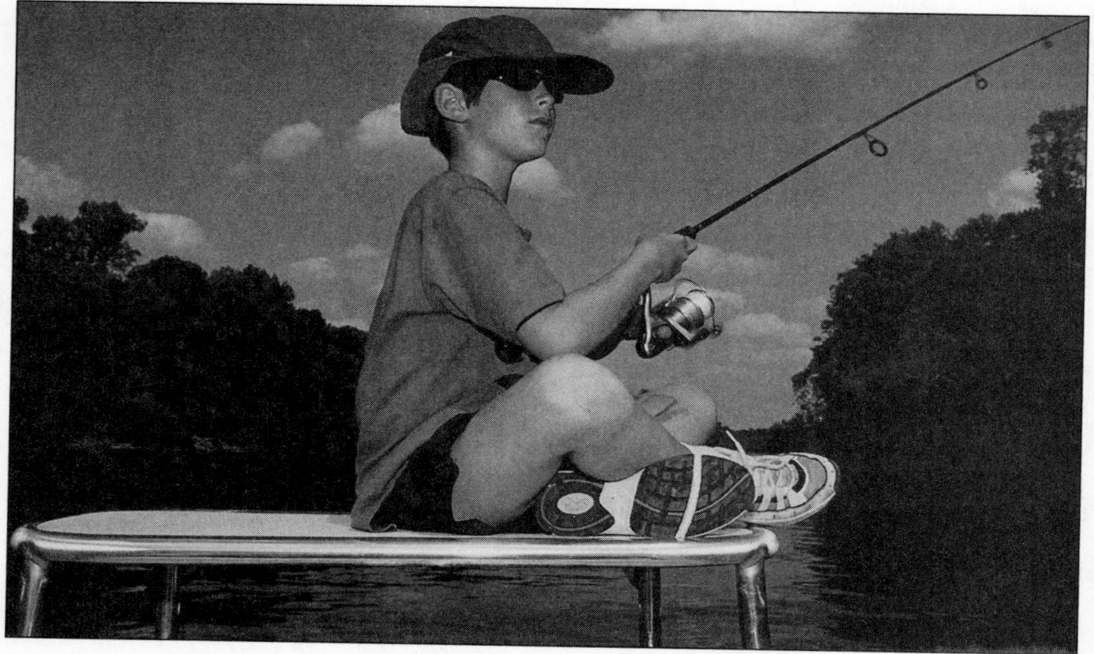

A poling platform is not just for poling, but it's also a great place to sit.

degrees or less), the pole can shatter, causing potential harm to passengers and your wallet.

Oars and Paddles

First the basics: Boats requiring oars are rowed, while canoes and kayaks are paddled. If you are the proud owner of a skiff, pram, or drift boat, you will need a set of oars in an appropriate length for your boat. The oars are placed in oarlocks, which rotate in oarlock sockets that are permanently attached to the gunnels of the boat. Oars are nothing more than levers with blades on the end. When oars are too short, a rower will have trouble reaching the water and getting enough leverage to power the boat. If oars are too long, they will not only be unwieldy, but they will be difficult to pull through an entire stroke, prematurely wearing out the angler. For many years almost every rowboat with which I was acquainted had six-foot oars, not because they were the right size, but because it was the size usually stocked by the local hardware store or tackle shop.

Although there is still no hard science that will help you choose the perfect set of oars, here are a few guidelines that may keep you from making a big mistake. Start by choosing oars that are each a little longer than one and one-half times the beam of the boat. Thus, a boat with a four-foot beam would require an oar between six and six and a half feet in length. A boat with a beam around four and a half feet would require oars between six and a half and seven feet in length. Also, please note that if the boat is low to the water (low freeboard), it will require shorter oars than the same boat with higher freeboard. If at all possible, try several lengths of oars with your boat before you buy. Again, if the oars are too short, you will have trouble getting enough leverage, and if they are too long, the rower may have difficulty clearing the water on the backstroke.

Remember, I described an oar as a lever with the blade on one end and the rower's hands on the other. The oarlock fitted into the oarlock socket acts as fulcrum. Although greater power can be applied by rowers with their backs to their destination, skiffs and dories easily can be rowed forward or backward when approaching fish or avoiding obstacles. Also, since oars are balanced in the oarlock, weight is not a significant factor. Although I know that there are some excellent oars available with aluminum shafts and tough plastic blades, the only oars that really stack up in a skiff or pram are wooden oars of the right length. With wooden oars you can row back in time with your modern tackle and challenge any fish that swims.

Paddles for Canoes and Kayaks

In the section on canoes we looked at canoes of various lengths, widths, and hull shape to evaluate their potential as fishing craft. The same must be done with paddles. In any shop specializing in canoes and kayaks you can be overwhelmed quickly by the variety of paddle lengths, blade shapes, grip shapes, and materials. You can choose from plenty of expensive Kevlar, graphite, and fiberglass paddles, or from inexpensive aluminum paddles with plastic blades. However, for toughness, weight, and appearance, it is hard to beat a wooden paddle. Today's wooden paddles are usually laminates held together by modern resins and protected by tough varnishes or epoxy.

You will see canoe paddles with broad blades in either a "tulip" shape or a "square-tipped" shape. Paddles with these broad, long blades are fine for experienced paddlers with the strength to move a significant volume of water. For the angler and everyday paddler, however, the old "beaver tail"–shaped blades are my choice for comfort of use. The beavertail blades are not as long or wide as paddles used for cruising or white water. You will also note that many of the wide paddles have a T-shaped grip as compared to the more rounded pear-shaped grip usually

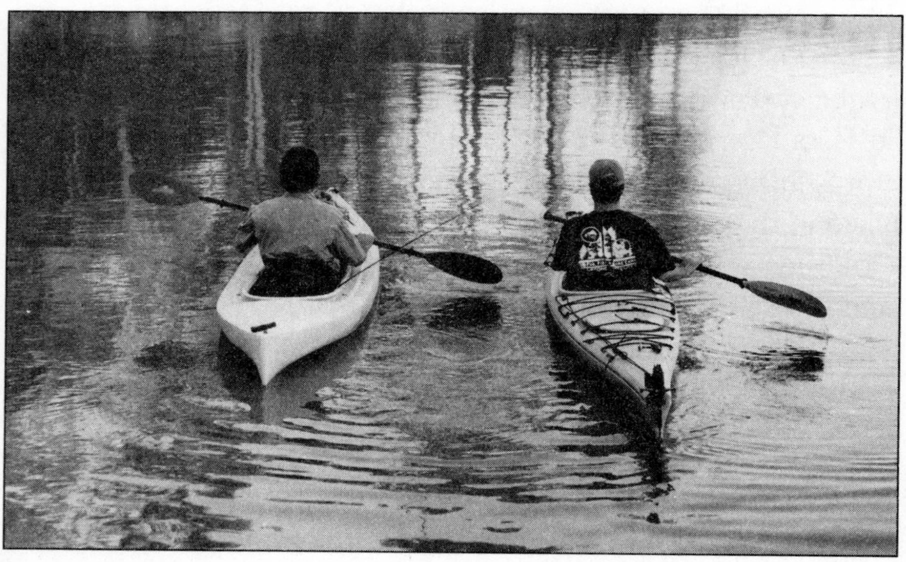

Paddle length and blade shape is important for anglers who use kayaks and canoes.

found on a beavertail paddle. T-shaped grips are for gripping in heavier water, while the pear-shaped grips lay more comfortably in the palm, and are my choice for calm-water angling use.

Choosing the right paddle length call be tricky. Over the years I have heard countless cockamamy "formulas" for choosing the perfect paddle. Most have something to do with a measurement somewhere between the distance between the floor and your navel, armpit, and eyebrows. Although I come from a school that says that the tall guy gets the long paddle and the short guy gets the stubby one, I have been convinced in recent years that there is some science to choosing a paddle. First, you must understand that it is inefficient for a significant portion of the paddle *blade* to be out of the water during a full stroke, or for much of the paddle's *shaft* to be submerged deep in the water. The shaft length of the paddle best suited for you should be approximately the distance from your chin to the waterline *when you are sitting or kneeling* in your preferred position. Add to the shaft length the length of the blade you have chosen. The total of the shaft length and your preferred blade length should add up to the right overall length for your needs. Again, however, I must emphasize that when fishing in small lakes and slow-moving rivers, I am not a picky paddler. I can make do, and even enjoy, paddling with almost any wooden paddle four to five feet in length.

When choosing a paddle for your fishing kayak, you will again confront many of the issues dealt with in choosing a canoe paddle. The main difference, of course, is that in kayaking, double-bladed paddles are used. Most kayak paddles are between seven and eight and a half feet in length. Although the length of the paddle depends in part on the width of the boat and the height of the angler's shoulders above the water, there is no hard-and-fast rule for determining paddle length. Generally speaking, long paddles (between eight and nine feet in length) with wide blades can cause muscle strain, especially in inexperienced paddlers. Shorter paddles (between seven and eight feet in length) with narrower blades are easier on the arms and shoulders of average paddlers and are, for fishing purposes, the best choice. First, the fishing kayaker is generally not interested in great speed or quick turns. Also, and even more important, longer paddles are more difficult to deal with in fishing combat. A shorter paddle, approximately seven and a half feet in length, with a fairly narrow blade will probably meet your needs. However, make sure that you try several paddles in different lengths and with different blade widths and shapes to find the one that feels best with your kayak and water conditions.

Electric Trolling Motors

No device or accessory epitomizes the modern fishing boat in fresh or salt water more than the electric trolling motor. It would be hard to find a modern bass fisherman who does not use an electric motor. Over the past twenty years, electric motors have also become a major feature on many saltwater fishing boats. Electrics can do many jobs for anglers. They can, of course, provide your silent propulsion once you have arrived at your destination. For many anglers, however, they provide primary propulsion when used with lightweight prams or, with brackets, on canoes. As primary propulsion they can take you considerable distances, help you catch fish, and then bring you home. Electric motors can also be used in conjunction with other forms of maneuvering and propulsion. For example, guides in the Florida Keys and on the striper flats of the Northeast have long used trolling motors and push poles together. Winds and stiff currents often can make poling a losing battle. Add the power of an electric motor, or even two electric motors, and the boat can still be moved quietly through the water and maneuvered easily with the push pole. In the last twenty years almost all of the tarpon fishing I've done in the Keys has been in boats equipped with both a push pole and an electric trolling motor.

Twenty years ago, a powerful electric trolling motor had 30 to 40 pounds of thrust. Now, trolling motors with 50, 75, and even 100 pounds of thrust are available. Electrics can be mounted on the bow or the stern, with hand controls, foot controls, and even remote controls. The most sophisticated electric motors have remote foot controls or "joy sticks" that can control the speed and direction of a trolling motor, or motors, from anywhere in the boat. Electric motors are also available that can be mounted on the cavitation plate of an outboard engine or on the trim tabs of a boat. The choices and options are endless.

Although most anglers agree on the benefits of trolling motors, there is still often considerable disagreement about whether they are most useful mounted on the bow or on the stern. Gen-

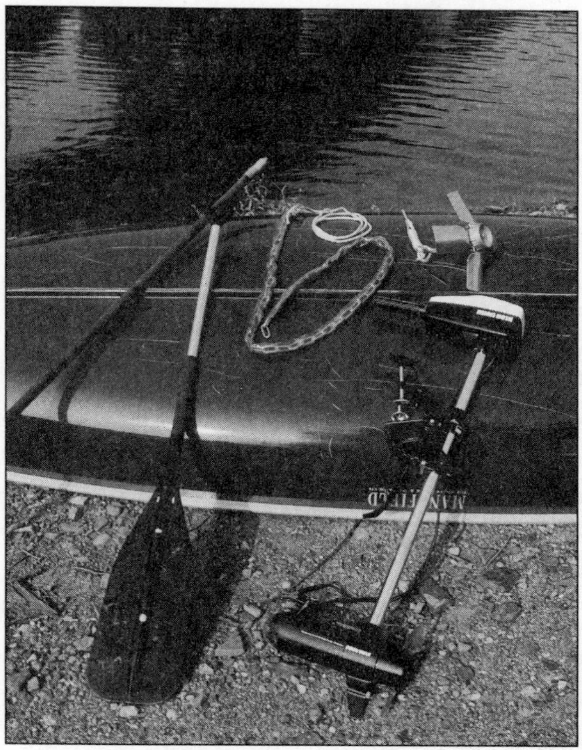

Ed Jaworowski

Push poles, paddles, and electric trolling motors can be used together to make a "silent boat."

erally, electric motors mounted on the bow allow for much quicker maneuvering. The bow can be pushed left or right quickly. For years, almost all bass boats have featured bow-mounted electrics. Now, many saltwater anglers are also opting for bow-mounted motors. Although I understand the advantages of trolling motors at the bow for bass fishing, I still prefer stern-mounted motors for most saltwater angling, especially saltwater fly fishing. In saltwater fly fishing there is often much maneuvering and lots of line on the deck. Bow-mounted trolling motors can be a major obstacle for saltwater fly fishermen. My fly lines always seem to gravitate toward them. Also, the larger wave action found in saltwater conditions often makes it difficult to keep a bow-mounted motor in the water. In rough weather conditions the bow of the boat can bounce up and down, causing an electric motor shaft to also bounce up and down. This will generally not be the case with stern-mounted electrics. Again, however, there are many conditions in salt water, especially for the spin and plug fisherman, where bow-mounted motors make perfect sense.

Twenty years ago the life of an electric trolling motor used in salt water was barely one year. Now, most of the major manufacturers of electric trolling motors offer models specifically designed for more demanding saltwater conditions. Saltwater trolling motors have specially sealed electrical components and composite or stainless steel shafts with special sacrificial anodes to protect metal parts. If you have a bass boat or johnboat equipped with an ordinary electric not designed for saltwater use, you may want to think twice before exposing it to the ravages of salt. If you decide to use your freshwater unit in the salt, make sure that you spray every inch of it with a moisture-displacing lubricant before use. After use in the salt, wash down your electric with mild soapy water. If you are an angler who, like me, regularly fishes in both fresh and salt water, make sure you spend a few extra bucks to buy a trolling motor suited to both the fresh- and saltwater environment.

Ed Jaworowski

Electric trolling motors can be mounted on canoes with brackets (top left), on the bow of a fishing boat (top right) or on the stern, as with these dual electrics on the trim tabs (below).

Unless you plan to use an electric motor only sparingly, then it is usually wise to have a separate battery, or bank of batteries of the deep-cycle type, to power it. As indicated earlier, deep-cycle batteries can be drained and recharged numerous times without damage. The same cannot be said about your cranking battery. Finally, most electric motors with 30 to 50 pounds of thrust are set up to run on a standard 12-volt system. Many of the more powerful electric motors delivering 60 to 100 pounds of thrust require a bank of trolling batteries to be configured so that they deliver 24 or 36 volts. Along with the proper power configuration, remember that trolling batteries are heavy, forty to fifty pounds each. Make sure that you work with your dealer in placing batteries for your electric motor so that your boat can maintain proper trim while at rest and under power.

* * *

With all of the methods of silent propulsion available to us, it is amazing that we as anglers are still a very noisy lot. Whether you use a push pole, oars, paddles, or an electric motor, learn to use them right. Place your push pole carefully and then retrieve it quietly to avoid making noise. Don't slap your oars or paddles in the water when approaching fish. Approach fish with the lowest and quietest speed available with your electric motor. Izaak Walton would applaud the silent propulsion options available to us. Unlike many of us, however, Walton would "study to be quiet" while using them.

VI

SAFETY AND ETIQUETTE FOR THE BOATING ANGLER

14

Angler Safety: More Than a Fire Extinguisher and Life Jackets

When I was sixteen years old I traveled with my father and one of his fishing friends, named Amos, to Lake Lure in the Blue Ridge Mountains of western North Carolina. It was mid-February and the water temperature was below 50 degrees. We were fishing for trout where the river flowed into the lake when we noticed another boat drifting in the distance. A couple of minutes later Amos said in a soft, worried tone, "There is no one in that boat."

With the air temperature barely above freezing and the water temperature too cold for extended survival, all of us jumped to the same conclusion: The unthinkable had occurred. Only after pulling even with the little boat did we notice that its engine was idling. Everything in the boat appeared in place, except people. Less than a minute later and perhaps a hundred yards away, we saw what appeared to be a head and hand barely above the surface. We quickly pulled a slender young man into our boat, a man lucky to be alive. Even though his voice and motor skills had almost been stolen by the cold water, he said that he was alone.

We got him into a warm car and helped him change into dry clothes. While insisting he did not need hospital attention, he told us that he had simply tripped and fallen out of the boat. He guessed that he had been in the water fifteen minutes before being rescued. Later that afternoon we helped him to retrieve his boat. In it were two life jackets, a thermos of coffee, a heavy coat, and his fishing gear.

Even though I had witnessed only a near-tragedy, and not the real thing, I wondered for many weeks about what the man could have done differently.

Since that day almost forty years ago, I have had three boats sink under me with no injury or loss of life. I once spent three days and nights on a deserted, mosquito-infested island because of a blown power head. And, like many anglers, I've had more encounters with high winds and lightning than I would like to admit. Although I've never considered myself foolhardy, like the young man pulled out of Lake Lure four decades ago, I have also been lucky. Because I'm older, but also because I have young children, I have given much thought in recent years to safety on the water, especially on fishing trips. I have reached a conclusion that is certainly not new to most experienced anglers: Safety is more a state of mind than a set of required equipment.

The items required on small boats by the United States Coast Guard—life jackets, a fire extinguisher, signal flares, a noisemaker, running lights—are all important and should be carried by every boating angler. I am completely convinced, however, that the vast majority of accidents, injuries, and deaths on the water can be prevented by "preemptive planning," also known as foresight. I know that many of us have cellular telephones and VHF radios to summon help, and GPS that can give the exact coordinates to the trauma center helicopter. However, injuries and accidents can occur so quickly that all that our electronic aids can do is help us to summon assistance

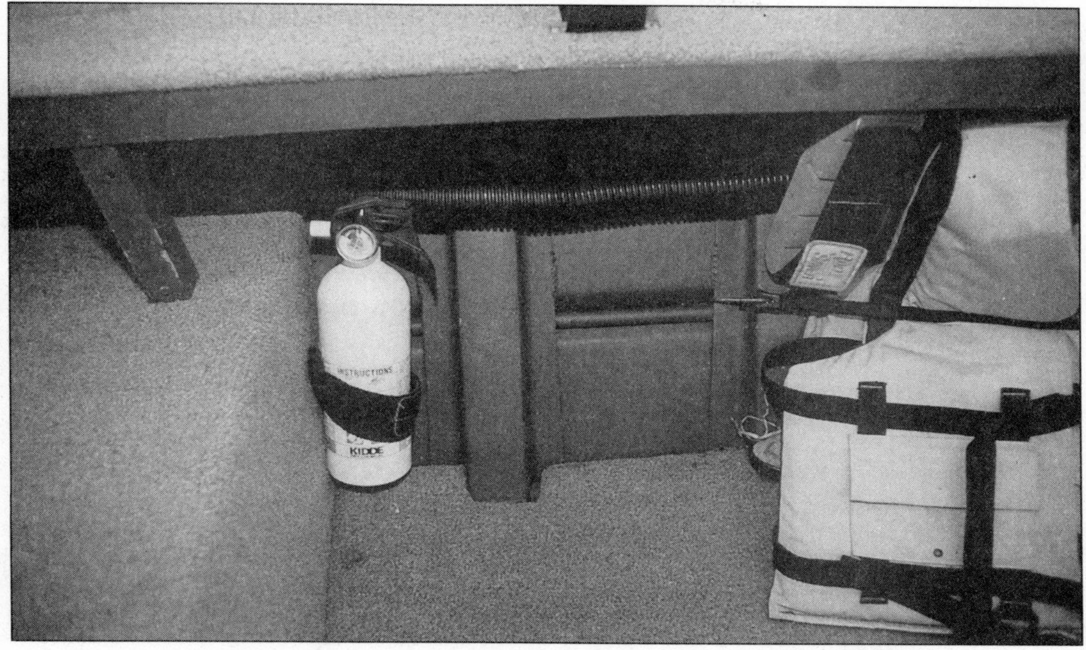

Ed Jaworowski

Safety equipment required by the Coast Guard and other agencies is important, but "preemptive planning" can prevent accidents from happening.

and pick up the pieces. Below I have listed several categories of problems that are at least in part preventable by a little planning and foresight.

Cold-Weather Fishing

When water temperatures are below 50 degrees, survival time is measured in minutes, not hours. We lose body heat up to twenty times faster in water than air. Even in "warm water" (70 to 80 degrees) hypothermia can still sap body heat over time. Although I love to fish alone, there are times when common sense dictates that I use the "buddy system." Take a second person in your boat, or even better, fish with a companion boat nearby. If you must fish alone in cold weather, or cold-water conditions, choose an area where other anglers are likely to be present.

I have spent many days on the water in late fall and early winter when the local weathermen predicted a balmy 75-degree day. Such predictions may be correct on land. However, when on a small boat, you'll often find the air temperature closer to the temperature of the water. At even modest speeds there will be a significant wind-chill factor. Running on top of 45-degree water at 30 mph will be very close to experiencing the wind-chill effect of a 30-mph wind on a 45-degree day. Both cold water and cold air can steal body heat, resulting in hypothermia. That is why it is so important on cold days to "layer up" when on the water. Warm clothing is important, but the most important part of any cold-weather-boating clothing "system" is top-quality water-and-wind-resistant foul-weather gear. It is the operator's responsibility to make sure that every passenger has adequate cold-weather clothing, or the day can end prematurely for everyone when a "popsicle passenger" has to be returned to the dock.

Don't forget feet, hands, and heads. It's very common to see anglers decked out in warm clothing and foul-weather gear wearing wet sneakers and a baseball cap. Make sure that your cold-weather fishing outfit is complete.

In cold weather you must "layer up." The top layer should be good foul-weather gear.

Sun and Dehydration

Not all tragedies from exposure on the water come quickly. I have lost two good friends to melanoma, an often fatal skin cancer. One of them, Capt. John Emery, was one of the finest saltwater fishermen of his generation. Even if I hadn't known victims of this horrible disease, I have still had ample warning from the news media and my doctor over the past two decades. In my files are many slides and photographs taken many years ago of angling friends and me wearing only shorts or a bathing suit, and sporting a dark tan. No more. When I'm out on the water for any significant period of time, I wear a long-sleeved shirt, long pants, and a hat that can cover my face, ears, and neck. I also use sunscreen several times a day, sunscreen with a SPF rating of 30 or more.

I have also concluded in recent years that shade is not for sissies. Although I have spent countless twelve-hour days on the water with no shade, I now look forward to time out of the sun. As indicated earlier, a Bimini top or good umbrella can help make your fishing trip. The blessed relief of getting under a

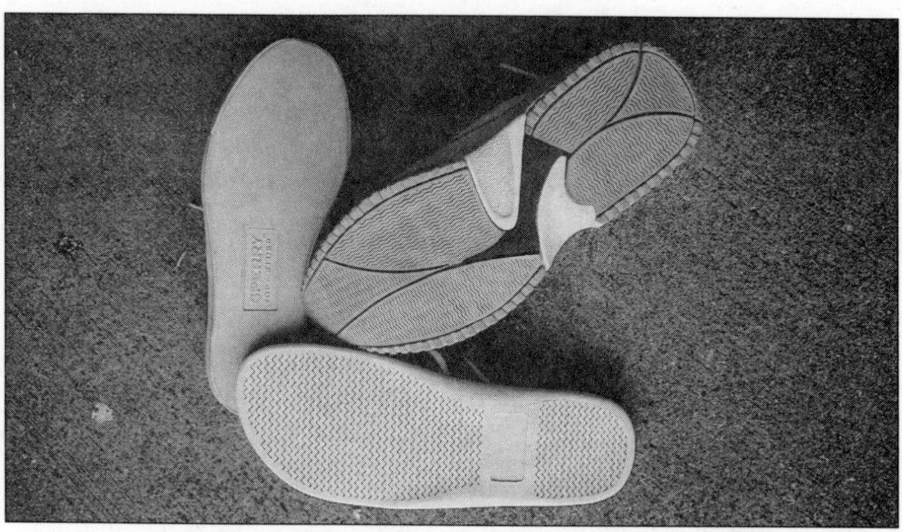

Proper clothing on a fishing boat includes nonslip deck shoes.

bridge or large shade tree is also a treat that should not be avoided.

Shade not only protects you from the sun, it helps prevent dehydration. Dehydration is another slow-acting and insidious villain on the water. I have seen numerous people get sick over the years because they did not drink enough nonalcoholic liquids during the day. Even though dehydration can occur on days when it is not hot and humid, every captain or operator of a fishing boat should make sure that enough liquid is on board for every passenger. The combination of heat and dehydration can lead to heat sickness, and even heat stroke. I often declare a "water break" on my boats when my passengers fail to drink enough water on their own.

Speed and Alcohol

At the risk of beating a dead horse, high speed on the water—especially on fishing trips—makes very little sense. Even at modest speeds of 30 to 35 mph, a partially submerged piling or a floating rope can cause operators to lose control of their boat. Even if your boat is designed to run at interstate highway speeds, you and everyone around you will be safer if you ease up on the throttle.

I feel funny writing about alcohol use in a book on fishing boats. However, nothing is more preventable on the water than an alcohol-related accident. Many states now have laws regulating the use of alcohol by operators, and even passengers, on powerboats. Unfortunately, not everyone has gotten the word. Alcohol and speed on the water can be just as deadly as on any highway.

Necessary Tools

When I think about necessary tools on any fishing boat, a good set of adjustable pliers, screwdrivers in several sizes, and a flashlight always come to mind. Over the years I have also found that a really sharp, substantial knife, not a flimsy bait knife or pocketknife, can be especially useful in cutting rope or tangled vegetation off of my propeller. There are also times, such as in heavy surf or currents, that you may need to cut your own anchor rope quickly.

Another item that has found its way on each of my powerboats in recent years has been a set of jumper cables. Several years ago the operator of a sea-towing service told me that a substantial number of calls to which he responded were related to dead or weakened batteries. It's nice to have cables available for your own needs or those of fellow anglers, since a set of jumper cables is much cheaper than a visit from a commercial towing service.

Polarized Glasses

Finally, I can think of no more important piece of safety equipment on my boat than polarized glasses. Yes, they help you see fish, but they also cut the glare so boaters can see rocks, stumps, shallow bars, and partially submerged debris. I've seen numerous boats run aground over the years, simply because the operator couldn't see shallow waters ahead. I don't care how much you

Polarized glasses should be on top of the safety "equipment" list for any boater. You may run over what you can't see. The left view of this sandbar is seen through regular lenses while the right is through polarized lenses.

paid for your designer sunglasses, if they aren't polarized, they shouldn't be on the water.

A good pair of polarized glasses will also help prevent eyestrain during a long day on the water. Your day will be safer and more enjoyable. This is one piece of "equipment" that can prevent accidents.

The list of issues and items above related to safety is not intended to be comprehensive. As you have reviewed my concerns I hope that you have thought of many more safety issues relating to your own fishing conditions. The things we carry in case of emergency are important, but anticipating or preventing an emergency is far more important. Again, safety is much more a state mind than a set of required equipment.

15

Angler's Etiquette: The Golden Rule

I once commented to an elderly resident of western North Carolina that the owners of a wonderful stretch of private trout water were "real gentlemen." I was surprised when the old mountaineer responded, "I could be a gentleman, too, if I didn't have to share miles of stream with anyone else."

That response pretty well sums up the major problem facing fishermen today, especially those using boats. With inland and coastal waters becoming more crowded, there is growing potential for conflict between various user groups. Even when you take commercial fishermen and nonangling boaters (water-skiers, sightseers, and jet sled jockeys) out of the mix, there is still plenty of room for misunderstanding. The rules and expectations are different for angling boaters using different techniques. Fly fishermen, trollers, live-bait drifters, and plug casters often have a different view of the world. What constitutes a breach of etiquette is a matter of perception and experience. For example, people who fish flats in shallow-draft boats know to give a wide birth to other flats anglers and to shut down their motors well before reaching the fishing zone. Anglers with no flats experience may be clueless, and run their craft across an entire flat without ever understanding that people using a push pole are trying to be quiet. On several occasions while poling my skiff as quietly as possible, I've watched in disbelief as fishermen in another boat motored across a half mile of two-foot water only to ask me, "Caught anything?"

Dividing good fishing water without conflict and hard feelings is a difficult task. Several years ago a friend and I left the dock at 5:15 A.M. to run to a wreck twelve miles off the beach. The wreck was in ninety feet of water and typically held king mackerel, barracuda, amberjack, and dolphin. Because the ocean was slick we had an easy trip in the 20-foot center console and arrived on station about 6:00 A.M. We rigged our fly rods and enjoyed a cup of coffee while watching dolphin (the fish) chasing a "covey" of flying fish. A couple of sinister barracuda rose from the wreck and began staring at us from behind the engine. Using large streamers on sinking lines we had just started to make our first drift when we heard the drone of engines in the distance. Within fifteen minutes four other boats chose the same location for their fishing pleasure. The wreck we had all chosen was prime habitat well known to anglers of the region. Two charter boats trolled a variety of lures and baits, fishermen in another small boat dropped live baits on the wreck while trying to maintain their position, and the anglers in the final boat, like my friend and me, wanted to drift. Soon, no one was happy. The trollers insisted on making their passes directly over the structure, the live-bait guys wanted to hog the center of the wreck, and those of us who wanted to drift and cast had little room to work. After an hour of no fish and no fun, I cranked the engine and left.

Because my friend and I arrived first, did we have rights superior to the latecomers? Since the charter boats had paying customers on board, did their captains have the right to run over those of us in small boats, the "mosquito fleet"? Did the live-bait anglers have the right to park their rig over the wreck, effectively stopping drifts and trolling patterns? This scenario has no genuine "bad guys" and no clear breaches of etiquette. There are also no clear-cut solutions. All of the anglers deserved a clean shot at the angling prizes over the wreck, but for that to happen, the operator of each boat had to acknowledge the needs of strangers and communicate with them, a tough thing to do. In such situations the Golden Rule—do unto others—can work, but it takes effort. More on that later.

Boat-to-Boat Courtesy

Unfortunately, there are situations in which uncaring anglers violate the rights and space of others. There are jerks who fish. When someone *knowingly* cuts off my drift, runs through fish I am working, tries to butt into the tight space I'm occupying, or casts directly over my lines, I get angry. At such times I have several options. I can sneer, call the offender dirty names, offer The Finger, threaten physical harm, or attack. All these options raise blood pressure and accomplish nothing. In the rare situations when I encounter jerks on the water, I depart when attempts to reason fail. It is better to retreat and waste part of a day than mess up your whole day by mixing it up with a jerk.

I'm sure you are wondering how to distinguish the jerks, the intentional violators, from the unthinking or uninformed boater who violates your fishing space. There is not an angler/boater alive who has not *unintentionally* run over another's space either while daydreaming, or out of lack of experience. However, those who commit unintentional breaches of etiquette will usually apologize, correct their mistake, or depart when politely informed of their transgression. The *intentional* violator of another's fishing space would rather fight than fish. He will generally ignore a polite request or protest vehemently: "It's a free country, and I can fish anywhere I want."

Infringing on the rights of other angler/boaters, as already hinted at above, can take many forms. Crowding other boats already in position is among the most common. If anglers in one boat, be it a canoe, rowboat, or high-tech powerboat, have already established their position in a limited area of fishing water, they have priority. Here I'm talking about anglers in a boat fishing a small cove, sitting on a rocky point, working a single school of fish, or poling a limited stretch of shoreline. In such situations "first come, first serve" applies. I have been disappointed many times after running several miles in a boat only to find my destination already occupied. It is far better for the second boat to exit, and head for an inferior location, than to crowd the first boat.

Just as bad as crowding is failure to share. Many locations can and should be shared by a number of boats. There is a rock jetty near my house on the North Carolina coast that regularly hosts dozens of boats during the speckled trout (spotted weakfish) run. Anglers using spin tackle, live bait, and fly gear can exist side by side and catch fish. The rules are simple: Enter, drop anchor quietly, and give adjacent boats adequate casting room.

Multiple boats can also work a variety of schooling fish in open water. It does, however, take some watching and a little communication before entering the game. I've often been a part of a small fleet of anglers that seeks white bass or walleye in freshwater, and false albacore, Spanish mackerel, or stripers in the salt. These are situations where fish are spread out over a large area. Here anglers don't cut in front of others, throw up big wakes, or knowingly put down fish. No boat has a right to an entire bay, inlet, or a long stretch of beach, and fishing can be good for everyone in such situations when operators are alert and courteous. I don't like fishing in a crowd, but when a number of boats are "dancing" well together, it can sometimes be pleasant.

Guest Courtesy

Courtesy must also be exercised in a boat. If you are a guest passenger, ask questions of the owner or captain before the trip. What time are we leaving? What tackle should I bring? Are we spin fishing or fly casting? Should I bring food and beverages? What time are we returning?

Such questions seem so simple, but unless you ask, a good day of fishing can be ruined for everyone. Nothing is more frustrating for a group of anglers than waiting for a straggler at the dock as the sun is rising or the tide is being lost. It is inconsiderate for a guest to arrive with many rods and tackle boxes and expect the host to store all of his mess. It is also unfair for a guest to dictate the tackle or technique—fly, spin, or conventional—unless the issue was discussed beforehand. I've been late, brought too much gear, and been inconsiderate in a variety of other ways. However, having been on the receiving end of similar breeches of etiquette, I now try very hard to be a considerate guest.

When sharing a boat with other anglers, fishing time must also be shared. Even though it is true that some of us with more experience like to watch others catch fish, there should be a discussion early in the trip about how time should to be divided. When there are two or more anglers on a boat itching to fish, dividing fishing space and time can be fun. My dad and I used to employ the "half hour, two misses, or one fish system." It's as simple as it sounds. In the best fishing spot on the boat, usually the bow, each fisherman got thirty minutes, two missed strikes, or one decent caught fish before giving the seat to the next angler. No matter how you divide space and time, try to make it enjoyable for everyone.

When invited to fish on another angler's boat, I firmly believe that that the guest should offer to pay or split the costs for gas, oil, ice, ramp fees, and other incidental expenses. Even though the host may decline the offer, fishing/boating etiquette requires that the offer be made. Anyone who owns and maintains a boat, no matter how small or grand, knows that daily out-of-pocket expenses are just a small percentage of the real costs of ownership, which includes the purchase price, storage, insurance, and mechanics' fees. At the end of the day it is also a courteous gesture to offer to take part in the cleaning and wash down of another's boat.

Final Thoughts

Federal, state, and local authorities try to legislate boating etiquette in many ways. There are rules setting aside "no-wake" zones, rules that tell those of us in powerboats to give way to nonpowerboats, and rules that are intended to stop us from throwing trash in public waters. To their credit, many fishing clubs, tournaments, and organizations have codes of conduct. For thoughtful and experienced boaters, most items covered in regulations and codes are common sense and second nature. However, for many of the thousands of new fishing-boat operators hitting the water each year, government- or club-mandated etiquette is useful and necessary, but it can cover only a fraction of the situations on the water where courtesy is required.

Ultimately, I believe there are two basic solutions to bad manners on the nation's waters. First, boating anglers must try to understand, and appreciate, the needs of fishermen who use boats, tackle, and techniques different from our own. We must talk with, not at, other anglers at club meetings, at the dock, and on the water. We must treat others with the same courtesy that we expect for ourselves, even if it means catching fewer fish. Yes, this is the Golden Rule, and it works on the water, even though there will always be a few jerks who will make you wonder why you should bother to work things out. Overall, I'm amazed at how few angry moments there are among fishermen running their boats in close proximity to one another. Most of us want to be courteous on the water.

The second solution to avoiding conflict on the water is to fish at times and places so as to avoid the crowds. Even though I'm still attracted to the hot spots and hot fish well known to everyone, I find myself more attracted to water that no one else wants, and seeking fish that are on few anglers' glamor lists. In recent years I've caught some monster carp fishing the shallows of some of America's finest bass lakes. They are great fun to catch, and I have hardly any competition. Even if you insist on fishing for bass and other marquee fish, try lakes and ponds that are not on everyone's top-ten list.

In salt water I also look for new challenges away from the crowds. A few years ago such fish as false albacore and spadefish were undesirables that drew few crowds. Now anglers love them. There are still many unappreciated and unfished critters in the salt. New challenges may mean smaller fish on lighter tackle, different fish, neglected waters, and leaving the dock at 5:00 A.M. Once you begin to look for less desirable fish at undesirable times and places, like the old mountaineer, you'll find that it is easy to be a gentleman.

A Boating Glossary for Anglers

This is not intended to be a comprehensive glossary of nautical, sailing, or boating terms. Along with a bare minimum of general boating terms, the entries below are intended to help the reader understand the terminology used to describe fishing boats, equipment used on boats, and characteristics of their design and construction. Virtually all entries are covered in considerable detail in the preceding chapters. These definitions are written with the angler and not the general boating community in mind.

Aft: Toward the rear or stern of the boat.

Anchor: Any device used to secure a boat to the bottom or to control drift. Some anchors work as deadweight, while others depend on their design to dig in and hold.

Ballast: Weight carried low in a boat, usually below the waterline, that increases stability. In a small fishing boat, the way that

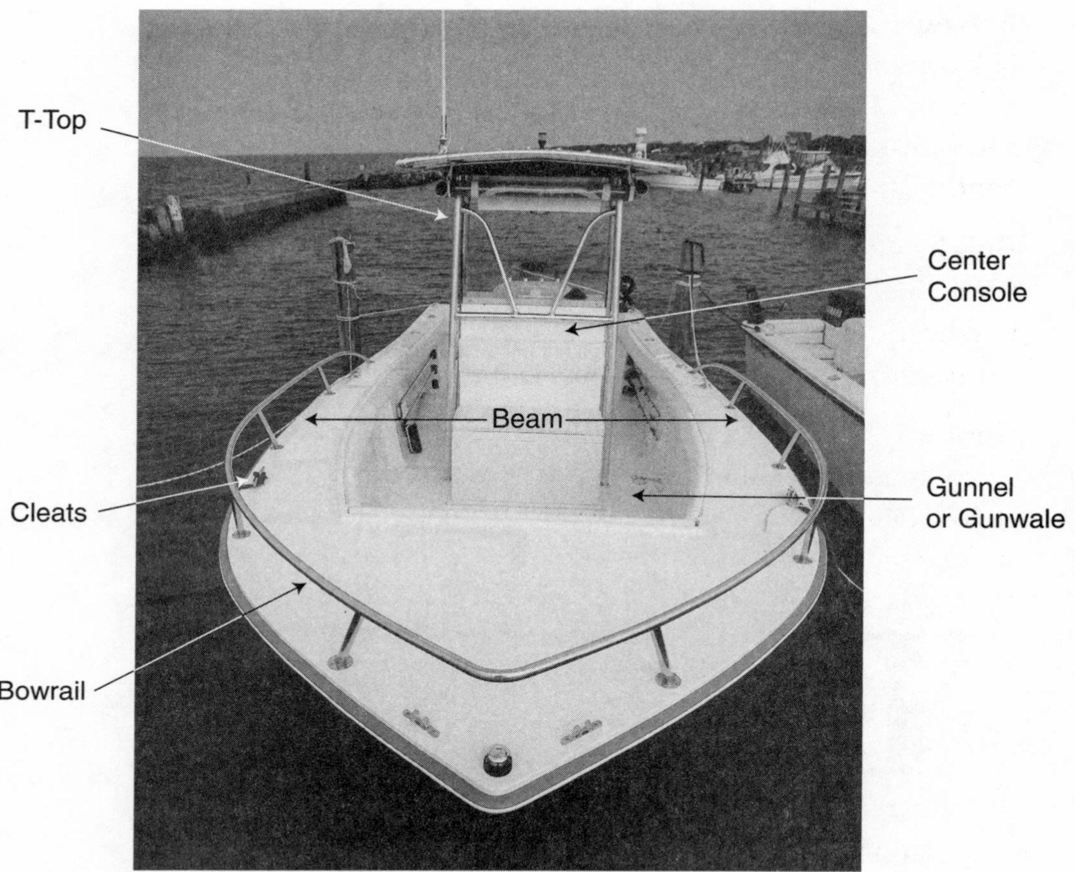

the batteries, fuel, livewell, and gear are arranged can determine the trim and seaworthiness of a small boat.

Beam: The widest point across a boat. Beam is important to anglers because width is an important factor in the stability of all boats—rowboats, bass boats, kayaks, canoes, or center consoles.

Bimini Top: A folding fabric sunshade on a metal frame, commonly used on family and fishing boats.

Bow: The forward or front end of a boat. It is often the best location for light-tackle anglers, since those on the bow platform get to make the first presentation to fish.

Bowrail: A large metal grabrail protruding from the gunnels (a.k.a. gunwale) at the front end of a boat. High bowrails can be a fisherman's worst nightmare since they tend to catch fly lines and lures. In a fishing boat, low bowrails or strategically placed handrails are generally more fishing-friendly.

Bulkhead: Any vertical partition to keep water from moving from one location in a boat to another. Many small boats have a bulkhead between the transom and the deck to keep water from sloshing around outboard-motor mounts and into the boat.

Center Console: A class of boat in which the steering and instrumentation are located on a console placed over the boat's centerline. Center-console boats are favored by many light-tackle anglers, especially in salt water, because there is plenty of room to move fore and aft around the console.

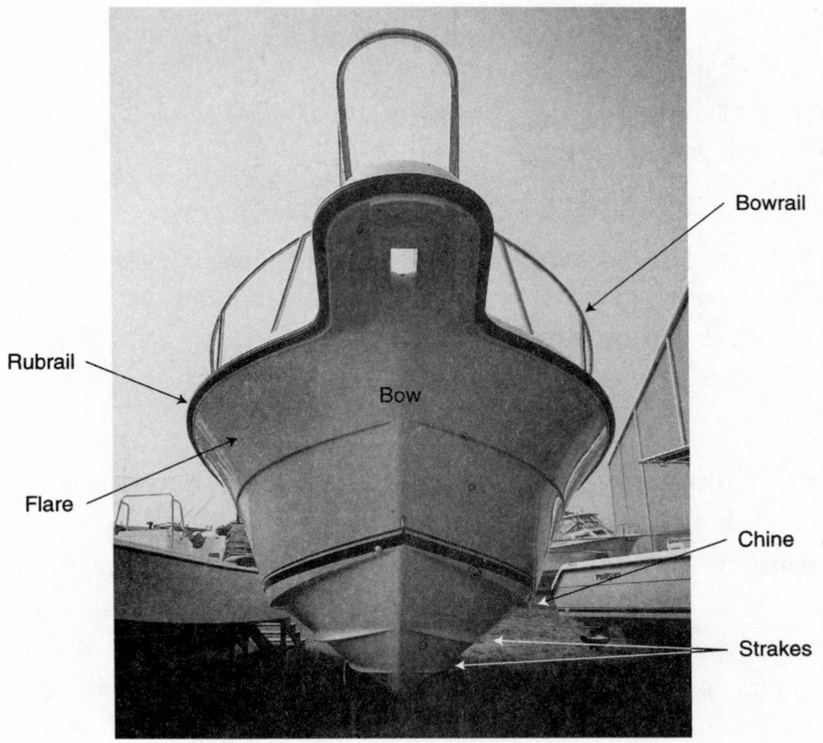

Chine: The edge or angle where the sides of the boat (topsides) meet the bottom of a flat or V-hulled boat. The chines on a fishing boat are extremely important because they affect how well a boat gets on plane and how dry a boat is while under power.

Cleat: An object in a boat or on a dock to which mooring and anchor lines are attached. Since cleats often have protruding horns, they can grab lines or shoelaces at inopportune times. Well-designed fishing boats often have recessed or pop-up cleats.

Compass: The simple, magnetic navigation device without which no boat should be on the water.

Cuddy Cabin: A small cabin, often with bunks, that allows passengers to escape from the weather. The walk-around cabin also provides privacy and protection, but is better designed for fore and aft movement by anglers.

Deck: The raised, flat area above the hull. The design of the deck space, open or cluttered, often determines how a boat works as a fishing craft.

Deep V: A hull design with significant deadrise at both the bow and stern that can provide a smooth ride in heavy seas. Although boats designed with deep-V hulls are excellent under power, they do not provide the stability at rest or at anchor offered by boats with less extreme deadrise, the modified-V boats. Modified-V hulls have a "flatter" V at the stern.

Depth Sounder: A sonar device that helps determine water depth. For fishermen, depth sounders and fish finders are often the same unit that not only shows depth, but also the structure below, whether the bottom is soft or hard, and whether fish lie between the surface and bottom. Those used on most small fishing boats are LCD (liquid crystal display) units.

Eye Splice: A method for putting a loop in the end of an anchor line or mooring line.

Flare: A design characteristic in which the topsides of a boat angle outward. Flared sides, whether on a dory or a powerboat, can help provide both stability and dryness.

Foredeck: The forward deck area, often raised, at the bow of a boat. The foredeck on many small boats—bass boats, flats boats, and johnboats—is often the cleanest and best laid out fishing space on a boat.

Freeboard: The distance between the gunnel and the water. When tipped to one side or fully loaded a boat should have adequate freeboard. Boats with low freeboard, like flats boats, have little profile to catch the wind, an advantage when poling. Boats used in open water generally have higher freeboard for safety.

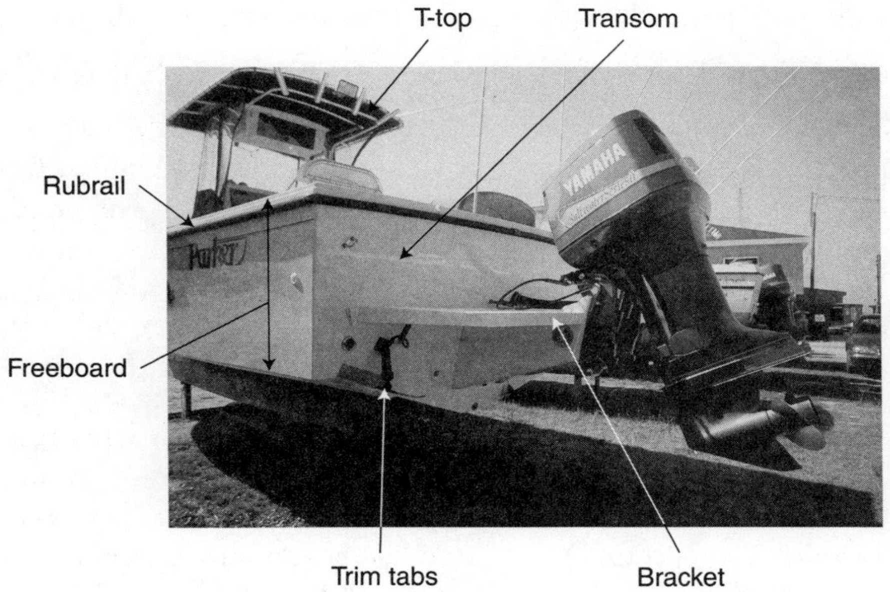

GPS: Global Positioning System. Handheld units or boat-mounted units available to boaters can receive navigation information directly from satellites orbiting the Earth. GPS units can provide a fisherman's exact position, course, and the location of previously entered "way points."

Grabrails: Low railings or hand holds used to move around a boat safely. Low, small railings are generally preferable to large bow and side rails often used on small fishing boats. High rails often make casting and movement difficult.

Gunnel: The rail or top edge of a hull or sides of a boat. Traditionally written as "gunwale." For fishermen a gunnel is a place to sit, and rods are often stored beneath it.

Gunwale: See "gunnel."

Outboard Motor: An engine and drive system separate from the boat that can be clamped or bolted to the transom or a bracket. Outboards now power most small fishing boats. Both two- and four-cycle outboards are now available to anglers.

Pilothouse: A small enclosed area around a console that gives some protection from the elements.

Planing Hull: A hull designed to run with the bow lifted out of the water when under power. Most small powerboats built for sportfishing have planing hulls.

Rocker: The curve in a boat's hull as seen from the side. Rocker can be found in the hulls of prams and drift boats, canoes and kayaks, and dories. A rowboat with rocker in the stern will not have as much drag, and a canoe with rocker will turn easily.

Rubrail: A rope, rubber, or metal fender around a deck of a boat that protects the hull from encounters with docks and pilings.

Self Bailing: The ability of a boat to drain without a manual or mechanical pump. Self-bailing boats have decks above the waterline angled from bow to stern that allow water to drain through drain holes, also above the waterline.

Skeg: A small keel-like appendage attached to the bottom at the stern end of a boat that helps a boat to track straight.

Stern: The rear portion of a boat.

Strakes: Raised longitudinal ridges or edges on the outer surface of a hull that help produce lift, reduce spray, and increase stability. Strakes help improve the performance of many fishing boats, especially those with V hulls.

Stringers: A fore and aft structural element attached to the hull usually made of wood or fiberglass. Stringers give a hull strength and stiffness, and also support the deck flooring.

Tiller: On outboard motors, the tiller is the metal bar or arm extending from the motor that is used to steer the boat.

Toe Rail: A low vertical rail found on the deck edge. They are especially useful for fly fishermen because they help prevent lines from blowing off the foredeck in light winds.

Topsides: The area of the hull between the gunnel and the chine, the visible sides of the boat.

Transom: The flat, usually vertical, back of a boat to which sides and the hull are attached. Outboard motors can be attached directly to the transom, or attached to a bracket that is bolted to the transom.

Trim: The proper attitude of a boat at the bow and stern when properly loaded. Boats are said to be "out of trim" when improperly loaded, or when propulsion is applied while the propeller is at the wrong angle.

Trim Tabs: Metal tabs attached to the transom on each side of the engine that can raise or lower the bow. Trim tabs operate much like the flaps on an airplane wing and can adjust the attitude, or trim, of a boat—left, right, up, and down—while under way. They improve performance and stability, and should be considered for any boat, especially those with V-hulls over 17 feet in length.

T-Top: A fixed metal frame with a cloth covering often installed in center-console boats. These tops provide some protection from the elements and often have rod holders and antennae attached.

Winch: A mechanical or electrical device used to pull a boat onto a trailer.

Index

Page numbers in italics indicate figures.

abrasion resistance, 79
ABS plastic, 198
accessories, 2, 33, 115–16, *117*, 136–38, *137*
  batteries/battery systems, 133–36, *134*, *136*
  fish finders, 124–27, *126*
  navigation aids, 127–30, *128*, *129*
  onboard communications, 130–33
  protruding, 118–21, *118–24*, 124
accessory plugs, 137–38
accidents, 130
alcohol, 230
algae, 146, 147
aluminum boats, 76–78, *77*, 135
  canoes, 197–98
  compared to wood, 78. *See also* johnboats
anchor bend knot, 169, *169*
anchor chains, 173, *175*, 176
anchors, 87, 162, 199–200
  noise and, 78
  storage of, 59
  types of, 172–76, *174*
antennae, 121, *122–23*
anticavitation plate, 63, 65
artificial reefs, 52
Ashley Book of Knots, The (Ashley), 163
automobile engines, 98

back splices, 163, *164*, 166
backing, 109, 157
bag anchors, 176
baitwells, 90
ballast, 70
bass boats, 11, 75, 138, 211
  freeboard of, 82
  with "pad" modification, 49
bass/walleye boats, 25, *26*, *27*
bateaus, 30
batteries, 55, 133–36, *134*, *136*, 221
  dead, 142, 231
beam (width), 3, 193, *194*, 215
belly boats, 187
bilge pumps, 12, 13, 92, 133
Bimini tops, 90, *91*, 229
boat shows, 17, 68, 115
boat storage, 142–45, *143–45*
boat-to-boat courtesy, 235–37
boating-supply houses, 149, 156
boats, 1–4, 7–16, *9*
buying, 32–33
  cleaning, 145–48, *146*
  form and function in, 17–33
  oar-powered, 180–81
  protecting and maintaining, 141–58
  sinking, 13, 226. *See also* specific types of boats
Boston Whaler fiberglass boats, 68
bow, 57, 61, 84, 93, 119
bowline knot, *170*, 170–71
bracket motors, 110, *111*
buddy system, 227

cane poles, 29
canoes, 17, *21*, 55, 132, 191, 193–200
  aluminum, 76
  beam of, 193, *194*
  outboard motors and, *195*, 205

canoes (*continued*)
 paddles for, 215–18
 with poling platforms, 205
 in rivers, 29–30
 rocker and, *192,* 193
 rod protection and, *196,* 197, *197*
 trolling motors and, *221*
capsizing, 43
carbon buildup, 149
carbon fiber. *See* graphite
cargo canoes, 20
Carolina Flare, 24
catamarans, 52–54, *53, 54*
catch-and-release fishing, 52
cathedral hulls. *See* tri-hulls
cathode-ray tubes (CRTs), 125
cell phones, 131, 132, 138, 226
center consoles, 17, 31, 82, 138
 lean posts and, 120
 modified-V, 24–25
centerline, *60,* 99, 211, 212
children, 119
chine walking, 46
chines, 46, 48
chop, 41, 90
chopper guns, 72
cleat hitch knot, *167,* 167–68
cleats, *74,* 118, *118, 119, 120*
clothing, 228, *228*
clove hitch knot, *166,* 167
clutter, cutting, 124, *124,* 127
Coast Guard, 13, 131, 132, 226
coastal waters, 22, 76, 126, 182, 212
coffee cans, 8, 12
cold-water flats, 19
cold-weather fishing, 227–28
comfort, 54, 138, 188
communications, 130–33
compass, 83
Compleat Angler, The (Walton), 207
compromise boat, 22, 32
computers, 127, 130
consoles, 83
conventional drive systems, 97, 98–100, *99*
corrosion, 152–54, 156
costs, 12, 32, 54, 99, 141
 boat storage, 144
 fly tackle, 159
 push poles, 211
cotter keys, 97
cotton ropes, 160
covers, 143, *143*
cranking batteries, 135
croakers, 14
cross members, 72
cuddy cabins, 92
cutting hull, 41

Dacron ropes, 160, 161
Danforth anchor, 173, *174,* 176
deadrise, 25, 45–46
 on flats boats, 50
 modified-V hulls and, 47, *48*
decks, 52, 54, 93
deep-cycle batteries, 135
deep-V hulls, 38
dehydration, 229–30
depth sounders, 14, 133
diesel engines, 99, 107
Differential Beacon Receiver (DBR), 130
dinghies, 55, 184–85
displacement hulls, 37
dock lines, 162–63, 166
dories, 28, 40, 185
 initial stability and, 41
 oars and, 215
 powered, 43, *44,* 45
double-enders, 184
down riggers, 121
drag, 8, 19, 180
drain holes, 93
drift anchors, 173, 175–76
drift boats, 19, *20, 27,* 27–28, 185–87, *186*
driveshaft, 61, 98
dry-stack storage, 144, *144*

E-boats, 138
E-glass, 67, 70–73, *71, 73,* 75, 78
electric trim tabs, 61
electric trolling motors, 113, 218–21, *219, 221*
electronics, 1, 157–58
elements, protection from, 90–92, *91*
emergency situations, 131, 132, 172. *See also* safety
engines. *See* motors; outboard motors
environmental standards, 101, 105, 147
etiquette, 233–39
Euro transoms, 110, *111,* 112
external fittings, *74*
eye splices, 163, *165,* 166

family boats, 84
farm ponds, 22, 23
Federal Communications Commission (FCC), 132
feet, keeping dry, 92–93
fiberglass boats, 2, 11, 24, 50, 198
 E-glass, 75
 graphite, 75, 76
 kayaks, 204–5
 Kevlar, 75, 76
 lifespan of, 67–68
 punt design, 40
 S-glass, 73–75
 skiffs, 31
fire extinguishers, 226, *227*
fish boxes, 90
fish finders, 124–27, *126,* 135, 157
fishability, 2, 33
flat-bottom boats, 39–41, *39–44,* 45

canoes, 191, 193
in rough water, 77
skiffs, *30,* 30–31, 50
flats boats, 17, *18,* 19, 75, 138
batteries and, 135
freeboard of, 82
hulls of, 50–51
line containment and, 93–94, *94*
push poles and, 121
shallows fishing and, 28–29, *29*
float tubes, 187
fly fishing, 3, 55, 187–88, 189
canoes and, 196
T-tops and, 92
foam flotation, 72, *73*
folding anchor, 173–74, *174*
food storage, 90
four-cycle engines, 101, 102, *103,* 104–5
freeboard, 25, 48, 76, *183*
child safety and, 119
interior design and, 84, *85–86,* 86
oars and, 215
freshwater, 76, 113, 127, 154
FRS (Family Radio Service) radios, 132–33
fuel filters, 142
fuel injection, 101
fuel tanks, 55, 57–58, 64, 110, 148–49

gadgetry, 14, 83, 116
galvanic corrosion, 152–54, *153*
garages, 142, *145*
garveys, 30
gas tanks. *See* fuel tanks
gasoline, 10, 99, 101, 142, 149
gel coats, 147, 148
Global Positioning System (GPS) units, *128,* 128–30, *129,* 135, 137
LCD (liquid crystal display) and, 126–27
preemptive planning and, 226
protection of, 157
grab rails, 25, 84, 119
Grady-White fiberglass boats, 68
graphite, 75, 76, 216
grapnel anchor, 173, *174,* 175
guest courtesy, 237–38
gunnels, 25, 58, 84, 87, *181*

handrails, 84, *85–86,* 86
hatch covers, 86–87, *87, 89,* 90
Heddon Sonics, 10
Hewes fiberglass boats, 68
hickory shad, 22
"holes," 61, 102, 191
hour meters, 137
hulls, design of, 37–55
hydraulic trim tabs, 61
hypothermia, 227

ice chests, 59, 90
inboard/outboard motors. *See* stern drives
initial stability, 38, 40–41, 47, 191. *See also* reserve stability; stability
inlets, 93, 129
interior designs, 81–83
consoles and seating, 83
dry feet, 92–93
handrails and freeboard, 84, *85–86,* 86
line containment, 93–94, *94*
protection from the elements, 90–92, *91*
storage areas, 86–87, *87–89,* 90

jet propulsion, 97, 112–13
jet skiers, 113
johnboats, 22–23, *23,* 28, *40,* 76
as flats boats, 50
freeboard of, 82
horsepower and, 43
interior design of, *89*
jet propulsion and, 112–13
mushroom anchors and, 174
outboard motors and, 105
push poles and, 121, 211

kayaks, 17, 189–91, 202–5, *203*
as "get there" boats, 200, *201*
light traveling and, 132
paddles for, 215–18
keels, 42, *43*
Kevlar, 75, 76, 78, 198
kayaks made of, 204–5
paddles made of, 216
knives, 231
knots, 159, 163, *164–70,* 166–72

lakes, 108, 112, 126, 130, 162
lateral trim, 58, 63
launch line, 161
LCD (liquid crystal display) units, 125–27, *126*
leaks, 8
lean posts, 120
leverage, kayaks and, 202
life jackets, 87, 226
light-tackle angling, 3–4, 41, 43, 47, 55
bracket motors and, 110
canoes and, 196
modified-V hulls and, 48
power trim and, 61
quiet tools for, 208–22
lightning, 226
line containment, 93–94, *94*
line endings, securing, 163
liquid corrosion inhibitors, 149
liquid silicone, 156
livewells, 13, 52, 55, 90, 158
loops, in line endings, 163, *164–65,* 166
Loran navigation systems, 127–28
lubricants, 149, 156
lures, 10–11

McKenzie drift boat, 27, 185

maintenance, 71, 142
  of motors, 148–49, *150, 151,* 151–52
  of ropes, 162–63
  of wooden boats, 79–80
Manila ropes, 160
marinas, 12, 130, 141, 144, 149, 157
marine supply houses, 132–33
marshes, 52, 200, 212
Mepps' spinners, 10
millponds, 23
mini rudders, 64–66, *65,* 152, *153*
modified-V center consoles, 24–25, 31
modified-V hulls, 46, 47–49, *48*
  adaptability of, 55
  on flats boats, 50
  in rough water, 77. *See also* V-hulls
motors, 97–98
  brackets and Euro Transoms, 110, *111,* 112
  conventional drive systems, 98–100, *99*
  jet propulsion, 112–13
  maintenance of, 148–49, *150, 151,* 151–52
  stern drives, 107, 107–8
  twin engines, *108,* 108–9, *109. See also* outboard motors
muscle boats, 27
mushroom anchor, 174, *174,* 176

National Oceanic and Atmospheric Administration (NOAA), 132
navigation aids, 127–30, *128, 129*
Navy anchor, *174,* 174–75
neglect, 141–42
noise, 78, 197–98, 222, 234
nylon ropes, 160, 161

oars, 180–81, 214–15
ocean, 22, 91, 108, 130
oil, 101, 155
onboard communications, 130–33
outboard motors, 7, 8, 11, 100–102, *103–4,* 104–5
  bass boats and, *26*
  canoes and, *195,* 205
  contemporary boats and, 98
  cotter keys/shear pins and, 97
  flats boats and, 50
  high-altitude waters and, 77
  horsepower, 25, 27, 29, 51, 101, 102
  in johnboats, 22
  maintenance of, 148–49, *150, 151,* 151–52
  tiller steering and, 105, *106*
  twin, 52, 54
  walk-around cabin boats and, 32. *See also* motors

"pad" modification, *49,* 49–50
paddles, 215–18
paper-chart recorders, 125
peapods, 184, 185
performance hulls, 49–50
personal boats, 3
Pflueger Medalist reels, 10
pilothouses, 92
pirogues, 30
piston rings, 149
pitching, 38
planing hulls, 37–38, 57, 102
planing wedges, 49–50
plastic tarps, 143
plowing, 63
polarized glasses, 231–32
poling platforms, 53, 205, 210, *210, 214*
poling towers, 50
polyethylene, 205
popping bugs, 29
porpoising, 61
powerboats, 32, 33, 188
  accessory plugs and, 137–38
  etiquette and, 238
  hull designs, 37–55
  interior designs, 81–94
  trim, 57–66
prams, 17, 23–24, *24,* 182, 187
propellers, 50, 61, 64, 97
  jet propulsion and, 113
  maneuverability and, 100
punts, 30, 40–41
push poles, 121, 208–14, *209–10, 213,* 218

quartering seas, 63

"rabbit," 172
Rabolo fiberglass boats, 68
radar, 14, 115, 124
radio direction finders (RDFs), 127
radios, 14
rails, 119–20
rain gear, 87
Ranger fiberglass boats, 68
reefs, 52, 129
reels, 10, 59, 87
reserve stability, 38, 41, 47
  canoes and, 191, 193
  of dinghies, 184
  modified-V hulls and, 47. *See also* initial stability; stability
reservoirs, 19, 22, 90, 91, 174
resins, 70, 71–72, 76, 80
rivers, 22, 23, 28, 90, 130
  anchors for, 174
  fish finders for use on, 126
  jet propulsion on, 112–13
rock anchor, 173, *174,* 175
rocker, 8, 19, 40, 180, 182, 191
rods, 10, 69, 75, 84, 86
  storage of, 87, *88*
ropes, 159–63, *171,* 172
round-bottom boats, 54–55
round-turn/two-half-hitch knot, *168,* 168–69
rowboats, 179–88

rudders, 97
running lights, 121, 226
rust, 147

S-glass, 73–75, 78
safety, 2, 109, 119, 225–27
  cold-weather fishing, 227–28
  delegation of responsibility and, 12–14
  necessary tools, 230–31
  polarized glasses, 231–32
  speed and alcohol, 230
  sun and dehydration, 229–30. *See also* emergency situations
sail effect, 25
salt water, 76, 113, 127
  boat cleaning and, 146, 147
  corrosion and, 152, 154
  electric trolling motors in, 220
  fly fishing in, 190
  motor maintenance and, 152
satellites, 127, 129, 138
sea anchors, 173, 176
sea cats. *See* catamarans
sea-gasket coil, *171,* 172
Seacraft fiberglass boats, 68
seating, 59, 83, 120
self-bailing boats, 12, 92
semi-V hulls, 55
semidisplacement hulls, 37
shear pins, 97
shoals, 93
shoes, 228, *229*
shoving poles, 208–9
side thrust, 64–66
signal flares, 226
skeg, 41, *183*
skiffs, 1, 67, *68,* 120
  construction of, 179–80, *180, 181*
  features of, 182, *183,* 184
  flat-bottomed, *30,* 30–31, *42,* 50
  light traveling and, 132
  outboard motors and, 8, 182
  push poles and, 211
skinny water, 19
sliding turns, 41
slow roll, 55
snap, 5
sonar, 115, 125
speed, 3, 11–12, 38, 102, 124, 126, 200
  alcohol and, 230
  wind-chill factor and, 228
speedometers, 14, 115
spray, 52
spring line, 161
spring protectors, 155–56
squatting, 63
"squirrelly" boats, 57
stability, 39, 50, 54, 94, 202. *See also* initial stability; reserve stability
staking out, 213–14
stern, 57, 61
stern drive, 97, *107,* 107–8
stiffness, 69–70, 77–78, 78
storage areas, 59
  interior design and, 86–87, *87–89,* 90
  outboard motors and, 101
strakes, 46, 48
stringers, 72, *73, 77,* 77–78
stripping baskets, 93
sun, safety and, 229–30

T-tops, 91–92
tachometers, 14, 115, 137
tackle boxes, 97
technology, 3, 14, 67–69, 125
temperatures, 78, 92
test running, 33
throttle, 83
tie-downs, 87
time difference (TD), 127
toadstool seats, 120
toe rails, 93
torque, 64–66, *65,* 105, 109
towrope, 162
trailer protection, 154–57
transoms, 13
  motors and, 98, 99, 110, *111,* 112
  rocker and, 180
trim tabs and, *62*
trimming motors and, 61
trawler yachts, 37
tree sap, damage to boats, 141, 142
tri-hulls, *51,* 51–52, 55
trim, 57–59
  mini rudders, 64–66, *65*
  outboard motors and, 101, 105
  trim tabs, 61, *62,* 63–64
  trimming the motor, 61
trim tabs, 46, 50, 61, *62,* 63–64
  on flats boats, 51
  modified-V hulls and, 49
tripping canoes, 195
trolling batteries, 50
trolling motors, 109, *109,* 121, 135
  electric, 113, 218–21, *219, 221*
trout, 28, 200
tuck, 180
tunnel-drive hulls, 50
turning, 41, 109, 212
twin engines, *108,* 108–9, *109*
two-cycle engines, 100, 101, *104,* 105

umbrellas, 90, 229

V drive, 98
V-hulls, 25, 31, 38, 41, *45*
  aluminum, 76
  canoes and, 193, 195
  modified, 46, 47–49, *48*
  pros and cons of, 45–47

V-hulls (*continued*)
  trailers and, 156. *See also* modified-V hulls
vacuum-bagging, *75*, 76
VHF (Very High Frequency) radios, 121, *122–23*, 131–33, 135
  preemptive planning and, 226
  protection of, 157
visibility, 53, 83

walk-around cabins, *31*, 31–32, 82, 92
walleye boats, 82
water
  depth of, 124
  height from, 52
  temperature of, 124, 126, 137, 225, 227
water skiing, 14
waterline, 99, 202
waves, 38, 39, 78
weather conditions, 143–44
weather information, 132
weight, 38, 39, 69–70
  distribution of, 41, 55, 57–59, *58–60*, 66
wheel bearings, 154–55
whipping, 163
white lithium grease, 156
width. *See* beam (width)
wind, 81, 84, 94, 160, 226
  anchors and, 162
  wind-chill factor, 228
winterization, 148, 149
wooden boats, 8, *9*
  juniper skiffs, 67, *68*
  strength and durability of, 78–80, *79, 80*
wraparound rails, 84, *85*